KUSHANAVA CHOUDHURY grew up in Calcutta and New Jersey. After graduating from Princeton University he worked as a reporter at the *Statesman* in Calcutta. He went on to receive a PhD in Political Theory from Yale University before returning to Calcutta to write a book about the city. *The Epic City* is his first book.

THE
EPIC
CITY

THE WORLD ON THE
STREETS OF CALCUTTA

KUSHANAVA CHOUDHURY

BLOOMSBURY CIRCUS
LONDON · OXFORD · NEW YORK · NEW DELHI · SYDNEY

BLOOMSBURY CIRCUS
Bloomsbury Publishing Plc
50 Bedford Square, London, WC1B 3DP, UK

BLOOMSBURY, BLOOMSBURY CIRCUS and the Bloomsbury Circus logo are trademarks of
Bloomsbury Publishing Plc

First published in Great Britain 2017
This edition published 2018

A catalogue record for this book is available from the British Library

ISBN: HB: 978-1-4088-8888-9; eBook: 978-1-4088-8890-2; PB: 978-1-4088-8883-4

2 4 6 8 10 9 7 5 3 1

Typeset by Manipal Digital Systems
Printed and bound in Great Britain by CPI Group (UK) Ltd, Croydon CR0 4YY

To find out more about our authors and books visit www.bloomsbury.com and
sign up for our newsletters

To my friend, Sumitro Basak (1975–2017)

He llegado a la conclusión de que aquél que no encuentra todo el universo encerrado en las calles de su ciudad, no encontrará una calle original en ninguna de las ciudades del mundo. Y no las encontrará, porque el ciego en Buenos Aires es ciego en Madrid o Calcuta ...

Roberto Arlt, 'El Placer de Vagabundear'

I have come to the conclusion that he who does not encounter the whole universe in the streets of his city will not encounter an original street in any of the cities of the whole world. He won't encounter them because those who are blind in Buenos Aires are blind in Madrid, or in Calcutta ...

Roberto Arlt, 'The Pleasure of Vagabonding'

Contents

Midlife Crisis

Of all the people who came to Ellis Island in the first decades of the twentieth century, more than half went back. They never told us that on our seventh-grade class trip.

The American immigrant myth says that migration is a reset button. The New World offers deliverance from the past, liberation from the Old World's limited horizons. The myth states: 'The past is gone. The future awaits. Start over.'

It never really works like that. That was the story no one ever told about America. The past is never left behind. It haunts every world you live in. Sometimes it drags you back.

By the time I visited Ellis Island on that class trip, I had already migrated halfway around the world four times, flipping back and forth between continents like a dual-voltage appliance. My parents were Indian scientists, torn between nation and vocation. Twice they moved to America, twice they moved back. They were unwilling to leave their country and they were unable to stay. When he was around forty, my father quit his cushy job at a government research institute in Calcutta. He wanted one more chance, he said to his boss, while his 'blood was still warm'.

'How many more times will you move that boy?' his boss asked.

He said this was the last time.

So, when I was almost twelve, my parents and I moved to Highland Park, New Jersey.

Our move carried no Emma Lazarus cadences. We certainly had not arrived tempest-tossed, beating at the golden door. Our coming was equivocal, always tied to return. Living in New Jersey, we hardly saw ourselves as immigrants. My parents expected to go back to India, like many of their Bengali friends, someday, eventually. On Saturday nights, they gathered at each other's homes, ate fourteen-course meals brimming with various types of fish and meat, and derailed each other's sentences in locomotive Bengali, their conversations full of memories of Calcutta. Return, the duty of return and the dream of return, were spoken of endlessly while eating platefuls of goat curry and hilsa fish. Few, of course, actually went back. There were too many good reasons not to. Nationalism and nostalgia did not pay the bills, raise children or advance careers. And yet that dream of a return to the great metropolis cocooned them like a protective blanket from the alien world all around.

As for me – my friends, my neighbourhood, my Calcutta life was gone. In New Jersey, I was in seventh grade in a public school that had almost no Indian students. Cocooning was not an option. I had to fit in fast. I wasn't assimilating as much as passing. So much of what went on inside my head was from another place. I had happy childhood memories of mid-morning cricket matches during summer vacations, of games played in gullies, rooftops, courtyards and streets. When I moved, it was the streets of the city as much as my childhood that I left behind.

We had not had an easy few years in America. The man who had offered the job to my father had made promises he did not keep, and so my father was forced to find other work, work he grew to despise. From time to time, there would be talk of another move, to Georgia, to Colorado, and I would pull down the posters in my room and prepare. We stayed put, the three of us adrift in the treacherous shoals of the lower middle class, a world of chronic car trouble and clothes from K-Mart. In the fall of my senior year, a piece of good news finally came to our two-bedroom apartment. I had been accepted early to Princeton University.

Every immigrant who has lugged worthless foreign degrees through customs knows that where you go to college, the seal on that sheepskin determines your lot in life. When the acceptance letter from Princeton arrived, my parents acted as if someone had come to our door with balloons and a giant cardboard cheque. It was their happiest day in America. But it wasn't mine.

It is probably universally true that education drives a wedge between us and our hometowns, our families, our earlier selves. But for the immigrant the gap is greater, that divergence in mentality more extreme. My trajectory was taking me farther afield, to Princeton, while a part of me was elsewhere, in another country, in another city. Through all my sojourns I had carried memories on my back like Huien Tsang's chair, until at seventeen, I felt hunched over with nostalgia like a middle-aged man. When the Princeton letter arrived, I had what my friend Ben called a 'premature midlife crisis'.

At night, I couldn't sleep. By day I sleepwalked through classes. Each evening, while my friends assembled at Dunkin' Donuts, complained about how there was nothing to do in our little town and roared together into the night on long aimless drives, while they enjoyed the languor of spring and that sweet American affliction called senioritis, I stayed home and stewed. In my mind, I hatched a plan. I would go back.

India lives in its villages, Mahatma Gandhi had said. So, even though I was a city boy who had never spent a night in an Indian village, I wrote letters back home to arrange to teach in a village school. Instead of Princeton, I would take a year off and head to rural Bengal, I told my parents. But in our two-bedroom apartment full of shared immigrant striving, such a detour was out of the question.

Instead I just drove. The black night, the shimmering yellow lines on inviting ribbons of asphalt, the radio jammed loud. Enveloped by night and noise, the mind gave way to a deeper calling. Just drive. It was the mantra of our Jersey youth, an exhortation, a command, an ideology, something hardwired in us as teenage boys. Night after night, I took out my parents' Toyota and just drove, without destination, without purpose, to escape.

Down Route 27, past New Brunswick towards Princeton, were farms and wooded pockets not yet sullied by the florescent glare of strip malls. Back then, there were still a few miles of dark solitude. When the cop pulled me over, I was doing 74 in a 45 zone. He had been following me for quite some time.

It would be four points and a hefty ticket, he told me. 'My parents are going to kill me,' I muttered. He took my fresh license, my father's insurance and registration cards, and went back to write it up.

He came back with a reduced ticket. Two points.

'Where were you going in such a rush?'

'I was just driving – just trying to clear my head – to Princeton,' I said. 'I'll be going there in the fall. Sometimes I go there just to see what it is going to be like.'

He went back to his car again. I waited. A few moments later, he came back.

'Don't drive angry,' he said. 'And don't believe everything those liberals teach you at that school.'

He let me go.

***

'Princeton in the nation's service,' university president Woodrow Wilson had said nearly a century before, and when I arrived on campus, that motto had been amended by the sitting Princeton President, to include 'and in the service of all nations.'

In Highland Park, rich people had been the tenured Rutgers professors with two-storey houses on the north side. They were Volvo-rich. At Princeton I saw the real American aristocracy. I was going to join them. I could graduate from college and within three years be making more money than my parents combined. In a decade, I could be a millionaire. As incoming freshmen, we soon learned about the two true paths to prosperity: investment banker and management consultant. No one told us these things at orientation. It was in the ether and we breathed it in.

Princeton was an amazing social experiment. The search committee scoured the fifty states each year for the most diverse, overachieving and interesting students they could find, then put them in a social blender for four years and poured them out in two moulds. More than half of each graduating class was being siphoned off into banking and consulting. It didn't matter if you majored in psychology or chemistry, philosophy or art history. As long as you had a Princeton degree, you were cut out for sitting in a corporate office staring at spreadsheets all day. The sheer drudgery of it!

Beyond Wilson's motto, on campus, 'service' was generally preceded by the word 'community', and together they suggested a version of what in earlier days was called charity. To serve the nation meant merging and acquiring companies for seventy hours a week, fifty weeks a year in a downtown temple of finance and ladling soup up in Harlem during the holidays. The workplace somehow lay outside the community or the impulse to serve it.

The summer after my freshman year, I taught at a summer school for 'underprivileged' children – a euphemism for poor black kids – in Trenton, New Jersey. The essence of teaching schoolchildren was repetition and disciplining, the same lessons and rules enforced over and over until they are learned. I don't know what I managed to teach in those months, but I spent a lot of time telling kids they couldn't go to the bathroom. It was not the career for me.

I had worked in newspapers in one form or another since I was fifteen, fed on their energy and variety, the constant novelty of the game. When we went to Calcutta on a family visit the following summer, I worked as an intern at the city's leading English daily, the *Statesman*. It was a fateful choice. Henceforth, I sleepwalked through Princeton, marking time. My education was happening someplace else.

After graduating from college, while friends set up their apartments in New York, Boston and Los Angeles, I headed to Calcutta, to join the *Statesman*.

***

Before we moved to America, we had lived in Sir's house in Calcutta. Sir was my parents' professor. As graduate students, Ma and Baba had met and fallen in love in Sir's lab. His real name was Rajat Neogy, but like most professors in India, he was addressed as 'Sir' by his students. As a kid, perhaps not knowing this was not his name, I took to calling him Sir as well.

When I came back to Calcutta, I moved back in to Sir's house. His wife had long since passed away. His only son lived in Boston, and Sir shuttled between continents, dodging Boston's snowy winters and Calcutta's monsoons. Sir was a father figure to my parents, a revered teacher. To me, he was a grandfather, teacher, confidant, friend. We ate together, watched cricket together, and he read anything I read. When I woke up early in the mornings, he would send me down to Niranjan's sweet shop to fetch *kochuris* and *jillipis* – a Bengali fry-up – for breakfast. On days when I slept late, he would say: 'Are you taking drugs?' I sometimes felt like we were a premise for a sitcom: two bachelors separated by two generations, living under one roof.

Sir had an idea that I had come to Calcutta to find a wife. There seemed to him to be no other reason that I would be living with a seventy-five-year-old man, watching cricket and working at the *Statesman*. After all, everything that could possibly be wrong with a city was wrong with Calcutta. The city is situated between a river and a swamp. Its weather, Mark Twain had said, 'was enough to make a brass doorknob mushy.' For six months out of the year, you are never dry. You take two to three showers a day to keep cool, but start sweating the moment you turn off the tap. The dry winter months, when I arrived, were worse. I woke up some mornings feeling my chest was on fire. Breathing in Calcutta, Manash, the neighbourhood doctor told me, was like smoking a pack of cigarettes a day. Keeping the dust and grime off my body, out of my nails, hair and lungs was a daily struggle. Then there were the mosquitoes, which arrived in swarms at sundown and often came bearing malaria.

I could look forward to the monsoons, of course, when floodwaters regularly reached your waist in parts of the city. When they weren't flooded, the streets were blocked by marches, rallies, barricades and bus burnings, all of which passed for normal politics in the city. Staying cool, dry, healthy and sane took up so much effort that it left little enthusiasm for much else.

Nothing had changed since my childhood. The *paanwallas* still ruled the street corners, perched on stoops with their bottles of soft drinks and neatly arrayed cigarette packets. On the streets, the pushers and pullers of various types of carts still transported most of the city's goods. The footpaths were still overrun by hawkers selling bulbous sidebags, shirts, combs, peanuts in minuscule sachets, onion fritters and vegetable chow mein. The mildewed concrete buildings, the bowl-shaped Ambassador taxis, the paintings on the backs of buses, the ubiquitous political graffiti, the posters stuck onto any flat surface, the bazaars full of squatting fish sellers, the tea shop benches on the sidewalks, the caged balconies of the middle classes, the narrow entrails of corrugated slums, nothing had changed, not even the impassive expressions on the faces of clerks. The city was in its own time zone.

It was not a happy time. Calcutta was in its twenty-third year of Communist rule, its third decade of factory closures. Until the 1970s it had been the largest and most industrialised city in India but had now been eclipsed in population and prosperity by Bombay and Delhi. The only reason politicians seemed to visit the city any more was to pronounce its death.

Since the early 1990s, life in other parts of India had been improving for people like us, the educated few. The government had loosened its hold over the economy, and dollars were flowing into the American back offices and call centres located in Bangalore and Hyderabad. Countless college-educated young men and women, including many of my cousins, had fled Calcutta for these boomtowns. On my mother's side, none of my cousins remained in the city. Our ancestral house in North Calcutta had once been filled with the voices of children; now my two middle-aged and widowed uncles occupied one floor each with hardly a soul to argue with. My grandmother, Dida, occupied the middle floor. I was the only grandchild in the city, and I enjoyed a monopoly on her affections. She was half-paralysed and had been confined to a bed for years, but her spirit was always cheerful in spite of it all. She still read books and the newspapers. She stayed up in the afternoons watching Bengali soaps and into the night to keep up on the international cricket matches.

I feared visiting most of my other relatives, however. My generation had gone missing, leaving behind a city of geriatrics who busied themselves with bilirubin levels and stool analyses. Their blood-test results were kept in plastic bags as if they were examination mark-sheets or graduation certificates, to be presented to visitors along with tea and biscuits.

Why had I come back? everyone asked.

It would be one thing if I had come back to take care of my ailing parents. But my parents lived in America.

Maybe I did not get along with my parents? asked the bank officer when I went to the local branch to open an account.

Could I not get a job in America? asked the man who ran the copy shop in the bazaar.

Had the Americans, for some reason, thrown me out? wondered a colleague at the *Statesman*.

Well then, if I must stay in India, they all advised, I had better clear out of Calcutta. If I had any career ambitions at all, I should go to Delhi, Bombay or Bangalore. After all, even if I had been booted out of America, I had that magic wand that opened all doors in India: a foreign degree.

I knew why I was back, though I did not tell people this, fearing they would scoff at my noblesse oblige, or worse, laugh at my naiveté. Like the revolutionaries of my parents' generation, I wanted to change things. There was no revolution for me to join, no ideology I could adhere to, no dream left. My best hope for making a difference was to work at a newspaper.

***

I'd joined the *Statesman* in 2001, when it was already over a hundred years old. At the turn of the last century, when India was ruled by the British and Calcutta was the capital of their Raj, it had ten times the circulation of any paper in Asia. Now it was barely beating its younger competitor across Chittaranjan Avenue, the *Telegraph*. In the decade before, a dozen cable news channels had appeared. Other newspapers, like the *Telegraph*, used the front pages to feature cleavage and product placements. With each new subscription, they doled out free tchotchkes. But the *Statesman* was the *Statesman*. It may no longer have been the largest paper in Asia, or even in India, but in Calcutta it was still, tenuously, king. The offices of the *Telegraph* had cubicles with glass partitions and an electronic security system, but that did not change the the fact of their humble location. Like the nouveau riche who rented antique furniture and passed it off as their own, the building's new frontage boasted alabaster columns, but it still hovered over a shabby little side street off Central Avenue. The *Statesman*'s Doric columns loomed above Chowringhee Square in the heart of Calcutta.

When I first started at the *Statesman*, a co-worker told me this story about my new boss, Michael Flannery. He and Mike used to work the newsroom nightshift together. One night, as they were leaving the office, a drunk grabbed the co-worker by the collar and began to accost him, swaggering with the taunt, 'I've murdered someone tonight.' Mike walked up to the drunk, and without a word, knocked him down with one punch.

Newspaper men were divided into desk and beat. The beat guys were streetwise; they went out every day covering the dirty rotten world around them. By sundown they were at the

Press Club, drinking. The desk sub-editors came to work in the late afternoon and stayed past midnight. They turned the beat reporters' filings into palatable prose, designed and laid out the paper, and produced headlines. They never left the air-conditioned office. The subs saw the reporters as no better than the wild monkeys that sometimes laid siege on Indian cities. The reporters saw the subs as house plants. Mike was an assistant editor at the *Statesman*, a desk man with the heart of a beat reporter. His education was on the city's streets; he had barely lived anywhere else.

Every evening Mike's office was given over to the sweet Bengali pastime of aimless digressive conversation called *adda*. To call mere conversation an adda is like confusing a jazzy ring tone with Billie Holiday. There was the bureaucrat who ran the city's malaria-control unit and wrote Kafkaesque short stories from the perspective of the mosquito. His name was Debashis, but we called him Mosha (mosquito). Mosha was often accompanied by young Debjit, who wanted most of all to be a journalist and hoped to accomplish this by hanging around editors' offices instead of writing articles. Next to him sat the admirers: the dancer, who always smiled and never spoke, and occasionally the Amazon, whose boom was heard across the newsroom. Then came the 'race men' with their pamphlets full of numbers and prospects, their talk full of conspiracies and false hopes that reliably turned into disappointments every Saturday afternoon at the Calcutta racecourse.

In this configuration of unlikely persons, Mike would largely keep quiet, a lit Gold Flake between his fingers as he edited away, paring down the turgid prose on screen. He was a master whittler, and while his name never appeared in a byline, many a hapless writer's articles were buoyed by what he called 'my gift of language'.

When I first met Imran in Mike's office, he had just written an article about a bar that had illegally opened in proximity to a school. After the article appeared, the city was forced to close the bar. One evening at the adda, Mike told us that the bar's owner had come to see him. 'He had a suitcase full of money. He said, "Mr Flannery please type a retraction. I will pay." He had twenty-thousand rupees in his briefcase.

'I said, "Are you aware that this room is bugged? Everything you have told me has been recorded." You should have seen the face of that bugger.'

Henceforth the 20,000 figure would climb to over 200,000 with each telling, as an ever-swelling testament to the power of Imran's pen. Imran had grown up in a village in north India and now lived with his uncle in Calcutta. We were the same age, far from home, both new and hungry. Naturally, we became fast friends.

There are no jobs in this city, Mike told me in one of our evening addas, so every guy on every street corner is running some small-time hustle to survive. It might simply be stealing power from the overhead lines to run a paan shop, or paying off a cop to look the other way while you squat on the pavement selling aphrodisiacs. Then there were the big-men's scams: surgeons charging for bogus operations, builders constructing high-rises with sand passed off as cement, or medical suppliers reselling used syringes to hospitals. The most poignant were the cases of government callousness: the retired schoolteacher reduced to begging on a railway platform because his pension was never paid, the schools where no teachers ever appeared at all, or the babies who died in the children's hospital because not enough oxygen cylinders had been allotted.

Calamity could befall you at any moment in Calcutta. A century-old portico could fall on your head on the way to work, or you could plummet into an unmarked manhole, or be hit by a runaway bus. The only power people had in such moments was in the fury of the mob. If a road accident happened, the driver could be yanked out and lynched, his vehicle doused in kerosene and set ablaze. If a pickpocket was caught, every passer-by would get one free thwack, a consolation for all the everyday tragedies for which there was no justice, no recourse.

As a reporter at the *Statesman*, sometimes I wrote a few hundred words to make sure that an accident victim's medical bills were paid by the reckless driver who struck him. Sometimes, all it took was a phone call, identifying myself from the *Statesman*, and things would happen: justice, fairness or, more often, the water supply would be restored. In a sea of helplessness, newspaper work made you feel like you could be, as the motto had said, of service.

***

A group of students from Princeton arrived to spend their spring break volunteering with the Missionaries of Charity, the order established by Mother Teresa. I met them for beers at their hotel, the Kenilworth, just off Park Street. Even around the Kenilworth, political graffiti covered the walls, hawkers sold goods on the pavement, taxis blared their horns incessantly among crowds and stray dogs nestled in the garbage piled up on the street. Where are the nice parts of Calcutta, they asked me.

You are in the nice part!

In the days when the city was the capital of the British Raj, Park Street had been the heart of the old White Town. In theory, the White Town was manicured, administered and didn't stink. In its institutions, dogs and Indians were often not allowed. All around the White Town was the overcrowded Black Town. There the natives – both the elite and their minions – lived to serve the White Town. Even then, that division was imperfect, for the white sahibs lived with retinues of personal servants, just like the native elite. Now, White and Black Town were all jumbled together. There were no neighbourhoods that were 'gentrified', that is, cleansed of filth and the poor. The rich and the poor lived everywhere on top of one another, amid the roadside hillocks of garbage, the baying of stray dogs and the ubiquitous stench of urine. The city offered few of the escape hatches of a typical Third World metropolis. There was no historic district in Calcutta, frozen in amber and packaged to lure tourists. The whole place simply looked old. Its colonial buildings were mostly just falling apart. Even the new concrete boxes looked mildewed and ancient. For a global elite, the city had neither the comforts of modern leisure nor the easily digested 'character' that is available even in other poor cities. Calcutta was clueless about the global aesthetic – which is the same in Berlin or Shanghai – of urban cool. Its strangeness was truly strange.

The Princeton students were amused by the apparent anachronism of the city's Communist politics. It was so old school. They had interpreted the red flags across neighbourhoods, which demarcated area control, as kitsch. The students had cut their teeth volunteering in inner-city Trenton, as I once had. We never went to Trenton to walk the streets, idle on corners, to hang out. The Third World became Trenton writ large, a place without any redeeming qualities, full of people who were by turn to be feared and pitied, understood only as the recipients of redemption. Beyond the tourist sites, the places themselves, the people and their ways of being were defined by failure, by what they lacked. For the Princeton students, when they left and resumed their lives in America among the powerful and the well-intentioned, Calcutta would only be the city of poverty and Teresa, suffering and its redeemer, and nothing more.

***

Imran and I were hanging out at the pavement tea shop outside the *Statesman*, drinking sweet tea out of clay cups and smoking Filter Wills cigarettes. Imran was complaining: Every day you make the rounds of phone calls, buttering up bureaucrats and then stretch out your beggar's bowl: *Dada kichu ache*? Brother, have you got something for me? Meaning, a story to leak?

Most of the news that filled the paper emanated from government reports and press briefings. The 5 p.m. daily round up at Lalbazar police headquarters, the daily dose from Calcutta Corporation and Writers – city and state governments – the daily declarations of the ruling Communist Party of India (Marxist) (or CPM) and the non-existent opposition, the politics of he said, she said, then fires, accidents, crime. We attended the daily press briefings, noting down what the public relations officer said, and regurgitated it back in the newsroom, all digested into 400-word pellets.

The rote of newspaper work, I said, could be done by monkeys.

Meanwhile, the worlds of the city went on. Millions toiled in workshops and on pavements, never ate enough, shat outdoors, slept ten to a room or under the night sky. The stories of those people could not make the news, because they did not hold briefings or employ press relations officers. You could not call them from the cool comforts of the office to stretch out your beggar's bowl. Their everyday lives fell into no beat. They only appeared in our pages when they marched in rallies or barricaded roads, as bit players in a production of political theatre. Their voices were only heard in the fury of the mob.

In the afternoons, increasingly I joined Mike and his coterie at Chota Bristol in Esplanade, across the tram lines that ran down Lenin Sarani, for their 'liquid lunch'. No one has their own table at Chota. Instead you sidle up next to any party that has a few empty chairs and order your drinks. You pay first. Then the waiter fetches the drinks from the bar. There are other waiters at Chota who come around with trays full of snacks which are slung around their necks like hawkers on local trains. In fact, Chota has the feel of a place of transit, not repose, a waiting room to delay returning to the places you wished you did not have to go.

Chota is the last bar in Calcutta where only men are allowed. There are stories of female journalists attempting to infiltrate Chota in disguise, but none to my knowledge has ever breached the gates. It is a place full of men who are avoiding the women who await them at home. In the bustle of waiters serving Old Monk and ferrying trays of fish fingers, there is the appearance of a hall full of activity, of things happening. The shared tables at Chota are full of whispers, insider talk. And a first-time visitor may mistake this for intrigue – for back-room banter among dons and thugs, journalists communing with their sources, traders paying off pols. There are other bars and restaurants for such clandestine matters. The talk at Chota is among strangers who know each other's predicament, which does not bear talking about. No deals, no business, no work, no home – talk is of booze, and jokes about booze. Maybe a bit of banter about betting pools, cricket and races, a little wagering by men of small means who have given up hopes of ever making it out. I met a man in Chota once who had been cuckolded by his own brother. The brother was a bachelor who lived under his roof. Everyone knew the score, but they kept living in the same home – a triangle of unhappy souls, none with any hope of escape.

***

From time to time, Sir needled me slyly for not having a girlfriend. 'Go see a movie,' he would say, when I hung around the house on a Sunday afternoon. 'Poor thing. You don't even have anyone to go with.'

Whenever my mother called from New Jersey, he would say, 'When are you going to marry this boy off? He seems to be taking no initiative at all.'

He was right. I was taking no initiative. If I had returned to find a bride, then I was doing a very poor job. On some nights, I would ride the late bus home from work thinking of as many of the hottest girls from New Jersey as I could remember. At each stop – Ganesh Avenue, Ram Mandir, Girish Park – I would try to remember a face, a body, as if to remind myself that I had had another life too, another reality, which seemed to have slipped away. While I came to Calcutta and fell off the map, those of my friends from Princeton who did not become bankers or consultants were becoming doctors or lawyers. I was twenty-four years old, single and earning less than $200 a month. What was I doing with my life? Many nights I had fantasies of a life without Calcutta, of exorcising this part of myself and becoming the corporate conquistador I'd been trained to be. I had no idea what this work entailed, but in my imagination it involved cracking open emerging markets for multinational firms, assessing the creditworthiness of Latin American plutocrats, and merging and acquiring anything in sight.

In time, Sir left Calcutta for Boston, to spend a year with his son's family. My confusion became compounded by loneliness. Each Sunday I cooked rice and chicken curry and stowed it in the freezer. In the evenings I came home from work and chiseled away a couple of pieces and made do for dinner. I ate the reheated rice and chicken curry in front of the television, to fill the house with voices. It felt better than eating alone. The ghosts of my high-school midlife crisis returned to haunt me. Some nights I lay awake till dawn. On such nights I would get the food cravings of a pregnant woman from New Jersey, for cheese steaks, Sicilians and sushi, the tastes of the inaccessible America. Soon, I stopped going to work.

Manash, the local doctor, sat in a windowless room in the back of Shyamal's pharmacy. He was in his sixties, an old-style medic who still made house calls. I told him I couldn't sleep. He did the requisite check-up, measured my blood pressure, my pulse, my deep breathing under a stethoscope.

Then he said: 'When one can't sleep, does one watch things one should not?'

Manash was referring to the after-midnight fare offered by the neighbourhood cable operators on local access, the guilty pleasure of every man from fifteen to ninety-five.

I confessed to all charges. The windowless chamber began to feel airless. I felt panic that he would telephone all my geriatric relatives to rat me out straightaway.

'At this age, it's most natural,' he said. 'Those images excite the mind and make it even harder to fall asleep. Think happy thoughts instead.'

He prescribed a bottle of 'tonic', a rosewood-coloured syrup that looked like something Queen Victoria may have been prescribed by her royal physician if she complained of insomnia and confessed to impure thoughts.

Colleagues at the *Statesman* insisted I visit a psychiatrist for my woes. The shrink sized me up for about five minutes and jotted down the details of my biography. Then he asked: 'Why have you come here?'

He was wondering why anyone in their right mind would return to Calcutta.

I wasn't sure any more.

It took two monsoons in Calcutta to wash away all the idealism that I had brought across the seas. Calcutta grinds you down. There is so much to which you have to react that you have little time or energy left to act. You arrive with grand plans, and soon you are merely surviving. All around were shells of men who had given up, and given in to tedium. What I was doing was not enough, I knew. But I did not know how to do any better, or protect myself from being indifferent about the difference. I could feel myself becoming deader by the day. I felt like one of those characters in an R. K. Narayan short story, who returned home with blueprints of schemes whose absurdity in Indian conditions was somehow never detected when they were formed in America.

I took a vacation and went home to Jersey. My parents, always anxious to see me back home, asked that I stay on. After two years in the city, I had no real reason to go back. I had done my time in Calcutta. I had tried to change things and I had failed. The *Statesman* had no future. The city had no future. It had no place for me.

I entered a PhD programme at Yale University. My scientist parents were relieved. I was no longer falling off the map. Princeton, now Yale – that was a narrative that made sense, which could be explained to friends at Bengali dinner parties. For them, I had returned to the trajectory of my real American life.

PART I

Umbrella Park

One of my first memories of Durba is of seeing her in a coffee shop in New Haven, curled up in a big armchair, reading a novel. We had met as PhD students at Yale and become friends. She was studying anthropology while I studied political theory. Among our closest friends were Colombians, South Africans, Turks and Spaniards. Durba had grown up in New Delhi. Her father was Bengali and his side of the family all lived in Calcutta. Yet when we eventually became a couple, in the cosmopolitan cocoon of graduate school, our common background seemed almost incidental.

In the fall of our fourth year of graduate school, Durba went to India to do a year of field research for her dissertation on how globalisation had changed the Bengal countryside. That winter, she was living with her grandparents in Calcutta, so I planned a visit to the city. Her grandparents did not know of our relationship. So, after many months apart, we reunited in Calcutta on a street corner. She was wearing a fitted T-shirt and tight jeans. I watched her as she came up the sidewalk to where I was standing. Any public display of affection, or even holding hands, was socially taboo. We just stood there, looking at each other lustfully. In Calcutta, Durba and I felt like actors who had wandered off the set of an indie romantic comedy and onto an instructional video shoot for the Taliban. In the few zones where romance was allowed, guards were on the prowl to offset any hints of an excessive public display of affection.

'Sitting and touching are forbidden here!' a guard barked at us at a shopping arcade that seemed to exist precisely so that couples could sit in pairs and whisper sweet nothings to each other. In most places, a kiss or a caress could get you booked for indecency or, more commonly, could be used as a pretext to extort a bribe. Instead, in designated areas like Rabindra Sadan, you could sit two by two on benches with your arms around one another, feeling lustfully constipated.

One day, we were passing by what looked like an ordinary city park, except it had a ticket counter at the gate. 'What's inside the park?' I asked the ticket seller, wondering why he charged admission. 'Inside,' he said with a meaningful smile, 'is a park.'

We paid and strolled in. Sure enough, there were trees, shrubs, trails, a lake. It was a hot afternoon and initially we seemed to be the only ones there. Then, everywhere we looked, we noticed umbrellas. They were resting against the boundary wall, among the shrubs, along the lakeside – all opened up like shields. Occasionally a man would stand up from behind one such shield, zipping up his pants, followed by a woman.

Durba looked at me, amazed: 'My uncle comes here for his morning constitutional!' she said.

In fact, by late afternoon we spotted a few old timers at the park benches; some were even pretending to read the newspaper. Probably their families were entirely unaware of their voyeuristic perambulations in what we took to calling 'Umbrella Park'.

Umbrella Park typified what we felt was Calcutta's conspiracy against romance. Sex outside marriage in any form still remains unseen and is unspeakable in the drawing rooms of the *bhodrolok,* i.e. the city's dominant Bengali middle class. If you are an unmarried couple, no one will even rent you a house. Group sex, hooker sex and premarital sex are all more or less equivalent and all consigned to the netherworld of illicit activity. Just as most men smoke cigarettes, but not in front of their elders, lovers are free to do as they like, so long as they keep it out of sight. Prop open an umbrella in the middle of a public park, and well, anything goes. Or hire a boat on the Ganga, which comes with a bed and a boatman and can be booked by the hour. Or slip into one of the city's old restaurants which still have 'family cabins' – booths which can be closed off with a drawn curtain. Like lovers the world over who are desperate with longing, most couples in Calcutta seek recourse in hourly hotels. There a young unmarried couple is on the same footing with a boss and his secretary or a prostitute and her john. When police raid such places, all are equally vulnerable, because none are married.

The great Indian family remains the organising principle of modern Bengali society. It stands on two pillars: get married, have a child. The 'get married, have a child' formula is applied as widely as penicillin. Depressed, unemployed, gay? Get married, have a child. Once you have taken steps one and two, society will absorb you as a recognisable unit and extend its myriad protections. No matter the situation, a marriage can always literally be arranged between strangers, with the express objective of making babies. Defy the social structure and you may find yourself with your pants down in Umbrella Park. In New Haven, monogamy, not marriage, was the defining norm. For Durba and I, the lack of a marriage certificate had had little bearing on our shared life. In Calcutta it made all the difference.

***

It is fair to say that Durba despised Calcutta. Her hometown, New Delhi, is the India of 8 per cent GDP growth. A massive subway system and new roads and highways were being built as the metropolis readied itself to be a 'world-class city' for the upcoming Commonwealth Games, Delhi's answer to Beijing's Olympics. New Delhi is India's capital, the hub of a rapidly modernising nation state. Calcutta lacked what Durba considered the basics of her Delhi-ite life. To her, Calcutta felt closed, impenetrable, provincial. It was a city without street signs, and with many unwritten rules.

Delhi is a city where I once overheard two twenty-something women at a doctor's office debate whether Lee or Levi's jeans feel better when you squat. Until twenty years ago, Delhi was downright sleepy. The new money and power has coalesced there, but Delhi has no distinct urban culture, no sense of its own swaggering particularity, no heart. Its broad avenues and countless identical traffic circles were built on a scale fit for giants. To me, Delhi is not so much a city as an agglomeration of 'enclaves', as many of its gated neighbourhoods are literally called. Its rich residents turn inward into the privacy of their own atomised lives; its poor are largely shunted out of sight. Stop and ask for directions in Delhi and no one knows, because no one is truly of the city. Ask for directions on any Calcutta street corner and a half-dozen mustachioed men will appear out of nowhere, determined to direct you somewhere. They may offer radically divergent views on the matter, a street fight may break out as a result, rival political camps may emerge, and traffic may be barricaded for the rest of the afternoon. But it is their city, their streets, their neighbourhoods.

Since I had left, the city kept drawing me back. Each summer, I had returned to Calcutta for months at a time, without a project or a purpose, just to be there. The *Statesman* looked worse with each passing year. Most of my *Statesman* friends – those who weren't lifers like Mike – had fled to the *Telegraph* or one of the national papers that had opened up offices in Calcutta. The times were changing. India's corporate boom was trickling into the city. New jobs were emerging. Some friends had left journalism altogether to work in back offices, writing content and doing design for American corporations. On the verdant eastern edge of the city, a whole planned suburb called Sector Five had sprouted to accommodate them. Next to grazing fields dotted with palms and cows, the likes of IBM, GE and Pricewaterhouse-Coopers had built glittering glass temples to global capitalism.

Premodern and postmodern India headbutted each other as if waiting to deliver the punchline to a cruel joke. A peasant and a programmer walk into a bar ...

I met a friend who had found such a position in an American firm at Sector Five. As she was showing me around her glass temple, she took me to a room full of rolled-up mats. They reminded me of the mats that some of the Muslim waiters used to spread out during prayer times at the *Statesman* canteen.

'Are the mats for *namaz*?' I asked.

'No,' she said, 'they are for yoga.'

It was the first time I had heard anyone in Calcutta utter the word. She didn't say *joge*, which is the Bengali term for the breathing exercises and body contortions that we had all been forced to practise as kids, exercises that were the realm of old geezers, much like consulting astrological charts, performing exorcisms or taking snuff. *Joge* to us was some grandpa forcing you to sit still for fifteen minutes and pretend to 'meditate'. This avatar of grandpa's *joge* as yuppie yoga was part of a prepackaged global lifestyle imported from America.

At six o'clock, Sector Five was lined with more coach buses than South Point School. As those glass temples emptied into the streets, throngs of twenty- and thirty-somethings all lit Filter Wills cigarettes and fired off that last text message. And new masses replaced them, for another shift would start soon enough. It may have been quitting time in Calcutta, but somewhere in New York or California, the day had just begun.

Sector Five was staffed by my people, my generation of the middle class. It employed thousands of men in Moustache jeans and women in Fab India salwars, the types that in my time would idle for years, having passed their college exams, offering tutoring, writing Charminar-fuelled poetry before finally giving up or moving out of the city. Those multitudes represented something unprecedented in my lifetime. Before, I had only seen such crowds of the young middle classes at cricket matches and during student demonstrations. This was new. They were not jeering Pakistani cricketers or attacking tuition hikes. They were working. In Sector Five, on parade was Bengal's new bourgeoisie.

Sector Five was part of a larger planned suburb of Salt Lake, where Durba's grandparents lived. Salt Lake was an anti-Calcutta of identical traffic circles, unnamed streets and neighbourhoods identified only by block numbers. Its tranquillity made it a desirable area for some of the city's middle class, who moved there and were then rapidly bored to death. In 2004, after I had left Calcutta, the Indian architect Charles Correa built a mall there to ameliorate their tedium. The mall has ample steps around an outdoor fountain, ideal for sitting two by two, sipping cold drinks and dating on the cheap. It also has several 'multi-cuisine' restaurants, a Pizza Hut, a Kentucky Fried Chicken and a multiplex. On the top floor of City Centre is its food court, Hangout. There you can buy chow mein, shish kabab, pad thai and other inedible fare from half a dozen countries, just like in Menlo Park Mall near my parents' house in New Jersey. At Menlo Park, only tired shoppers would opt to eat at such a place. In Calcutta, Hangout was the capital of yuppie love.

With nowhere to go and nothing to do, Durba and I began hanging out at Hangout. I imagined the indefinite future of our relationship, at Hangout every night, sitting on brightly coloured chairs, eating bad Thai food, the jangling of blue balls drowned out by the *dhichak-dhichak* soundtrack of the new shining India. Picking at her red-curry chicken in disgust, Durba turned to me and said: 'I will never live in Calcutta.'

We had to get out, out of Salt Lake, out of the oppressive straight lines and traffic circles. One day, I mentioned to Sir in passing that a friend of mine would drop by the house. Durba arrived straight from the field, at the end of a day of interviews with bus drivers. She was dressed in a mud-coloured salwar kameez, a heavy bag over her shoulder. She looked like the kind of woman who comes to your door in India with information on how to prevent tuberculosis by consuming vitamin-fortified wheat. This was the outfit she preferred while working so as not to draw attention to herself.

The disguise had little effect on Sir. 'Make some tea,' he commanded me, 'and bring some biscuits.'

He led Durba into the drawing room and regaled her with stories of driving around in his Studebaker, and steak and whisky dinners from his post-doc years in Minnesota in the 1950s. We had tea and biscuits. Sir invited Durba back for dinner. When she got up to leave, he made sure I dropped her home. After he was rid of me, he called Ma in New Jersey and asked, 'When are they getting married?'

A few days afterwards, Sir and I were having lunch together. While nibbling his fried okra, he said, 'I'm going to a friend's house in Alipur for lunch tomorrow. I won't be back till six. There's enough food for you in the fridge.'

'Yes, Sir,' I said.

He paused. 'Enough food for two, in fact.'

'Yes, Sir.'

'You could invite a friend over.'

I nodded.

'You could invite Durba.'

'OK, Sir.'

'I'm going to a friend's house in Alipur for lunch,' he said. 'I won't be back till six.'

'Yes Sir! Yes Sir!' I repeated vociferously. I feared he would next write me a set of detailed instructions on the art of courting.

So it became easier, our Calcutta life. We began to take walks through the city. I took Durba to College Street, the book neighbourhood. We walked along the used-book stalls, looking for bargains and ended up at Coffee House, where people came not for the coffee but for adda. I had heard that writers and revolutionaries used to meet there to argue over Marx and Mao, but that was all before my time. No one had fomented a revolution over chicken cutlets in a generation. But the waiters still wore turbans, their manner was still brusque, their speed still glacial, and at Coffee House, they never ever asked you to leave. Durba and I drank cold coffee and talked politics, like lovers in a Satyajit Ray film who arrived on set thirty years too late. Then we weaved through the old North Calcutta neighbourhoods – Badurbagan, Parsibagan, Hedoa, Chaltabagan – with intimate lanes and century-old houses with beautiful wrought-iron balconies. She had never seen those neighbourhoods before. They seemed to her impossibly exotic. Peering through gullies, Durba was reminded of the Castelo section of Lisbon, which we had visited together a year before. While we had wandered the Castelo together, I told her, I had thought only of Calcutta. The jangling streetcars of Lisbon had made me ache for a tram ride through College Street.

Years before, when I had been in Córdoba, Spain, I told her, I had relished *croquetas* because they tasted so similar to our Bengali 'chops'. Upon discovering the towering legacy of Antoni Gaudí in Barcelona, I drew mental parallels to his contemporary, Rabindranath Tagore. I had been in Polokwone, South Africa and the sight of a barber buzzing hair across from a stall frying chickens had made me feel like I was back in Bowbazar. In tiny St George's, the cadences of the bus conductor's call transported me to the Jadavpur Airport minibus as it wound through Convent Road. I had stood on a street corner in Singapore at rush hour, and the sound of its silence had filled me with horror. In New York, the no-go areas of the Bronx disturbed my Calcuttan's prerogative to wander any street. I found solace in Chinatown, where they sell fresh fish just like at Maniktala Market.

As Durba and I walked together through the lanes, I wanted to make sense of the city that had escaped and defied me as a journalist, the city that exercised its magnetic pull. I wanted to walk these lanes press conferences, without deadlines. The journey down its gullies would take me into rabbit holes, each telescoping from one to the other to the other. In a city with no street signs, there is no other way to tell a story but to follow the lanes. I wanted to move back to Calcutta.

Durba is a sceptic by temperament, and about this scheme especially. Even though she did field research in Bengal, she did not have any great desire to live in Calcutta. We could certainly not spend a year living as we were, we agreed, treated like outcasts and subjected to the indignities of Hangout and Umbrella Park. If we were to live in Calcutta at all, we both realised, we would have to get married.

The first person to whom I told the news was not my parents or friends but Sir. One morning, Durba arrived at our house wearing an elegant salwar kameez, her long black hair cascading over her shoulders. Sir took us in a taxi to my grandmother's house. Like most old North Calcutta houses, the entire facade of the second floor is a beautiful wrought-iron balcony. Above it are portholes along the terrace wall, like you would find on a ship. 'What a magic house!' Durba said.

We walked past the courtyard and up the smooth, broad steps. Dida was reclining in bed, watching her soaps. Upon seeing Durba, she sat up: 'Where have you been hiding her all this while?'

Durba sat on the bed next to Dida while a servant brought tea and sweets.

Sir pulled up a chair next to the bed. 'These two,' he said to Dida, 'are going to get married.'

'*Amar tow dekhei bhalo legeche,*' Dida said, laughing. 'I liked her right away.' She repeated it several times. Then she turned to me and whispered, 'Have you given her an engagement ring?'

'An engagement?' I asked. 'Since when did we follow such American customs?'

'Don't be smart with me,' she said. 'Do you think I don't know what goes on these days?'

I led Durba up the wooden steps to the fourth-storey terrace. From there you could see the two bridges over the Ganga, the TV tower in Tollygunge, and the rooftops of almost all of the city. Maniktala, Sealdah, Moulali, Esplanade, the landscape of my former life stretched before me. For the first time in days, I felt like I could breathe. I took out a ring and asked Durba to be my wife.

Flat Hunt

In less than a year, we were back in Calcutta. I had finished my PhD at Yale. Durba and I married in New Jersey. We moved back so that I could write a book about the city, while she finished writing her PhD dissertation on transformations in rural Bengal.

Oh, to be newlyweds in India! The difference between simply 'going around', as they say in Calcutta, and going seven times round the sacred fire is quite literally feast and famine. I had been cadging meals from Sugato and Jayanti for years, abusing neighbourly affection by arriving unannounced at lunch and dinner times. On one of the first times I met Sugato, in my *Statesman* days, he was holding forth with his father on Hannibal, the ancient Carthaginian general who had crossed the Alps with elephants to attack the mighty Romans. As a student of history, Sugato was well versed in the sagas of Hannibal, Alexander, Napoleon – figures he greatly admired. All this dead learning, I had said, just to rile him. I bet he couldn't find Carthage on a modern map. Why not bet a plate of mutton biryani on it, he countered, unable to fathom how an upstart could challenge him on his Hannibal.

The general came from what is today Tunisia. My biryani came from Shiraz in Phoolbagan.

Now that I was a married man, Sugato wanted to feed us, properly. The plate was set with the standards: rice, dal, fritters and greens. Sugato had also prepared the great Bengali delicacies: a rich goat curry, thick and brown, which I loved, and hilsa fish in mustard sauce, Durba's favourite.

Sugato's wife, Jayanti, had recently loaned me Ingmar Bergman's *Wild Strawberries*. I had been mesmerised by Bergman's clarity of vision, I told them. 'That man makes Satyajit Ray look like Swapan Saha,' Sugato said, referring to the prolific Bengali director of hits like *Baba Keno Chakor*, or *Why Is Dad the Servant*. Ray had died almost two decades earlier. His son made films now. But the sons of great men were always doomed, we agreed. When was the last time we heard from Tagore's offspring?

Didn't Bengalis all suffer that stunting fate, I said. Weren't we all unable to transcend the unquestioned glorification of our dead ancestors?

'The modern Bengali has three deities,' Sugato had once declared, 'Tagore, Netaji and Vivekananda.' The poet, the liberator, and the missionary. Without the trinity, he argued, the Bengali is without a world view, culturally lost.

Stomachs bursting with goat and hilsa, our talk turned to girth. Durba was telling us all about a Roman senator who needed two slave boys to carry his overflowing belly around with him. When they had met as history students almost thirty years before, Sugato and Jayanti were both featherweights. As Jayanti pointed out, Sugato swelled with each promotion in the police service, while she, even after two decades as a college professor, remained preternaturally slim. Her husband did not protest. He went to the bedroom and returned with a volume by the seventeenth-century French writer, François de La Rochefoucauld.

'We all know it's bad to talk too much about your wife,' he read. 'It's worse to talk too much about yourself.'

***

In suburban Salt Lake or the more fashionable parts of South Calcutta there are real-estate agents and 'houses for rent' posted in newspaper classifieds. In the rest of the city, there are neither agents nor listings. There is only word of mouth. One night, as I bought a packet of biscuits from Tonoy, the grocer, I mentioned to him that I was looking for a flat. A tall man in a golden *panjabi* leaped from the darkness into the light like a lumpen genie.

'What square footage?' he asked. 'How much per square foot? How about a place in Baguiati? Want to live in Kestopur?'

'I don't want to buy,' I said. 'I want to rent. And I want to live right here in our neighbourhood, our *para*.' As quickly as he had emerged, the shimmering genie melted back into the darkness.

The next morning Tonoy called me over. 'The Party guy you saw last night,' he said, meaning a cadre of the ruling Communist Party. 'He said he can help. Those guys know every vacancy in the neighbourhood.'

'Do I have to pay him?' I asked, wary of demands from Party coffers.

'No, no. Don't get caught up in that!' Tonoy warned. 'Such touts are around by the dozen.'

The Party guy would give me the landlord's name and I was to speak with him directly. If a deal was struck, the Party would extract its gratitude from the owner. The next morning I stopped by the shop to see if Tonoy's Party guy had come through. He knew of a nice flat, 'Two bedrooms, facing the park,' Tonoy said, and would come around later with the address.

Jayanti was forever complaining about the encroachment in our para by the pavement bazaar and the ceaseless street festivities put on by the people who lived in the slum that ran alongside Tonoy's shop. 'Two bedrooms facing the park,' said Jayanti, imagining its relative tranquillity. 'How perfect!'

I, too, began to contemplate living in front of the park, taking leisurely walks and enjoying cups of tea from the nearby shop. I even began wondering if I should join the weightlifters who assembled at one corner of the green and start pumping iron.

Every evening I dropped in on Tonoy to catch up on para gossip, buy a packet of biscuits and subtly ask for the address of the two-bedroom flat facing the park. 'Tomorrow,' he always said, 'Tomorrow.'

After this routine had been repeated for a week, Tonoy became more embarrassed as I grew increasingly annoyed. It became clear that the Party was not coming through.

'How long will I wait for Tonoy's two bedrooms facing the park?' I asked Jayanti.

'Why don't you ask Shombhu?' she suggested.

Shombhu sold cigarettes, soft drinks and paan. From morning till night, he sat cross-legged inside a wooden box on stilts, which was his shop, and resembled a mini watchtower. Nothing escapes the gaze of men like Shombhu, they are a para's closed-circuit cameras.

Shombhu was sitting at his stall, making paan when I dropped by. 'Come tomorrow at ten,' he said, having heard me out. He would introduce me to someone who could help.

The next morning I went to Shombhu's paan stall. Seeing me, he sent for his guy, Ghoton, who arrived, sweating and panting, from the para club.

'Don't talk business here in front of the shop,' Shombhu said. 'Take him to your house.'

I explained to Ghoton our specifications – the number of bedrooms, the range in square footage, price and location. Did he know of any flats that would fit?

Sure, he said. There was one that would be perfect. It had two bedrooms facing the park. He could show it to me tomorrow. Of course, a month's rent would go to him, he explained, as a finder's fee. He would call us to arrange a viewing.

Durba and I grew eager with anticipation. The next morning we were having tea at the roadside shop when we ran into Ghoton. Next to him stood Toton, the handsomest fishmonger of the para.

A line of blades rose up like sails on our street each morning as the fishmongers set up shop, squatting in front of their choppers. In that formation of men shooing away gluttonous cats and adjusting their privates, tiptop Toton always looked the odd man out. Tall and lean with a strong chin and a thick moustache, he was an Omar Sharif among the hilsa sellers. Surely one day a Bollywood talent agent would turn up shopping for some pomfret, Jayanti used to say, and Toton would be whisked away to stardom.

'Toton,' I called out with pleasure, 'It has been a long time!' Toton flashed an Omar Sharif grin. Some male-pattern baldness was setting in, but otherwise he looked the same.

'You don't need a house,' he declared. 'You already have a house.'

'I'm married now,' I said, introducing Durba. 'We would like a place of our own.'

We arranged to meet Ghoton at the tea shop that evening to see the two-bedroom flat facing the park.

At 6 p.m., Ghoton was nowhere to be found. There again was tiptop Toton. He wore a black turtleneck, khaki trousers and white sneakers. His hair was oiled back, his moustache trimmed. He was gleaming. Dr Zhivago would have withered in his company.

I walked up to him to say hello. 'Let's go,' he said.

'Where's Ghoton?' I asked.

'I came instead,' Toton said.

'But ... you're a fishmonger.'

'That was long ago,' Toton said, laughing at my absurd remark.

How long have you been showing houses? I asked. Toton just walked on. He marched us to Phoolbagan, grinning all the way. In front of the Bata shoe shop, Toton asked us to wait. 'I have a nice place to show,' he said. 'Two bedrooms, next to the jute mill.'

'I don't think we want to live next to the jute mill,' I said. 'Show us the flat Ghoton mentioned, the one with two bedrooms facing the park.'

'Well, there's a cheaper flat near the railroad tracks.'

'I would rather not live near the railroad tracks, Toton,' I said. 'I want to see the flat facing the park.'

'How about one here in Phoolbagan? Just a look.'

I relented. Toton brightened, if that were possible.

A glass-eyed hunchback in a white dhoti cycled past. He looked like a character one might cast in an Indian *Alice in Wonderland*.

'Wait here,' Toton said, and went to track him down.

The glass-eyed man produced some chits of paper for Toton and then cycled off. Toton began dialling. In minutes, an energetic man appeared. The newcomer and Toton had a huddle. Toton came back to us to report: 'The Phoolbagan flat cannot be seen presently.'

'That's fine,' I said. 'Onward to the two-bedroom flat facing the park.' Toton reluctantly headed toward the elusive apartment. The newcomer accompanied us. 'Do you want to see a three-bedroom flat near the graveyard?' he suggested. 'How about a large one-bedroom next to the nursing home?'

'No, I do not want to live facing the graveyard,' I said, 'and I do not want to live next to the nursing home. We are interested in the flat Ghoton promised: two bedrooms facing the park.'

As we neared the park, I grew hopeful. The duo led us into an apartment building and trailed the caretaker up the stairs.

'This is the flat,' the newcomer said, pointing to an entrance.

Finally! Durba and I thought, as we stood with anticipation outside our two-bedroom flat facing the park.

'But you can't go in,' he said. 'The caretaker doesn't have the keys.'

Despite all of his preparation for a starring role in real estate, Toton had neglected one detail: he had no flats to show.

The next morning, Ghoton came with a little man named Babon.

'You are foreign-returned, isn't it?' said Babon. 'Why don't you buy a flat? There's one next to the jute mill I can show ...'

'Please show us the two-bedroom flat as we discussed,' I said to Ghoton, ignoring his friend.

'Can you pay six months' rent up front?' Ghoton asked.

'Can you pay two months' commission?' Babon asked.

This went on for quite some time, until the duo had exhausted their arsenal. Then I said, 'Let's stick to the agreement: one month's commission for the two-bedroom flat facing the park.' Babon agreed to show us the flat the next day. We were to meet him at the Bata shop in Phoolbagan, and we were to be on time, he insisted, so as to catch the owner before he left for work. Durba and I once again began imagining morning walks and evening tea, waking up to the luxury of green space in our two bedrooms facing the park.

The next morning, we cooled our heels outside the Bata shoe shop for forty-five minutes. When Babon arrived, he spotted us from the State Bank across the street, waved us over, and started off in the opposite direction. Weaving through the rush-hour crowds, we followed him like ghouls in a Pac-Man game. When he stopped, we were a long distance away from the park.

'This is not the flat facing the park,' I said to him, stating the obvious while panting from playing catch-up.

'No, but it is in a nice area,' he said, which was true. We stood outside a four-storey building with large balconies while he darted inside, then around the corner, then back out. 'Actually, the owner has left for office.'

Never mind, Babon said, he had a better two-bedroom flat in Beleghata.

'I don't want to live in Beleghata,' I replied.

'Oh it's not in Beleghata. Just up the road here. Please come. As it is you have walked all this way.'

As the sun rose higher, we walked deep into Beleghata and entered a nondescript apartment complex. Babon huddled with the caretaker. 'This complex has a generator, its own deep tubewell, twenty-four-hour security . . .' Babon narrated. 'The flat is a thousand square feet, and the rent ten thousand rupees a month.'

He led us up the stairs, and into a shoebox.

'This flat is not a thousand square feet,' I said.

'Oh yes. A thousand square feet.'

'It is no more than six hundred square feet.'

'Of course, it is one thousand "Superbuilt".'

What are you saying?

'Superbuilt,' he repeated, meaning counting the stairs and the common areas, it all added up to 1,000 square feet.

'This flat is no more than six hundred square feet,' I said.

'Without the stairs it's eight hundred and fifty.'

'No more than six hundred.'

'Well perhaps it is seven hundred and fifty.'

'It is at most six hundred and fifty square feet,' I said.

'Well, yes.'

'The rent cannot be more than seven thousand bucks.'

'Well, OK,' he said. 'You liked it then?'

We did not like it at all.

'Would you like to see one which is twelve hundred square feet?'

He led us to another flat in the same building, which was 700 square feet at most, and declared that we could pay 9,000 rupees a month to live in it.

Perhaps these were the only flats we would find, Durba and I began to mutter to one another. We were no longer even in our para. Our hope of a two-bedroom flat in front of the park seemed a distant memory.

Babon made some calls. Then he said, 'I have the keys to the first flat. Let's go.'

In the noonday heat, we followed him back to the original apartment. Reprising his cameo, the glass-eyed man rode into our lives again. He mercurially cycled past us, doubled back, retrieved some papers from his breast pocket, and slowly cycled offstage. Durba and I have since developed many sinister theories about him, but little is known of his true provenance. Babon scurried first to the cyclist, then into the building, then to a group of men lingering at the bus stop. We waited.

'Actually, the caretaker has gone to lunch,' he said. There would be no viewing today. 'But I have a nine hundred square-foot flat just around the corner for fifteen thousand bucks.'

One of the men at the bus stop planted himself before us. He had a 1,500 square-foot flat next to the nursing home for 7,000 bucks, he said.

'I don't want to live next to the nursing home,' I said.

We were surrounded by a group now. Various voices came at us:

'How about twelve hundred square feet for fifteen thousand next to the graveyard?'

'Fourteen hundred square feet for seven thousand in Beleghata?'

'One thousand square feet for nine thousand facing the park?'

'Facing the park?' Durba perked up.

'Two bedrooms, all marble,' a moustachioed man said. 'I can show it right now.'

We had been wandering the streets for a couple of hours. We were hungry, hot and more than a little disoriented.

'Durba,' I said. 'Let's go home.'

'But he has a two-bedroom flat facing the park ...'

We went home.

In the evening, Toton called several times, pledging to show us flats next to the graveyard, the nursing home and facing the park. A month's rent in commission would have paid for a lifetime's supply of his hair products. We began screening his calls. Men I did not know started following me when I crossed the main road yelling, 'Brother,' followed by various combinations of square footage and house rent. They all had two-bedroom flats facing the park.

Even Jayanti's teenage daughter seemed wiser than I. Sipun shook her head sagely and said: 'How did you ever fall into the clutches of brokers!'

***

I am a North Calcutta guy. When my foot touches down on Maniktala More, no matter how late at night or how much flooding there is, when I see the familiar clock tower of Maniktala Market and the naked bulbs of the vegetable sellers squatting on the footpath outside, I know that I am home. From the clock tower, a couple of blocks west past Amherst Street is Dida's house. Go the other way, past Raja Dinenda Street and across the Beleghata Canal and you are in Bagmari, where we used to live with my other grandmother, my father's mother, until I was six. Three more bus stops and you are in Kankurgachi, at Sir's house. In Calcutta, my life is circumscribed by that one-mile radius from Maniktala More. But Durba and I gave up on trying to find a house in that radius. We began to look south.

South Calcutta, as everyone knows, is more hep than the older North. It was built later than the North and so became poor later than the North. It is true that the women get better looking the farther south you go. But otherwise South Cal is no less dirty or diseased than the most pestilent corners of the old Black Town. The thought of shifting to South Calcutta left me cold. We would have to start over, find a new tea shop, a new sweet shop, new neighbours, a new para in which to dwell. It was something unnatural. In Calcutta, it is not as if we have an India Gate like in Delhi, or miles of beach as there is in Bombay or Madras. Our riverfront is full of warehouses and crematoriums. There is no place to relax, but in our own paras. In Gariahat, Gol Park and other desirable parts of South Calcutta, we were shown apartments by brokers who acted recognisably like agents in the US. But to plant anchor in Gol Park, to seek all the reference points anew, would be to almost start afresh in a new city. It did not appeal to me at all.

One afternoon, I noticed an ad online for a flat that was in our para. The rent well exceeded our budget, but I called anyway. The man who picked up spoke in English. He had come from Canada he said, and wanted to find a tenant in two weeks while he was visiting his mother in Calcutta.

'Durba, please let us charm these people,' I said, when we went to see their flat. When we met, Abhishek was wearing shorts like a tourist. He had grown up entirely in Zambia, where his father had worked as an accountant at an emerald mine. During all that time, his father had nurtured the exile's fantasy of return. He had bought an apartment in one of the new buildings in Kankurgachi and fitted it with end-to-end marble, air conditioners in every room and extensive custom-built woodwork. After a lifetime abroad, he and his wife had planned to retire in style in Calcutta. Then he had a heart attack and died. The flat had never been lived in.

Abhishek had an elder brother, who lived in New Jersey. Their mother, Mrs Bhattacharya, now lived alone in their family house in Beleghata. She looked like a woman thrust into the public sphere far too late in life, with no forewarning. When we met, she said to me: 'You remind me of my elder son. I keep telling him to find a nice Bengali girl and get married.'

Then to Durba, she said: 'You're so lucky to have found each other.'

Mother and son showed us the recessed lights and the hideaway bookshelves that Abhishek's father had built in the apartment. The flat was much bigger, and snazzier, than we wanted. But they were willing to rent to us for far below their asking price. We were very desirable tenants in Calcutta, since we could be counted on to leave.

As the son turned over the keys, he said, 'Please. Take good care of this place.' He had placed his father's legacy in our trust.

Nimtala

D ida had just returned home from the hospital on the day we went to see her, having sailed through perhaps her hundredth heart attack. Her eldest son Ashoke was visiting from California. My own parents had come from New Jersey. Jayasree, my eldest aunt, had come down from Ballygunge in South Calcutta. The house was full of people and Dida was in fine form. All afternoon, we laughed and swapped old stories about the family. I had always heard that the Kerrs had once owned fourteen houses, three gardens and umpteen ponds – or was it fourteen houses, three ponds and umpteen gardens? – indeed all of DL Roy Street.

'Was it true that the family once really had fourteen houses?' I asked Dida.

'Oh, that's true,' she said. They really did own everything around here once.

'Did you ever see any of that wealth?'

'Me? No, that was before me.'

On the walls of her room were full-length portraits of our ancestors: my grandfather, his illustrious brother the barrister, who had changed the family name from the Bengali 'Kar' to the Scottish 'Kerr' to attract more British clients – and their parents.

'What did *he* do for a living?' I asked her, pointing to the stern studio photograph of my great-grandfather.

'What do they ever do, those rich men's sons?'

So his father – my great-great-grandfather – had been a rich man?

'So, I've heard. He was dead by the time I arrived.'

At some point in the 1800s, the Kars must have migrated from their native village in Burdwan to Calcutta, and amassed a small fortune by doing business with the British traders in the new capital. The family lore was that we had a shipping business, which ended when an English client insulted one of our ancestors. The proud Kar kicked the Englishman's cargo – all thirteen boatloads of salt – overboard. Perhaps that boot was the beginning of our downfall. Dida was certain that the house she came to no longer had a thriving business. In fact, it was only half the size it is now. The family's fortunes improved after her marriage, Dida said, when Dadu and his brother's law firm prospered. She said that when his brother won a landmark case for the Star Theatre, his father went straight to the Star's proprietors and collected payment in cash before his son blew it on booze and dancing girls. That was how the second floor of the house was completed, and a third floor built.

At that time, Dadu even owned two cars. Then his brother suddenly died, and the British left India. As Dadu's fortunes dwindled, he sold one car, then reluctantly the second, an Austin. He could not countenance it being driven by someone else, so he sold it for scrap, and kept the steering wheel. When I was a kid, the Austin's steering wheel gathered rust on the terrace, where we would play with it.

We kept talking until it was dark outside, and the evening cricket match had come on the TV. As Dida grew distracted by the action on screen, I crossed the threshold and said, 'I'll come back tomorrow, Dida, and we'll talk about the game.'

The next morning, my uncle called. Dida was dead.

* * *

A caravan of cars followed the hearse down Beadon Street, to Nimtala. The great poet Tagore had gone home this way by open car in '41. Mobs of Calcuttans had flooded the streets, snatching at his corpse. By the time he reached the crematorium, he hardly had a hair left on his head. In my childhood, lesser mortals were carried on foot. *'Bolo Hori, Hori Bol, Bolo Hori, Hori Bol,'* the carriers chanted in rhythm with their footsteps as they nimbly wove through traffic, like stretcher-bearers from the wars of yore. *Bolo Hori, Hori Bol, Bolo Hori, Hori Bol.* In the name of God, in God's name. In the name of God, in God's name. Now the poor hire lorries and flatbed trucks. For the middle classes, there are air-conditioned hearses.

I followed the hearse in the office car of the city's chief engineer. In the back seat of the air-conditioned sedan, the hearse's siren became a pleasant muted muffle. The chief engineer called the crematorium to let them know we were coming, and arranged for us to cut in line. Our grandfathers had been cousins, it turned out. 'If I can't do such a thing for my own grandmother,' he said to me, 'Who can I do it for?'

The crematorium at Nimtala looked like a post office. Located on the banks of the Ganga, it was a squat one-storey red building with clumps of people trailing out to the street. Each group carried a corpse covered with a white sheet but for feet and face. Eyelids were blanketed with basil leaves, nostrils plugged with cotton wool, mouths taped shut.

Aside from Chief Engineer, there were dozens of moustachioed men in our party whom I did not recognise. There were only three of us from Dida's immediate family: my two maternal uncles, or *mama*s, and I.

We unloaded Dida's body from the hearse and hoisted the cot on our shoulders. Chanting, *'Bolo Hori, Hori Bol,'* we skipped past the corpses of the less well-connected to jump to the head of the queue. The funeral pyres, like the one where Tagore was cremated, were built of wood upon the riverbank. In wind, hail or rain, the corpses would not burn. The electric ovens are more reliable, at least in theory. There were four such furnaces at Nimtala crematorium, but as at any government agency in Calcutta, two of the four counters were always closed. You had to line up and wait.

When our turn came, we hunched down and lifted the cot to our shoulders. The great ugly machine opened its maw to show its red insides. We set my grandmother on the guiding rails. *Bolo Hori, Hori Bol.* I put some shoulder in to push her through, and said goodbye as they shut the oven door. Five thousand years of Hindu ritual, I thought to myself, have come down to this monstrosity, bereft of both the solid comforts of tradition and the merciful euphemisms of modern life.

The incinerator would take forty minutes. Lining the roadside were shops for buying bed sheets, garlands and other necessities for a Hindu funeral. Between the funeral-provisions shops were tea shops, each beckoning us with benches laid out on the road. Mejo Mama – my middle uncle – bought a round of tea for everyone in our cortege. Mejo Mama was once the 'right hand' of the local member of parliament of the Congress Party. The MP had died a few years ago and Mejo Mama had whirled out of politics. But his friends and former underlings in the Congress were still his social world. The Congress guys slurped tea out of clay cups and reminisced about so-and-so's time, when there was a queue of a dozen bodies and only one furnace running, or the time they had to wait three hours in the April heat, or another time, when it was pouring monsoon rain and the middle of the night, when no one went home till 3 a.m. For these men, 'giving shoulder' to the dead was like a profession. Everyone had a wealth of stories of this sort, except me, the cremation virgin.

I was the only grandchild present to lend a shoulder when Dida died. In Delhi, Dubai, London, Chicago and California, my cousins would be woken up with phone calls to be informed of her death. You never knew how to act or feel when the phone rang in America with news of a death on the other side of the world. You went to the office, the gym, the grocery store, had dinner with friends – the world went on despite your private loss. You kept going as if nothing had happened, as if the papers you had to grade or the meeting you had to attend were more important than death. In your quiet moments, you felt only solemnity and guilt, thinking you should be feeling something, doing something, weeping maybe, lamenting without knowing how. That is how my cousins would be mourning, staring at computer screens, going through the motions, not knowing how to feel. I felt sorry for them. I was sipping tea in Nimtala, present in the moment at the centre of our world.

The eldest son performs the last rites to ferry the soul to the next world. Dida worried that when she died, the body would have to be kept in an icebox in Taltala until Ashoke, my Boro Mama or my eldest uncle, arrived from California to do the last rites. It was a common fear of the middle classes, for whom the city had become a retirement home, and worse, a necropolis that the young had abandoned. But when Dida died, Ashoke was down the *dalan* in Dadu's room, just as she would have wanted. You might even say, as my mother did, that she had willed it that way.

After tea, we returned to the crematorium and descended the steps at the back of the furnace. There, the ashes and the navel were handed over in a clay bowl. The navel is the only part of the body that does not burn, the source of life carried forth into the afterlife. Bowl in hand, my uncles went down the steps to the Ganga. It was midday, low tide, and marigold garlands, plastic cups and Coke bottles were all caught in the muddy riverbank. Ashoke folded his hands in prayer amid the detritus. The silent chimneys of Howrah stood solemnly across the broad river. In the distance, passengers were boarding a ferry to cross over to the other side. The navel floated into the river. Our cord to Calcutta was cut. Dida was going home.

***

Calcutta is ten and a half hours ahead of New Jersey. The morning after the cremation, jet lag jolted me awake before the muezzin's first call. In the years when I worked as a reporter at the *Statesman*, on countless nights my bouts of insomnia would be calmed only by the distant call to prayer. The azan would lull me to sleep.

Dawn breaks in an instant along the Tropic of Cancer, as darkness transforms to glaring haze. At 7 a.m. the city is bright but still manageable. The sounds of the street are muted and your clothes do not yet adhere to your body like duct tape. I set off to walk the streets.

A collection of 'morning walkers' had gathered outside Niranjan's Sweet Shop. Their broomstick legs rested on a bench barely holding up their lollipop bellies.

'One boy, dancing with two girls,' one said. '*Eeesh.*'

'It feels so . . .' said the other, searching for an English word to express the gravitas of the Bengali sentiment, 'uneasy.'

They were having tea out of clay cups served from the cubby underneath the cigarette stall, debating the merits of the various dance competitions now on Bengali cable TV. They lamented the rise of Bollywood's Hindi music over Bengali standards. Why not more of Tagore's songs? one said, and the others nodded. Their shorts suggested they had left home with the stated purpose of walking, while their bellies suggested that they often succumbed to the pleasures of adda at Niranjan's Sweet Shop.

Niranjan had just lit incense and was saying morning prayers to the deities hanging on the shop walls. That meant the frying was about to begin. 'It will be ready soon,' he said, recognising me. 'The vegetables have already been cut.'

I had a *bhaar* of tea and watched the street. On that February morning, mothers in fluttering saris marched their doddering progeny to the bus stop. The mothers carried the backpacks, hoisting them by the shoulder straps like Lyndon Johnson used to lift his cocker spaniels. The children's heads and faces were covered with ski masks, which in Calcutta are called 'monkey caps', their bodies tightly wrapped in full-sleeved sweaters.

When I was a kid, there was a persistent old beggar on this stretch of Kankurgachi. He had a stubbly beard and a square five-paisa coin plugging one ear. The man would leap on and off buses at the stop, asking for change. There were no beggars here any more. How did that man die, I wondered?

Had it happened right at the bus stop? Who had carried him to Nimtala?

The vast pot of potato curry arrived from across the street. Niranjan's son-in-law squatted down next to it and set up the burner and the *karahi* on the sidewalk. He rolled the dough for *kochuris*, first between his palms into little balls, then into flat circles with a rolling pin. One at a time, they went into the fryer. Flat and flimsy like paper, initially they folded into themselves. In the hot oil, they slowly straightened out, floating like loungers in a swimming pool. As the oil crackled underneath, they swelled to become pot-bellied, like ourselves.

'To eat or to take home?' Niranjan asked. To eat. His son-in-law scooped four *kochuris* out with his strainer and placed them on a steel plate, ladled a serving of potato curry and passed it to me. With my index finger I perforated a belly. Steam rushed out. I waited a few moments, savouring the aroma. Then I tore a crunchy piece off, ambushed a potato in the curry, and ate.

Kochuris were the saving grace of my insomnia spells when I worked at the *Statesman*. At 6:30 a.m., the *Statesman* would be flung through the balcony like a baton. Sir would bring in the paper, and seeing me awake, would send me to fetch *kochuris*. Off I would go to Niranjan's, tramping through the bazaar, past the line of fishmongers, feeling a great sense of superiority for being up before the morning fish-buying crowd. In a half-hour's time, I was triumphantly walking home through the hubbub of the morning market. On my person were twenty of those air-filled round *kochuris*, stuffed with dal, and a half-dozen *jillipis* curled and bright like neon signs, warm and stuck together with syrup. When you got it to go, Niranjan put it all in a paper bag, the potato curry in a clay bowl covered with newspaper and sealed with a rubber band. By the time I reached home, the curry made stains on the newspaper like the faded maps of empires.

***

Mejo Mama had had a premonition that this might be Dida's final winter. It was at his urging that Ashoke came to see his mother from San Francisco. Now his ticket would have to be extended till the funeral. In Boro Mama's time, indeed, even in mine, the foreign airline offices were clustered around Park Street and Theatre Road, the heart of what had been 'Sahib Para', or White Town. The Lufthansa office was now in one of the glass towers that had emerged as if out of nothing in the last ten years in Sector Five. Even a decade ago, the traffic there comprised cycle vans and water buffalo. Now, when offices vanished in Cleveland or Kalamazoo, they sprouted up in such towers in Gurgaon, Bangalore and Sector Five, Calcutta.

Sector Five was not my uncle Ashoke's Calcutta. He was a creature of the north – North Calcutta, the Black Town – of neighbourhoods nestled in lanes and alleys, where the old Bengali business families had built houses with long verandas, courtyards and dalans. In Sector Five, where were the paras, the lanes, the double-decker buses? Where could you, while waiting for the bus, catch a whiff of roasting meat, dodge into a gully and emerge with a scrumptious beef kebab roll? Boro Mama looked up at the towers and said, 'This might as well be Singapore or Syracuse.'

He had heard that his fellow architect Charles Correa had built a mall in Salt Lake and wanted to see it. After my summer sojourn with Durba at Hangout, I was well acquainted with City Centre. I remembered that there was a café on a terrace of the mall. The view from up there is all water tanks and traffic circles, but among the swaying palms there was a pleasing late-afternoon breeze. We sat down at a table on the terrace, ordered cold coffees, and felt more human.

Correa had called upon the city fathers to develop a waterfront on the Ganga, I told my uncle, but no one seemed to have heard his call. 'The city that was built in British times is crumbling,' I said. 'Along the Ganga, the old British warehouses are shells of empire, reminders of an age when we were needed by someone somewhere.'

The old houses in the north, like ours, with verandas and dalans, are being bulldozed. And everything everywhere that is coming in their place is concrete box upon concrete box upon concrete box. A metropolis crumbles, and what rises instead are pigeonholes of 650 square feet. Boro Mama sipped his cold coffee through a straw and listened quietly.

The Bengal Renaissance, Tagore, Vivekananda, Netaji, I thundered. Was there a movement or an idea that had shaped modern India which had not been forged in the furnace of Calcutta? Here we were, in the twenty-first century, latecomers to India's back-office boom, seeking solace in the tasteful construction of a shopping mall! Where was the vision to imagine the future of the city in a new way?

'Do you know, in my childhood there used to be a traffic sergeant stationed at the Vivekananda Road crossing near our house?' he said. 'It was always a white sergeant. That is what we grew up with.'

It was that way with his whole generation. A white sergeant always stood guard at the intersections of their minds, always checking that their thoughts were in order. How could such a generation dare to dream differently?

'It will happen,' he said, 'but it will take time.'

The Ambassador crawled through traffic as we made our way back into the city. As we passed Maniktala Market, Boro Mama looked longingly down Amherst Street toward his alma mater, and said: 'Do you know that I didn't have a first name until I started going to St Paul's, in class six? That's when they named me Ashoke. But I wanted a different name.'

Up till then he had been called Khoka – kiddo. From a young age, Khoka had a talent for drawing.

'I wanted to be called Chitro,' he said. 'Chitro Kerr.'

Chitro Kar. '*Chitrokar*' meaning 'artist.'

'Did you ever make your desire known? To name yourself?' I asked.

'*Bah bah!*' he said, tilting his head back with laughter. 'In what world are you living?'

Young Ashoke, not Chitro, started school at St Paul's on Amherst Street and went on to Bengal Engineering College, which had just started an architecture department to meet the needs of newly independent India. Art was not a form of self-fashioning that was acceptable, not for the first-born son needed to prop up an edifice of declining fortune. Architecture was more practical. Soon thereafter, he would be on his way to the University of California, Berkeley. The year then was 1959, when my mother was still in frocks.

***

When Boro Mama went to Berkeley to study architecture, Indian students were rarer there than vegetarian restaurants. There, he became renowned for his red convertible, called Rosinante, in which, the story goes, Alice Waters bummed rides to visit a boyfriend who was in prison for his activities in the Free Speech Movement. Ashoke was young, single and in Berkeley throughout the whole of the 1960s, swept up by the dervishes of change. He lived in America for fourteen years, we were told over and over as kids, just like Ram had spent fourteen years exiled in the forest in the Hindu epic, the *Ramayana*. Then, like Ram, he returned to his rightful place at the head of his kingdom in Calcutta. Ashoke was our ideal immigrant. He went, and better yet, he came back.

His masters thesis at Berkeley had been on building affordable middle-class housing in Calcutta. He packed his bohemia into wooden crates and headed home. His plan was to ride the double-decker bus to Jadavpur University twice a week to teach while he started his own firm. Boro Mama moved into the third floor of the family house. His first renovation project would be his home.

Presiding over the ancestral home was his father, who had not worked regularly since the 1950s. Instead he wore pajamas and an undershirt all day, arguing against the headlines in the newspaper. First Independence, and then Communist rule. For

Dadu, history was going in the wrong direction. The dark and dank of a rustic Bengali existence was preserved in that house. In the courtyard, water was collected in open storage tanks and then hauled in buckets for baths. When the monsoons came, rain poured straight through the house, the winds sweeping water into the bedrooms.

Above the courtyard, Ashoke built a fibreglass cover that would keep the rains out and let the light in. He sequestered the water tanks behind arches that looked like a Roman aqueduct and refinished the courtyard with bright yellow mosaic floors. He created an overhang above a part of the courtyard and built a narrow kitchen where natural light filtered through a wall of latticework. He broke down walls in Dida's room to let in more air. He decorated the house with mirror-work vases he had brought back from Mexico. He installed new beams to create a garage with a grand entrance. Its red wrought-iron gates were installed across the facade of the house. Stenciled in wrought iron was the house number, 12, in a font reminiscent of Charles Demuth's *I Saw the Figure 5 in Gold*. There was no other entryway like it in all of Calcutta. At each point – the fibreglass, the mosaic, the beams – Dadu fought him. At each point Boro Mama prevailed. Dadu's room he left alone.

On the third floor, he built a study with narrow windows that looked as if they belonged to a medieval turret. There he planned to draw blueprints, and to paint. This was the capstone of his efforts: a room of his own. My mother finished writing her PhD dissertation in biochemistry in that study. Soon thereafter, with Boro Mama's support, she married a fellow graduate student in that house.

The study Boro Mama built soon merged into the entropy of the house. In the monsoon it leaked; in the summer it baked. He had neither the energy nor the calm to draw blueprints there, much less to paint. It quickly became another area of the house that was overtaken by the detritus of sprawling decline, the place where you would find a rusted steering wheel, or a full-length mirror of Belgian glass. In short, it became another corner that the adults had abandoned to our enchantment. There were piles upon piles of things: things collected at auctions Dadu used to frequent – toys, figurines, photographs; things given as gifts, bought by relatives who were long dead, forgotten or excommunicated. Just as Dadu had assiduously collected the hand-me-downs of the British, amassing a trash heap of empire, so too we revelled in his hand-me-downs, the rejects of a Bengali bourgeoisie in decline.

In my childhood, the garage Boro Mama built remained empty. He never bought a car. Other sisters had to be married off and architectural commissions came slowly. The kitchen, where my aunts laboured, was cramped and airless. It had clearly been designed by someone who had never cooked in Indian conditions. In time even the fibreglass roof began to tear, unable to withstand the monsoons. For nine years, Boro Mama fought with his father, his brothers, his wife, his colleagues, his city, his society. Then he gave up.

Calcutta had changed. The Communists were now in power. Contracts became ever more beholden to politics. By the early 1980s he was thoroughly defeated by the nexus of developers and politicians in Calcutta. The money had also dried up. There was no work for him to do.

When Ashoke left Calcutta for good, out of a locked closet emerged life-size canvases, vast Rothko-esque works which he had painted during his Berkeley years. They were the first abstract paintings I had ever seen. They were a vision of the life he had imagined in that study. They went back with him in a wooden crate, back to Berkeley where they belonged.

***

'Pushed out, that's what it was. What else would you call it?' Dida used to say. Dadu wouldn't let Ashoke stay. From the start, with each window replaced, each beam moved, each gate installed, there was resistance, reproach, and always in that house, the reverberations of men yelling. She always blamed

Dadu, but it wasn't just that. The city had become less hospitable for our kind – the educated, the ambitious and the mobile – and once we leaped abroad, we seemed to develop amnesia about the reality of Calcutta's conditions. This was why Ashoke left again, why my parents left. It was why I had left, and thousands of others were shown the door.

Among Dida's seven children only Mejo Mama and Jayasree, my mother's eldest sister, were left in Calcutta. They were barely on speaking terms. Periodically they would launch complaints to Boro Mama in California to settle their sexagenarians' feuds. When I had been in the city the previous summer, Jayasree sat me down on the day bed in their Ballygunge house and said her brother had threatened to kill her. 'Right there in front of Ma he said this,' she said to me.

'He's probably not going to kill you,' I had offered.

'Who knows, with his political contacts.'

Within days of Dida's cremation, Shampa and Joy, Jayasree's children, arrived from New Delhi. Joy and I were a year apart. Over the years, we had competed against each other in hundreds of rounds of 'hand tennis', table tennis and bare-knuckle fights. He came up the stairs and embraced me in the dalan. We had shared a magical childhood in that house. Dida's room, which was the family gathering place, was about 25 feet long, with ceilings that were at least half as high. In our childhood, it felt like a great hall. There, we played hand tennis, a game of our own invention, kneeling and swatting rubber balls with our bare hands on a court drawn out in chalk. On the same floor, during family feasts we would sit in rows and eat elbow to elbow, our mothers crouching to serve us food. After we had finished, Dida and her daughters and daughters-in-law would sit together with all the pots around them – for there was no one to serve them – the *handis* of rice and dal tottering on the craters of the moonscaped floor.

Most of our days in that house were spent running all through the three floors, as if the running was an end in itself. The centre of the house was Dida, constantly in motion, cooking, clearing, cleaning, sending servants off to market, slipping a tenner in this one's pocket, in that one's blouse, for *singaras* from Ganguram's, for medicine to soothe a grandson's cough. It was a vast anarchic empire, which she navigated and kept afloat.

Our pictures of Dida's room are always formal: group photos of rows of brothers and sisters, one row seated on the floor, another on the bed, couples together, with Dadu and Dida in the centre. Where are the photographs of the graffiti we wrote in orange chalk on the pockmarked floors? Where are the pictures of the daybed that sat in the middle of the room, all mesh and tangled springs like a giant Brillo Pad, and a refuge to generations of mice? Where are the images of the late afternoons, with curtains drawn, when the grandchildren lay down on Dida's giant square bed like fish at Maniktala Market? The floor turned into a bed then too, with mattresses unrolled, pillows and bolsters for the mothers. No one napped, they talked instead, until perhaps at four a quick wink, and then soon enough, the curtains pulled back, the French windows opened to the cacophony of the veranda, hot tea and biscuits for the grown-ups, and for the kids the welcome sounds of wickets being planted on the street below, beckoning us to a cricket match. Why did no one photograph those moments, which exist only as fading images in my mind?

Joy and I went up to the terrace, away from the gaze of grown ups, to have a smoke. Joy took a drag of his Filter Wills and declared: 'This is the last time I enter this house.'

***

Soon the rest of Dida's children were back home at D. L. Roy Street, sitting together in her room for the first time in decades. Manjusree, my middle aunt, arrived on an early morning flight from Dubai. Jayanti, the youngest aunt, flew home from London. My parents were already there. Mejo Mama hosted the family uneasily. What could we have to say to each other?

Mejo Mama had assiduously memorialised the past. There were pictures of the whole family at my youngest aunt's wedding, the portrait in oil of my aunt, Parna, Mejo Mama's wife, who died in a road accident far too young. Dadu was featured too, in a black-and-white photograph with a colour touch-up. A picture from a brunch in my parents' New Jersey house had been transposed to Calcutta. Our IKEA table had been Photoshopped out and replaced with the round marble tabletop of D. L. Roy Street. In a Bhai Phota photo, taken in Dida's room, our English cousins had been Photoshopped into the back row from a photo taken in London. Stalin removed his purged enemies from old group photos to sanitise the past. Mejo Mama was like Stalin in reverse, adding instead of subtracting, to fashion a false memory of utopia, when we were all united together at home. In reality, that frenetic house of my childhood had long been emptied.

There were thirteen days between the cremation and the funeral, a sea of empty time. Durba and I drifted from room to room, unsure of where we belonged. Between the four sisters there was a loose bond forged from living in a house of male grandiloquence, though each now occupied a separate universe. Lounging on Dida's bed in various states between sitting and lying down, the four sisters spoke in overlapping conversations that fell on each other like untangled threads. The men sipped tea at the round marble dining table – where my cousins and I had played hundreds of games of table tennis – surrounding the space with silence. More tea, fitful bursts of talk in starts and stops, words to fill up the space, to pass the time. Stories began to slip out, of Manjusree jumping off the veranda onto bales of hay, of Jayasree unleashing cockroaches on house guests, the sisters sneaking out to the movies – tales long forgotten, and tales repeated countless times before. The house of mourning filled up with laughter. It was the one thing Dida had always wanted, my mother said, the family together and joyous.

The funeral took place in a Vaishnav prayer hall inside a gully off D. L. Roy Street. The prayer hall was older than our house, and Boro Mama remembered accompanying his aunts there when he was a boy. At the funeral, he sat next to the priest, dressed in a dhoti, to give offerings and mumble incantations. Those of us who were Dida's kin took turns, like a supporting cast, performing truncated versions of the same act. Then we ate in rows, sitting on the floor, elbow to elbow. The food was served the way it used to be in Dida's room when I was a boy. I am not a believer, and yet by the afternoon's end, I felt that lightness of which Hindus speak, a thing like detachment which is called *boirag*.

We carried the flowers, the wreaths and sweets from the prayer hall down D. L. Roy Street, up the stairs past the dalan and into Dida's room. Servants were beckoned to make tea. We lingered after tea, staying on into the evening, talking and sharing each other's company. There were two French windows that led from Dida's room to the long veranda that looked out onto the street. Between the two fluttering curtains was Dadu's portrait. On a side table below, Mejo Mama had placed a portrait of Dida. Each day, new visitors brought garlands to adorn the photograph. Each evening, a lamp was lit in front of the portrait while Dida's soul was still in transit from this world to the next.

'Ma will get us tonight,' Mejo Mama said, lighting the lamp one last time. 'All this laughing and joking. Tonight, Ma's coming for us.'

The next day would mark the end of a fortnight of mourning. After two weeks of abstaining from eating meat and fish, from wearing stitched clothes, the brothers would resume their normal diets, their normal lives.

'I'll die when you all go,' Mejo Mama said. 'What will I do with myself?'

When we left that evening, the family gathered on the long veranda. They were all there, my uncles and aunts, and my cousins Shampa and Joy. Everyone fitted comfortably, with their elbows resting on the balustrade, as they watched us go. I imagined all the times we had stood on that veranda anticipating arrivals and waving goodbyes, and wondered if Joy was right, if this would be the last time we shared this house together.

'Let me take a photograph,' I said to Durba, stopping in the street.

'Wait!' I yelled up to my family. I fished out my camera and clicked. It was too dark.

'Tomorrow!' Durba yelled. But of course, the next day the circle was broken, life was un-paused. Soon everyone scurried back, to Delhi, Dubai, London. My parents returned to New Jersey and my uncle Ashoke went home to California.

Flyover

Mr Basak was buzzed up to our flat by the guard downstairs. Sumitro arrived, wearing a T-shirt and trousers, green bag on shoulder, and ever more rings on his fingers.

'*Nomoshkar!*' he said, palms pressed together in salutation. He made himself at home and started talking about the new money in Calcutta, and their poor taste in furniture. They either want to return to feudal four-poster beds, he was saying, or this Delhi Punjabi fashion of covering everything in marble, indicating the decor of our flat. It is like we are incapable of developing tastes of our own.

Sumitro was an artist. We had become friends almost a decade earlier when he used to moonlight as an illustrator at the *Statesman*. The art market in India had exploded in the years since I lived in Calcutta, largely buoyed by the growing coffers of black money among India's new business class. The new money had been kind to him, enabling him to become a full-time artist.

When I was a reporter, on Sundays I often went to his house, to eat *luchis* for lunch, and have adda. His higgledy-piggledy paintings of that time were full of social commentary and cutting humour, with juxtapositions of mythology and the popular culture of the street. In those days, armed with a water bottle and a snack in his nylon shoulder bag, he would set out to uncover the hidden old worlds that made up the city.

Calcutta was a collection of the whims of the communities who migrated there and became rich – Bengali and British, as well as Armenian, Jewish, Marwari, Bohra Muslim, Haka Chinese, Punjabi, Gujarati, Portuguese, Greek and Dutch. In Phoolbagan, within walking distance from my house, there were graveyards of Jews and Greeks, Chinese and Bohras. Their tombstones told of men and women who had been born in Budapest and Constantinople and died of cholera in Calcutta. Sumitro and I had walked the city's streets, discovering airy Sephardic synagogues, Armenian churches, and temples to the Jain saint Mahavir. In the old Black Town, we had mingled with the deity-sculptors among the lanes of Kumortuli, communed at the annual chariot festival at the Marble Palace and witnessed clandestine human hook-swinging during the Raas festival.

Off Beadon Street, in Satubabu and Latubabu's Bazar, so named after the two nineteenth-century Bengali business titans who founded it, metal hooks were dug into the backs of penitent believers and then hung from what looked a great balance scale made of bamboo. Then the hooked swung high in the air around the pivot of the scale, like giant gliding birds. The practice had been banned for nearly two hundred years, but it still took place, surreptitiously, in the heart of Calcutta.

A few nights after his first visit, I received a text message from Sumitro: 'Going to Rath in Bowbazar tomorrow. Coming?'

The police had blocked off the intersection at Bowbazar. Powdered and bejewelled housewives ate noodles in neatly pressed saris under the naked bulb of a chow-mein stall at Bowbazar crossing. The local toughs were promenading in the garish panjabis that local toughs keep for special occasions. Parked on the road was a house-sized chariot – or *rath* – featuring the gods Balaram, Subadra and Jagannath. Two priests were seated inside, receiving offerings on behalf of the holy trio before their journey. The Rath Jatra festival was literally a chariot journey of the three gods to their grandmother's house. Among mortals, the festival was commemorated with a parade in which groups of men pulled chariots carrying the deities down city streets so the gods, too, could promenade. Those house-sized raths were accompanied by pint-sized ones too, made by children out of tinsel and wood and wrapping paper, built like two-foot-tall skyscrapers, and tugged along to the beat of a rat-a-tat drum.

Bowbazar was Sumitro's childhood para. As a kid, he had pulled his rath down its streets, and remembered the lanes by the houses of the girls who once lived there and had long since been married off. He led me down a lane to a sweet shop. It was a place so obscure that only a boy who grew up in that para would know it. The two shelves inside the shop's glass display case were lined with trays of various types of sweets. Two flies buzzed inside. The magnification on the glass made both the *shondesh* and the flies look bigger than they were. Try the *gujia*, Sumitro said, and ordered two. I sampled the sweet, and felt the bliss of those two flies in the showcase.

The lanes of Bowbazar were the entrails of the nineteenth-century capital. Once, these lanes were choked with magnificence, the spectacles of mercantile wealth. Sumitro knew which mansions brought out the biggest chariots. Together, we went inside mansion after mansion. One had green tile work, Italian mosaics, an altar with cupids and vines in relief. In its courtyard was a chariot decked in silver and gold, but the family did not have the wherewithal to organise a parade. We went into another house, in Crouch Lane, where the offerings for the gods also now took place indoors. 'Forty years ago, when I was a boy, they had cockatoos and macaws and beautiful pedigreed dogs,' a man with salt-and-pepper stubble staggered toward us to lament. 'This year they didn't even take out the rath. The whole house has been divided and subdivided.'

On Hidaram Banerjee Lane, the Deys' mansion housed a chariot with a silver throne for Jagannath. They were also not taking out their rath. But their cousins, two doors down, were readying their chariot. 'My father was one of seven brothers. From this corner to that corner was our homestead,' the scion said, showing a block of attached houses that stretched across half a football field.

At one time, the Deys used to have tea warehouses. But the British did not continue their lease and their workers made off with the loose tea in their sandals. The Deys used to have large marble platters with handiwork from Agra. All sold. Their remaining possession was a chandelier that they believed to be worth over $200,000. That too would soon be sold to a dealer on Ballygunge Circular Road. They could have been my uncles, these men, retelling the mythical past as if it were yesterday, holding on to appearances as all the accoutrements of status slowly disappeared. Are we perpetually in decline, I wondered, only so that we can lay claim to more glorious antecedents than our present status betrays? After all, on the face of it, they looked just like every other Bengali middle-class family, like us. When I was growing up, my family acted as if their wealth had been momentarily misplaced, as if until just the other day, we had owned the whole block on D. L. Roy Street. The reality that I saw was a family clinging to one house, kept afloat by remittances from California. And yet, as my aunts keep repeating, we come from declining Old Money, we are actually somebodies. For proof, simply look at our four-poster beds and Victorian wardrobes, and our grand old house. It was the same story we told ourselves as a city. You may only see squalor now, but *once*, once Calcutta was the fabled City of Palaces.

The Deys' rath had brass-domed turrets. The domes used to be made of copper, they told us, but the copper domes were stolen during a wedding a few years back by a servant, who purportedly used the money for an elaborate rice ceremony for her newborn son. Then the child died. 'We didn't put a curse on the child,' the scion of the family said. 'We didn't want him to die.' But it just went to show, he explained, that their deities were very potent.

The family lived in Garia now, on the southern edge of the city. But today, on Rath, they reprised their roles as feudal figures. They became somebodies. Their rath was fully bedecked and ready to roll. A brass band led the parade.

A whole procession of people followed, pulling the chariot slowly as it lit up like fireworks on Kali Pujo night.

***

I had put off the inevitable. It was time to go to the *Statesman*. From Kankurgachi, I clambered on to a minibus headed to Dalhousie. Our siestas and rice bellies notwithstanding, there is one trick that we all learned at a young age: how to get on a moving bus. First, I latched on to the handle with my right hand. Second, I started running till I caught up to the speed of the bus. Third, while running, I leaped with my right foot and clambered onto the foothold. A sea of hands, like octopus tentacles, dragged me inside, into a sponge of flesh. There was only room enough for me to stand exactly as I was, as the mass of bodies surrounded me like a coating, buffering me against all the jerking and potholes that were part of the commute. I surrendered to the mass.

I reminded myself to be vigilant of pickpockets. If you are pushed from the right, check your left pocket. Sudden jerks to the left, then check your right.

'Maniktala, Girish Park, Ram Mandir, Medical, Bowbazar, BBD Bagh,' called the conductor's helper to passers-by, banging against the bus as if it was a bongo. 'BBD Bagh! BBD Bagh! BBD Bagh!'

From another end of the mosh pit, the conductor ran his thumb repeatedly across the stack of tickets in his palm to make a familiar rustle, like the sound of a thumb being run along a deck of cards. The rustle was his calling card. 'Ticket, ticket, ticket.'

'*Dada,* ticket*'ta korun,*' I yelled to the conductor.

Above the passengers' heads, I saw his free hand lunging towards me.

'Dalhousie,' I said and paid.

The hand took my money and disappeared. Meanwhile the helper on the footboard kept wooing more passengers –

'BBD Bagh, BBD Bagh, BBD Bagh!' – as if the amount of squeezing you could do inside that metal box was infinite. On the bus we went from being individuals to a mass.

The conductor's headless hand lunged again with change and a ticket. The bus made its way up Central Avenue, past the Ram Mandir and the Calcutta Medical College, picking up speed. As it turned into Ganesh Avenue, I started my slow roll to the gate. '*Dada, nambo!*'

When I got off the bus, squeezing out through the narrow space with a throng of office-goers, I felt like I was being reborn.

'*Bah bah! Banchlam!*' we all said, as we dislodged from the mass and reverted back into being individuals again. We were sweating even though it was March, and momentarily disoriented, but only momentarily, because this is of course a lifetime's habit and soon even the creases on our shirts and saris recovered as we made our way back into the gentility of bhodrolok life. Every morning, but not before 10 or 11 a.m., thousands thronged to Dalhousie and Esplanade, the office para, jammed into passenger trains and buses. The hardest part of having an office job in Calcutta, my father used to say, is getting to work and back.

***

Dalhousie is big British buildings, the police headquarters at Lalbazar, the railways headquarters at Fairlie Place, the palatial Governor's House, the General Post Office, and Writers' Building, which takes up a whole city block. Writers' was the administrative centre of British India when Calcutta was its capital. From here they ruled their Raj.

In 1930, three Bengali revolutionaries named Benoy, Badal and Dinesh entered Writers' Building and shot dead the British inspector-general of prisons, a terrorist attack to strike at the heart of colonial rule. It was at a time when Bengali boys were throwing bombs and firing revolvers to make Bengal ungovernable. After India became free in 1947,

Dalhousie was renamed Benoy Badal Dinesh – BBD – Bagh. The governor-general's residence became the home of the governor of West Bengal. Writers' Building became the administrative centre of the state of West Bengal, and the office of the chief minister of West Bengal. As Orwell might have said, the pigs turned into humans.

It was inside Writers' that I was once trapped in the health minister's cabin by the health minister himself. My friend Esha and I were reporting on the conditions of the state's mental asylums – places where patients were abandoned like Spartan children on a mountainside. They were abysmal institutions, lacking medicine and with electro-shock machines which malfunctioned fatally. My crime had been to ask the minister, a medical doctor, how much of the health budget was devoted to mental health. The minister would not say. I then repeated the question and, realising the minister would provide no information at all, closed my notebook – apparently too noisily – to get up and go. The minister, who seemed unperturbed by the deaths of patients, was apparently insulted by my expression of impatience. He locked the door and called security.

There were two of us, Esha and I, and so it had been difficult to saddle me with a false charge or take me to a police station and rough me up. Besides we were reporters from the *Statesman*. He let us go. Instead, he sent a huffy letter to the editor saying I had insulted him. Esha could verify that the insult had comprised my asking the minister a basic question to which he had no response. To the editor's credit, after making some perfunctory enquiries, I was left to do my job. Nothing came of the minister's note.

Months later, when seventeen children had died in forty-eight hours at the Bidhan Roy Children's Hospital due to a lack of sufficient oxygen tanks, the same minister would preside over a press conference and say that the mortality spike was absolutely normal, statistically speaking. Didn't the press understand statistics?

It was amazing to think that this same Communist government, when it first came to power, had actually shut off the air conditioning to the minister's offices in Writers' Building. This same government whose ministers now rode in motorcades, who threatened reporters, and refused to take responsibility for the death of babies in its hospitals.

They had arrived from modest, monkish origins. A stone's throw from Writers' is Dacres Lane, home to the famous 'cabin'. There are four tables inside a dim cave of a room. A long bench is placed like a hurdle on the side of the street. There are two stoves on the street with kettles going. Back in the days when the undivided Communist Party offices were around the corner, Jyoti Basu – the man who would run Bengal as chief minister for the first two decades of Communist rule – used to haunt this shop. Outside, customers sat next to each other on the long bench, enough room between them to set down their teacups and saucers and plates of toast. The tea is strong and sweet, the toast is thick, buttery and sprinkled with sugar.

It is not clear where Dacres Lane ends and its legendary cabin begins. The lane is the cabin, and the cabin makes the lane. All of Dalhousie is like that. The sidewalk is literally a movable feast. Along Fairlie Place there is hardly any place left to walk. 'Chow-mein *hobe*, rice *hobe,* veg momo, chicken momo, fried rice …' hawk the pavement maitre-d's. The biggest draws are the fish curry and rice 'hotels'. A few benches and narrow wooden tables are laid out under a tarp. The food is served from metal trays full of crimson *kalia*, the big fish heads pointing upward like Aztec pyramids to the sun.

Just off Old Court House Street, hawkers sell black plastic wristwatches in shallow tubs of water, exactly as fishmongers keep live *magur* fish in the bazaar. 'Yashika brand,' the vendor announces, 'waterproof.' Next to him, at a pavement stall, is a wall of suits hung up for sale. Beside the suits, someone is selling pirated VCDs advertising bare-breasted white women on the covers; next to him there are sellers of packets of mothballs, colourful combs splayed like pick-up sticks, doormats, ashtrays, mugs, flashlights, immersion heaters, magnifying glasses, banned Chinese toys – every possible human need can be met during lunch hour.

Under blue and violet tarps, typists sit outside the railing of Bankshall Court. Touts ask 'Attestation? Stamp Paper? What do you need? I have it.'

In front of the General Post Office, spread out on the pavements, are forms of all kinds: employment forms, admission forms. Between them sit the *munshis,* or letter writers. They look like semicolons marking a long sentence.

The *Telegraph* office is on a side street on the way to the Chinese shoe stores on Bentinck Street. In its lobby, magnetised ID cards hung from everyone's necks, and security cameras abounded. The city's number-one English daily had a policy against adda. No one could come up into the newsroom, so all conversations took place below on narrow Prafulla Sarkar Street, which doubled as the paper's parking lot and café. The *Telegraph* was ascendant. The paper's owners had recently built white columns on the building's facade, which made it look like a stage version of the *Statesman*. The *Statesman*'s decline had only infused the *Telegraph* with talent. Every third person passing under the columns on Prafulla Sarkar Street was someone I once worked with at the *Statesman*. I could stand outside their office and be plied with endless free cups of tea.

Imran now worked at the *Telegraph*. He and I were hanging out on the sidewalk, drinking tea, resuming our addas of old. He was telling me about how the jute mill closings had affected the *munshi* business outside the General Post Office. The *munshis* used to write out the money-order forms for the illiterate Bihari jute-mill workers. But the workers had no remittances to send home any more. Maybe you could put that story in your book, Imran said.

***

From the outside, Statesman House looked the same. Its Georgian columns and wrought-iron gate were there, its grandeur intact. I noticed a new sedan in the sickle-shaped driveway. In the past, only the editor-in-chief, who had ruled the premises as a kind of feudal lord, had been allowed to park in the drive. But two years ago he had passed away.

I walked through the heavy revolving doors into the foyer and hit a wall of darkness. Where were the classified department's bustling counters to the right, or the counters to the left where officious receptionists signed in visitors and doled out passes? Where were the 'cash' counters, behind metal bars, where generations of dour Mullick men, frowning beneath their fair moustaches, had dispensed salaries at month's end? All that was gone. Behind what had been classifieds I could make out a banner covering the whole wall, which said 'Emaar', with an Orwellian slogan below. Emaar are the people who own Burj Tower, in Dubai, the tallest building in the world.

There were a couple of men at a table at the foot of the stairs, writing out visitors' slips. They looked like squatters in a zamindar's abandoned mansion. 'Only Michael *saab* and I are still around,' Topiwala, the liftman said, as he offered me a ride upstairs.

I took the unlit stairs instead. I remember those wide stairs from the first time I went to the *Statesman* as a teenager, and the impression they had made of institutional grandeur. I remembered, too, the days of union wranglings when I worked there, when these stairs would be plastered with posters and slogans which dubbed the management 'dogs'. Now cobwebs crept down from the ceiling. Red paan stains crept up from the floor. They were unswept, with empty cigarette packs strewn everywhere. No one was even keeping up appearances.

Each floor was like ascending a new circle of hell. Upstairs, where Advertising had once been, walls had been broken through. Doors had been torn down. Exposed brick was everywhere. There was no longer the halls full of clerks in accounts, nor the canteen where the waiters read *namaz*. There was no longer the office where the editor sat, nor the corridor where his peon polished his walking stick. The building was completely hollowed out. On the third floor, the photographers' room, the reporters' room, the library, the offices of the assistant editors, Mike's old corner office that doubled as an *adda khana*, nothing remained. It was all empty, exposed like the innards of an abandoned factory.

The blown-out walls opened up to another vast emptiness below. Behind the main building used to be the workers' residential quarters. Management had installed the presses below the quarters, I remembered, to try to drive out the workers. Now, the presses had been taken off-site; most of the workers had been offloaded too. The whole building was gone. An area as large as a softball field was growing wild. It was all turning back into jungle.

For two years, this place had been my home in the city. And now it was gone.

The top floor, where the editor had maintained a penthouse, had been converted into the truncated offices of the newspaper. Suku'da, the layout designer, was playing a video game on his computer. It was the game where a paddle slides along the bottom of the screen hitting a bouncing ball against a wall. The game is called Breakout.

'That game is so old,' I said.

'Everything here is old,' he replied, without taking his eye off the screen.

I ran into Mishra, one of the last peons, now on the verge of retirement. Mishra had always been a stock-market geek. He was explaining to me the effects of the American crash on Indian equities. It was too complex for me to understand, but he said he could make 300 here, 300 there and scrabble together about 10,000 rupees a month. 'You can't depend on the *Statesman* any more,' he said. They had not paid salaries for five months.

In the last few years, I was told, circulation and ads had dropped precipitously. The story was that management was waiting for a few more clerks and peons to retire before salaries could resume. But there is hardly anyone left to let go.

'Some people are affected by the recession,' one of the staff photographers told me, 'And others are making the most of it.'

Meanwhile, the bottom three floors of Statesman House had been leased out to the Dubai-based developer, Emaar, which planned to build a shopping mall there. 'Buy a newspaper and get two underpants free,' said the wags in the nearly vacant newsroom. But then, for some reason, the construction had stopped halfway through, creating Dresden instead of Dubai below.

Mike's office was locked. He was inside, smoking.

The AC was cranked up so high that it was freezing in the unventilated cabin. Mike sat in a frigid haze of smoke. 'I'm not supposed to smoke in here,' he said, 'but who can be bothered to go to the balcony every time?'

He was sneezing. He said he had had malaria the previous week, and then proceeded to tell me about the horses he had bet on over the weekend. 'JB and I were at the races ...' he said and he was off, narrating one of his equestrian tales that none of us ever understood.

Soon we were sitting in a bar called Relax, under pink and blue lights, in an alley off Abdul Hamid Street. Popcorn arrived and red-eyed men dug in. A skinny Marwari man with almond eyes was telling dirty jokes. At the table was a mix of Bengalis, Marwaris, Biharis and Anglo, drinking beer, whisky and mostly watered-down rum.

Behind us a table full of men had just come back from the races. When I worked here, the race men always returned to the newsroom on Saturday afternoon, having nearly won something. There was a race in Calcutta that Sunday. I mentioned I had read about races which were fixed.

'We've seen horses bleeding from the nose,' Suku'da said. No matter what anyone said, he was sure the jockeys sometimes pulled back the harness so tight that the horse was restrained, not allowed to go as fast as it knew it could.

Mike was telling a story about a 'Naxal psychopath' in his old neighbourhood who stabbed a player from a rival football team on Bright Street. Mike now lived in draughty quarters on Grant Street, above Dr Lama's Sex Clinic, by Chandni Chowk Market. It was within spitting distance of the *Statesman*. His wife's Burmese forefathers had stayed there since the 1800s, so the rent was less than 250 rupees a month. The landlord wanted them out. He was offering around 2.4 million rupees, Mike claimed, but they were holding out till he offered 3 million.

Like most Anglo-Indians, he had family in England. He went there once, years ago. When he came back, one of the peons asked why he did not migrate like most of his kin. 'Baba,' he retorted in Hindi, 'but who can I call *behenchod* there?'

He claimed he had a property in England, and received rent in pounds, hard currency. Who knows whether this was true. Mike's fibs never had malice in them as much as wishful thinking. They were a way to order the world as it ought to be. When I first started at the *Statesman*, Mike told me that every Sunday morning he took his two young sons on a tram-ride adventure to an unfamiliar part of the city. They would hop on any tram they wished, ride as long as they fancied, and then hop off to explore a new neighbourhood. And so, Sunday by Sunday, para by para, father bequeathed his legacy, his city, to his sons. It seemed wonderful, and of course it was utterly untrue. These days, Mike rarely ventured past Esplanade. Once an ex-colleague invited him to join the faculty of a journalism school in Thakurpukur, a forty-five-minute tram ride away.

'I'll need a bloody passport to go to Thakurpukur,' he said, turning down the offer. For him, it may as well have been Timbuktu.

Relax was a new pilgrimage place for Mike and Suku'da. When I worked here, my favourite bar was a place called Majestic which had high ceilings, French windows and liveried waiters, and felt to me like a continuum of the *Statesman*. Mike and Suku'da's favourite haunt was Chota, just across Lenin Sarani from the Statesman House, where women were not allowed and the booze was the cheapest in town. Until the 1970s, the great avant garde figures of their generation treated Chota Bristol like their office. I had heard that Ritwik Ghatak used to come to Chota, in the years before his liver finally gave way.

'I met Ritwik Ghatak once, in Chota,' Mike said, 'in 1975.'

'Ritwik said to me, "I like the look of this boy's face."'

'I said something back and he said, "*Dhamnami hocche? Bhalo bhalo.*" Playing smart, eh? Good good.' Mike did a surprisingly good imitation of Ritwik's slurred, gravelly speech.

Ritwik Ghatak was a contemporary of Satyajit Ray. But while Ray became internationally renowned as the colossus of Indian cinema, Ritwik completed only a handful of films, which were mostly commercial failures, and died of alcoholism. Ray and Ritwik: both brilliant, one buoyed by the city, the other broken by it.

Ray was from an august North Calcutta line. Ritwik was from the verdant fields of East Bengal, which the political logic of the twentieth century had made into East Pakistan and then Bangladesh. In the 1950s, Ray's first film, *Pather Panchali*, had run to empty theatres until Cannes anointed it with a prize. Then, seeing Ray's films became a form of middle-class sacrament. The city's public embraced Ray, to bask in reflected glory, for Ray had garnered awards in the capitals of Europe. No such luck for Ritwik. His final film, the semi-autobiographical *Jukti Tokko aar Golpo – Reason, Debate and Story* – trails a group of social castaways through contemporary Bengal, led by a 'finished-off' intellectual with a bottle of country liquor always in his shoulder bag, played by Ghatak himself. It is a film about failure, intellectual failure, moral failure, artistic failure. The city had been Ritwik's subject, the heartless city that never made him feel at home.

The door inside the bar marked 'Toilet' led to the back alley, where there were urinals installed against a wall, for peeing al fresco. We were in the open-air toilet out back and Mike was telling me about his family's properties in Saidpur, now in Bangladesh, in Whitefield in Bangalore, the wonders they once possessed, his great-aunts and uncles with names like Bernice and Reginald ...

The gulf between the world as it ought to have been, and the world as it turned out was so vast. This is the devil's city, I thought. We are ground down by frustration, our ambitions thwarted, left with nothing but tales of remorse. Ritwik was clairvoyant, and could not bear it. Who would have told Mike and Suku at age thirty – the same age as I was now – hotshots at the biggest paper in the biggest city in India, that this would be where their ship would run aground, at Relax, drinking Old Monk rum, peeing against the wall?

We teetered out through Crooked Lane and took the shortcut through the building that had two caged parrots. As always, Suku'da whistled into the darkness and the parrots whistled back. We were back out by the dazzling marquee of Paradise Cinema and into the careening headlights of Bentinck Street. Suku'da was already far ahead of me, nimbly leaping onto the foothold of a moving bus. The way Suku'da jumped on and off buses was the way they lived – instinctive, reactive, unplanned.

'Kush, come by often,' Mike called out behind me. 'You're writing about Calcutta; you'll learn more here than anywhere else.'

'When I enter the *Statesman* now,' I said, 'it breaks my heart.'

'Think of me,' Mike replied. 'I feel that way every morning I walk in. And I was eighteen and a half when I started.'

***

Sumitro and I were sitting in the last row of a minibus, bouncing from Ballygunge to Rajabazar, travelling northward up the city's spine.

'Who are you writing for? Why are you writing about Calcutta? And whose Calcutta?' Sumitro fired those questions away with his piercing intelligence.

The minibus was idling in the traffic snarl at Park Circus when Sumitro asked: 'Why is it that representations of Calcutta seem unchanged for centuries?'

The first Europeans who came to these shores had refused to get out of their boats. They called the settlement in the

swamp Golgotha. Most accounts of Calcutta since have hardly
varied. Calcutta to Western eyes was the epitome of urban
hell, the Detroit of the world, the punchline to a joke: your
room looks like the slums of Calcutta. Every visitor, even those
who came to slum it in Calcutta, seemed to take away the same
city, I said, the same crumbling mansions of colonial elites,
graveyards full of dead Englishmen who could not survive the
tropics, and everywhere, like a disease, the suffering of the
poor. Ultimately the slummers all fell back upon the idea of the
urban hellhole, the city as a place of darkness and death. Even
Louis Malle and Allen Ginsberg arrived as gleeful voyeurs and
headed to the cremation ghats at Nimtala, as if the last rites
were a morbid spectator sport, as if they came from places
where no one died. Had any of them ever been to Nimtala
to give shoulder to the dead? Had they any idea how it might
have felt to be on the other side?

'Where in the representations of Calcutta is the jumble-
tangle human clot of Baguiati?' Sumitro asked, its intersection
throbbing at every hour of the day with careening autos
and overtaking buses and people rushing away in every lane
clutching polythene bags from Ma Sarada Stores full of moong
dal and Surf Excel?

'Why not the Maniktala Market?' I said, 'With its
fishmongers seated on their concrete plinths like sultans,
surrounded by mounds of hilsa, pomfret and koi.'

'What about all the shops and little village-worlds in
Bowbazar, in the heart of Calcutta?' Sumitro asked.

At Sealdah, the bus roared up the overpass we called 'the
Flyover'. To our right, the suburban train station was bright
with fluorescent lights; its orange neon signs were flashing
SEALDAH, SEALDAH, SEALDAH, alternately in English,
Hindi and Bengali, as they have eternally in my memory. To
our left, the evening rush at Baithakkhana Bazar spilled out
onto Bowbazar Street. Three centuries ago, the English trader
Job Charnock, who is said to have founded the city, had sat
under a banyan tree there and turned it into his parlour, hence
the name Baithak Khana, Living Room. The street was barely

visible now, covered over by the evening vegetable sellers squatting with their goods spread out on tarps, backlit by the beckoning glow of the jewellery shops that lured in wedding shoppers. Under a canopy of sulphur street lights stretching all the way to Dalhousie, was the perpetual human parade.

From atop the Flyover, Sumitro surveyed the sweeping view of all that was revealed below, and asked, 'Where has anyone represented all this?'

PART II

PART II

College Street

When I worked at the *Statesman,* many of my Sundays were spent among the bookshops and stalls on College Street. One day, I leaped onto a moving tram bound for College Street as it crossed Vivekananda Road. All traffic headed northward, except for the tram. Like a matriarch who refuses to die, the tram tore through pedestrians, rickshaws, cycle vans, Tempos, buses and lorries, defying the whole march of progress set against it. It lurched past rows of jewellery shops, then rows of shops for machine parts, then the string of shoe stores, before finally reaching the permanent book fair of College Street. I had arrived.

I followed three cows as they sauntered into a lane, sampling the local garbage along the way. Like all Calcutta's cows, they belonged to someone, but right then it did not matter whom. I just stayed with them. A way down, a man was lifting his dhoti revealingly. I trailed him to the 'bathroom'. He stood in front of one of the two public urinals. To his left, where a third urinal would have been, was a gully, precisely the width of a urinal stall. I entered the phantom urinal. About ten feet in, the gully hooked left and extended into a long straightaway. From the other side, a bicyclist approached. Behind him were three other men. Now there were others behind me, blocking my retreat. Even in this straw of space, I was in a crowd.

The bike got stuck. The cyclist backpedalled; the three people behind him backtracked too. I followed them all the way to the other end and emerged on Tamer Lane.

In the late 1300s a lame descendant of the Mongols named Timur rode down from Samarkand to sack Delhi, Baghdad and Damascus, conquering most of Asia along the way. His exploits terrified and fascinated Europeans. In English 'Timur, the Lame' became bastardised as Tamerlaine or Tamerlane. 'Tamerlaine,' rhymed W. H. Auden, was once 'A synonym in a whole armful, of languages for what is harmful,' who now survives 'as a crossword anagram, 11 Down – A NUBILE TRAM.' In Calcutta the Tartar became a cartographical pun.

I walked past the presses to the dead end of Tamer Lane and took another gully, again L-shaped. At its crook was a publisher's office. A dark, old man sat outside on a stool. I walked straight past him through a doorless frame. To my right were three blue doors. I entered the second blue door into a windowless room. Every Wednesday afternoon for the last forty-eight years, writers and poets had been meeting there for the Wednesday afternoon or *Budh-Bikel* Adda. Ranjan Gupta, the nominal leader, was seated at the back of the room. He had oiled white hair combed straight back and a moustache so sparse that the first few times we met, I thought it was a whit of stubble that the poet in his absent-mindedsness had neglected to shave. In deference to age, everyone calls him, Ranjan'*da*.

'Ranjan'da, do you know what Bidhan Roy said about doctors?' asked Sabyasachi, poet, editor and perennial sufferer of the runs. Bidhan Roy was a famed Calcutta physician and Congress Party leader, who became one of Bengal's first chief Ministers. 'If you get sick, by all means, see a doctor. Because the medical profession must survive. If the doctor writes a prescription, by all means visit a pharmacist. Because the pharmaceutical industry must survive. And if the pharmacist sells you medicine, by all means avoid taking it. Because you too must survive.'

'You, me and Jyoti Basu have the same thing: irritable bowel syndrome,' an elderly woman said, referring to Bengal's first Communist chief minister. 'Jyoti Basu had chicken and whisky every night. And just see, still going strong at ninety-six.'

'Oh that,' said her friend, 'that's nothing but giardia. I take a course of Metrozil every three months. That's what you need.'

'Chicken and wheeskee,' IBS repeated. She said whisky like a wheeze.

'Jyoti Basu never drank anything below Scotch,' someone countered.

'And why should he,' asked Giardia, 'coming from such a prosperous family?'

'Well, I can't afford Scotch every night,' said Sabyasachi.

'Try aloe vera in a sherbet,' one man said.

'Have turmeric with milk,' offered another.

'But eat onion fritters one day,' said IBS, 'and you're suffering for the next three.'

'Oh that, that's nothing but giardia. I take a course of Metrozil every three months, that's what you need.'

'The doctor fixed my blood pressure, my cholesterol, my blood sugar. He's quite a doctor,' said IBS. 'But when it came to this, he said, "Madam, this disease I cannot cure. It will be your companion forever."'

'Oh, that's nothing but giardia—'

'Drink boiled water.'

'Try *isabgol*.'

'But brother, my problem isn't that it doesn't come,' said Sabyasachi, 'it's that it just comes and comes.'

'Sixty years after Independence,' said Giardia, 'and still our government has done no research into our indigestion.'

'It should be a priority, sister. But until then try chicken and wheeskee.'

'Give everyone some tea!' said Ranjan'da. A *cha*-walla had materialised, kettle in hand, from the gully. He poured a round of salty black tea into tiny, jiggling plastic cups which looked like hot Jell-O shots, and passed them out.

The room had filled up. Nilkashyap began reciting. He was in his sixties, neat in a crisp panjabi and gold-rimmed glasses, his moustache dyed jet black around his overbite. He looked like he always had his mouth full.

'*Tar shoriri bibhongey jorano thakto dagor shahosh ...*' Her physique was wrapped in great courage ...

'We've heard this before,' someone heckled. Nilkashyap persisted, unperturbed.

'*Shonkher moton tar gayer rong.*' Her complexion was the colour of a conch shell.

'Did she have a skin disease?' another whispered.

'*Bhanj kora muthoe dhorey rakhto gurh rohossher dana.*' In her fists she held concealed the seeds of mystery ...

Everywhere else, he was known as Panchanan Chatterjee, a retired State Bank assistant manager. At the adda he became the poet, Nilkashyap. He had three books of poetry, which were currently on sale on College Street.

'I went on a trip to Rajasthan and she was my guide,' he said. 'I had to write a poem about her.'

To meet Nilkashyap was inevitably to confront his poems. '*Montromugdher moton shey shonato Rajasthani doha,*' he started reciting without provocation, '*Jaisalmer, Chittor, Rana Pratap, Paddabatir golpo.*' She would entrance us with her Rajasthani verses. Tales of Jaisalmer, Chittor, Rana Pratap and Paddabati.

'I love history,' he said, 'See how I've taken her into the past, into the age of the Mughals, in the poem?'

And he was off: '*Tar ingitey kothar pakhira eshe boshto itihasher shiritey, ekantey akta chobir moto.*' At her signal, the birds of language would sit at the stairs of history, pretty as a picture.

Henceforth every time I went to the adda, Nilkashyap looked up at me after reading a poem, tilted his head sideways and said, 'You liked it, yes?' as if he had just guided me through the wondrous fortresses of Chittor and Jaisalmer and expected payment in awe.

The walls at Budh-Bikel are lined with wooden benches. Perch at your own peril; some of the benches are missing legs. Between the benches are red plastic stools. When the room is full, it looks like the inside of a Calcutta minibus. Many of the men and women there have travelled on trains and long-distance buses from neighbouring towns and suburbs. Like daily commuters, they have grown to know each other. Here they live a second life of literature. At the adda, they are recognised as their other selves, as artists. The need to talk and the need to be heard: what human desires are more universal than those?

Ashok Lakhdar was in his forties. His sparse stubble looked like sugar crystals flecked across his face. '*Moner moto mon jodi pai*' he sang, '*jurtey boshi mon tatey*.' If I find a soul mate for my soul, I stop to join myself with you.

'There isn't a person alive who hasn't written two lines of poetry sometime,' he said. 'You start writing as a teenager; perhaps it's the sight of a girl ...'

For most it stops there. Writing is a phase you grow out of. Those who persist start seeking literary contacts. Through legwork and chance, some land up at an adda.

'Here some will encourage you, some will laugh at you, but this is a step.'

The ultimate goal was to publish a book. But only the rare publisher gave book contracts on College Street. In many cases, no advance was paid at all. Most books were published with the writer bearing some of the cost.

'The joy and happiness from creating poetry can't be explained,' Lakhdar said. 'But poetry is very cruel.'

In the battle of attrition that is daily existence, the men and women of the adda were some of the survivors. Albert Ashok was also about Lakhdar's age, part of the younger cohort. He said he ran away from home as a teenager, travelled a thousand miles and somehow made it to Calcutta. His business card said he is a 'writer', 'artist', and 'human rights activist'. The card said Albert has written several children's drawing books and also has six blogs. Most of the attendees at the adda brought handwritten manuscripts on chits of paper or in old executive diaries. Albert Ashok always came with a printout.

'Are you on MySpace? Facebook?' Albert asked. 'It's very important for networking.' He had lots of online friends from the US, UK and Brazil. 'They want to see my writings and paintings.'

'Joy Goswami has the most online friends,' he said, referring to the best Bengali poet of his generation. 'He can reach a thousand people with one message.'

Ranjan'da opened his diary to read a poem: 'Each day, I live for ten minutes.' It was about the brief interlude in each day when he was able to read poetry. It was, in fact, one of the poems I liked best from the adda.

After all the poems were read, he said, 'If I have to say one poem today was very good, I should say it was mine.' Despite hearing piles of purple prose and poetry about women, flowers, fortresses, sunsets and Tagore, often in lethal combinations, he had a sense of humour. Then he said a word or two about several of the writers, encouraging all without regard to merit.

***

From Tamer Lane, along the gully that leads to the phantom urinal, there is a house with a mosaic mural of two birds with Bengali lettering. The letters read: 'Little Magazine Library'.

Sandip Dutta sat in the front room of his family home. He looked a bit glum, half asleep, just like a Calcutta doctor in his chamber. Not one of those hotshot cardiologists who rake in millions, but more like the para homeopath without much business.

Surrounding him were bookshelves piled high with stacks of documents. Behind them was a glass showcase covered with pasted magazine clippings, like in a teenager's room. They included cut-out pictures of Satyajit Ray, Ritwik Ghatak,

Ingmar Bergman, Vincent Van Gogh, Jibanananda Das, Mother Teresa, Nelson Mandela, two big red lips, one big eye, Salvador Dalí and Che Guevara. A cartoon read, in rhyming Bengali: 'Policeman, take off your helmet when you see a poet.'

On one wall was a taped computer printout: '"I have been following the grim events (in Nandigram) and their consequences for the victims and am worried." Noam Chomsky, Nov 13, 2007. 4:18:17 a.m. by email.'

Curios from local fairs were indiscriminately piled high on the desk. Cucumbers made of clay, pencils carved into nudes, tubes of cream that were actually pens, pens with craning rubber necks like swans, bronze statues from South Africa, masks from rural Bengal, a porcelain dancing girl from America. Behind them, Dutta looked like an alchemist in his lair.

'I went to the National Library in 1971 and I saw that they were throwing away a bunch of little magazines,' he said. 'I had a little magazine of my own then, and I took it as a personal affront.'

No one was archiving little magazines at the time. No libraries kept them. When Dutta finished his masters, he started collecting them. At first he had a job that paid fifty rupees a month, then another for one hundred rupees, teaching three days a week in a remote rural school. 'They were funny jobs,' he said. 'Jobs basically to buy magazines.'

In 1978, he got a teaching job down the road at City College School, he told me. That same year, in the two front rooms of his house, he began the Little Magazine Library. Since then he has been running this operation by himself – a bit like those heroes in Bollywood films who take on a whole band of ruffians single-handedly, he likes to say. His is a one-man effort to save the ephemeral present.

Every afternoon he came home from school and set to work at his library. A couple of days were devoted to maintenance, spraying to prevent bookworms and termites. The rest of the afternoons, he kept the library open to the public.

In Bengal, literary movements were usually connected to one little magazine or another. The heyday of the Bengali little magazine was probably the 1960s, when the poets Sunil, Shakti and Sandipan brought out *Krittibas*. No magazine today packs the same literary punch. Yet people keep publishing Bengali little magazines. By Sandip's count, each year 500–600 little magazines are still published.

The little magazine originated in early-twentieth century America. Many of the radical strands of modernism – like James Joyce's *Ulysses*, which was first serialised in the Chicago-based *Little Review* – first appeared in little magazines before anyone bet on their viability in the capitalist market. The early works of T.S. Eliot, Ernest Hemingway, Zora Neale Hurston, Tennessee Williams, Ezra Pound, Virginia Woolf, William Faulkner and many others were all published in the little magazines of their day. Unlike regular magazines, they relied on patrons and modest sales rather than advertising. Shielded from market pressures, they provided a place for writers to be read, even if by a small number of people, and they gave intrepid readers a way to discover new writers. In Calcutta, like so many other aspects of life taken from the West – the tram, homeopathy, Communism – once adopted, little magazines then took on a life of their own and became central to how we understood ourselves. In a proper capitalist system, these magazines would have vanished long ago, taking with them thousands of writers. But like those 1950s Chevrolets in Havana, the Bengali little magazine rolls on, patched up, creaky, a source of local pride, as if it were uniquely ours and as integral to Bengali-ness as a fish curry and rice lunch.

Tapan Ghosh had come from a small town about an hour and a half's train ride south of the city to drop off the latest issue of his magazine. Its topic: Simone de Beauvoir. Tapan was also editing a volume on the Sundarbans, the tiger-infested mangrove jungle in southern Bengal. He was compiling dozens of articles on the Sundarbans, he told Sandip. 'It's going to be a big, expensive book.'

We got to talking about the gods of the Sundarbans. There is one god for protection against crocodiles and another for protection against Royal Bengal tigers, called Dakkhin Roy. There was a temple to Dakkhin Roy, Tapan said, with a larger-than-life statue of the moustachioed deity in a dhoti, carrying a shotgun. 'Buy a seven-rupee ticket from Sealdah station to Dhopdhopi on the Lakkhikantapur line,' Tapan advised me. Then three rupees by rickshaw. 'Dakkhin Roy.' He said again. 'Go see it.'

Another man arrived, shirt tucked in, folio in hand, obviously on his way home from work. His neighbourhood club was having a short-story competition. Could they get the names of some little magazines to contact?

Sandip did not have a list written down. It was in his head. He suggested picking up a catalogue at one of the book stalls. The man noted down the name of the stall Sandip suggested. He did not get up.

'I didn't expect this place to be like this,' he said finally. 'You're also a collector?'

Sandip began to pick up each curio on his desk and describe it. He opened a diary the size of a thimble. 'I write something in it every day,' he said. 'Sometimes we don't pay enough attention to the small things.'

He opened a minuscule snuff box to reveal Ganeshas so tiny you needed a magnifying glass to see them. Inside a mini vase was a chili pepper with a curved stem. It looked like an umbrella in a stand. 'I don't know why I put it there,' he chuckled, 'Probably it's for flowers, but I just thought, why not?'

I have met many men in Calcutta like Sandip over the years, who devote their lives to obsessive, apparently useless pursuits. Some collect matchboxes. Others build wax statues, or cameras out of found objects. On the surface, they appear to share something with the American hobbyist, the comic-book nerd or the antique-car builder. Except hobbies are a leisure activity, something to do when you have more time and money on your hands than you can use. Here, the job is just a place where you have to show up for a few hours every day, do little work and draw a salary at the month's end. A job is more like a hobby. The obsession is the true vocation.

***

Hindu School, Presidency University, Medical College and the University of Calcutta all sit on the two city blocks that make up College Street. These four British-built institutions have carried countless Bengalis from short pants into middle age. Between them is College Square, the great public swimming pool at the centre of the swirl. In the monsoons the water is not only in College Square, but everywhere.

On College Street, the saying goes, it takes one pissing frog to cause flooding. Ten years ago, my cousin Joy and I trudged through monsoon waters to get his migration certificate from Calcutta University. Joy and I grew up together. I came and left and came back, oscillating between Buffalo, Calcutta, St Louis, Calcutta, New Jersey, Calcutta. Joy stayed put. From birth until he graduated college he lived in the same flat in Ballygunge. On summer afternoons there we played cricket, bowling underhand in front of the temple and round-arm fast in the dead-end lane. As happens in Calcutta, Joy's friends were all my friends too. On their roof, I learned to play soccer with a tennis ball, dodging defenders and clotheslines. On that same roof, I came back and learned to smoke cigarettes.

We were on College Street because Joy had been accepted into a masters programme at Jawaharlal Nehru University, in Delhi. Like so many of our generation, he was leaving the city for good. But not without a migration certificate. Like a bonded labourer, he had to be released by the University of Calcutta before he could join JNU. Getting the certificate can take weeks. Like Majnun seeking Leila in the desert, many have wandered in vain amid the university's vast Sahara of clerks. Its halls are full of rows of tables with men sitting among piles of discarded files undoing the top three buttons of their bush shirts and saying, '*Uff, ki* humidity!'

Bengali last names when transliterated into English often have multiple spellings. For instance, my name, Choudhury, can be Chaudhuri, Chowdhury, Chaudhry, and so on. These variations are used by aunts and cousins in my own family. Other Bengali last names even have varying pronunciations. As with Bob and Robert, so too everyone recognises that Banerjee and Bandopadhyay are the same name. Everyone, except the University of Calcutta. Each name has a prescribed university version. If your birth certificate says Choudhury when the university accepts only Chaudhuri, there will be forms you will have to fill out and get attested, clerks you will have to flatter and treat to tea while you wait to be renamed. Like Yahweh, Ellis Island and the slave masters from *Roots*, not only will the university play name-giver – on your certificate you will become Chaudhuri, of that there is no doubt – but whether they will recognise your life prior to your conversion is a matter left up to the fates themselves.

These are the fears that run through you on a monsoon morning as you wade waist-deep in rainwater and dog shit on the way to collect a migration certificate. Fortunately, Joy's father, as a retired professor, still enjoyed the goodwill of a clerk or two. With their munificence, it took only six hours for us to acquire Joy's release from the university, and from Calcutta.

Ten years later, the two of us were back in the same university building on College Street. Joy's mother, my aunt, had just had an operation and we had come to drop off about one hundred pages of hospital bills, pharmacy receipts and doctor's certificates, collated and photocopied in triplicate, to file the insurance claim. Joy was now a professor in Delhi. Dida's death had loosened our collective mooring to the city, and my ailing aunt and uncle were now leaving Calcutta to reluctantly join Joy in exile. The clerk inspected the papers. In one of the pages submitted, he noticed that the date of release had been incorrectly written by the nursing home. All the other documents had the right date. 'You're going to have to get this redone,' he said.

Mentally I quickly worked out the steps: It meant tracking down the hospital clerk who made the error, convincing him that he had in fact erred, creating a new 'hospital release certificate', then tracking down my aunt's doctor to sign off, before finding the university clerk who was before me now. This would easily take days of wandering through the various layers of Calcutta's myriad bureaucratic hells. Then the clerk had a change of heart – perhaps he remembered my elderly uncle, the retired professor – and changed the '4' to a '5' himself.

As we stepped out of the university gate, men hissed at us: 'What can I get you, brother? First year or second year?'

On College Street, shopkeepers sell books the way dealers elsewhere sell crack. The railings along the University of Calcutta, Presidency University, Hindu School and College Square are all lined with shops that look like large metal lunchboxes. The boxes open up into stalls full of books. There are over a hundred book shops on these side streets and lanes, making it the largest book market on earth. In Bengali, we call College Street '*Boi Para*', the book neighbourhood.

They say you cannot find good used books on College Street any more, but especially along the railings of Presidency University, there are still stalls that offer treasures that are worth a look. You can find second-hand gems, like early Naipaul paperbacks, nineteenth-century tomes on colonial law, and coffee-table books from the Chinese Cultural Revolution, in Chinese. The books are stacked high against the counters in no particular order. Sometimes I would see Graham Greene fourteen volumes down, and use all my Jenga talents to extricate *The Quiet American* so that all the other books above it did not fall. Then I would act as if the book was worthless: For this old thing, how much? The bookseller, who may not always read English, would quote a price and tell me what a 'famous' book it is, 'foreign', 'classic'. I would bid at half his price. He would demur. Even the pages are coming apart, I would say. He would resist. I would threaten to walk off. He wouldn't budge. I would walk off. He would call me back. We would settle on a price, and then I would probably end up buying two more books from him, which I would never read.

In those wanderings, I always scanned the towers of fraying spines for Maxim Gorky's *Mother*. I was in the middle of reading Joy's copy of *Mother* when I moved to New Jersey at age twelve. In Highland Park, hurled into the bewildering society of American middle school, the public library became my shelter, just as it was for the elderly, the homeless and the mentally ill. There, unprompted by parents or teachers, I read Thomas Hardy, P. G. Wodehouse, Agatha Christie, F. Scott Fitzgerald, Noel Coward, Ernest Hemingway, Oscar Wilde, Hermann Hesse, G. K. Chesterton, Somerset Maugham. There was no method to my reading, except that these were authors I had heard of and believed were important. It is no accident that books by these writers are still sold in Calcutta in the used-book stalls of College Street. In addition to the 'great books,' my reading had a second track. Like an autodidact, I picked up whatever 'Indian' name I could find on the public-library shelves. I read Nirad C. Chaudhuri and Mahatma Gandhi, R. K. Narayan and V. S. Naipaul, Anita Desai and Jiddu Krishnamurti, Raja Rao and Pico Iyer, and even the Inspector Ghote mysteries, which were set in Bombay and written by an Englishman who had not even visited India. Yet through all that reading in my new home, I never found Gorky's *Mother*. Neither the school nor the public library had a copy. Gorky had been a Soviet writer. *Mother* is a Communist novel about the revolutionary awakening of Russian factory workers, and such texts were still hard to find in early 1990s America. For years, as if by habit, I would search for *Mother* whenever I visited a new bookstore, but I never found the book.

Within weeks of returning to Calcutta, I tracked down a copy at a pavement stall. The cover had been torn off and replaced with a makeshift binding, and the book's title was written in with a marker pen. I bought it anyway. After more than a decade, a simmering private quest was over. I thought it was a homecoming.

The funny thing is, I never finished reading *Mother*. That loose end of my disrupted childhood remained untied. I was after something else.

***

When I was a student at Calcutta Boys' School, our academic year was marked by three term exams. The tests would be in at least a dozen subjects. Preparations would take over a month of mugging up. During exam time, a hush settled over Calcutta's families, as mothers fretted, cajoled and provided warm glasses of milk, while the little one prepared for his term exams. The SATs were a breeze compared to my Calcutta first-grade final exams. No test I would take in the US – not even the field exams in graduate school – ever required the amount of mindless memorisation, or produced as much competitiveness and anxiety, as those grade-school exams.

After each term exam we would be ranked among our peers. The status of the kid who topped the rankings, the 'First Boy', can be compared only to that of an American high-school quarterback. He was typically bespectacled, oily haired and a bit of a bore, but students revered him, teachers granted him the equivalent of diplomatic immunity, and other kids' mothers wanted to copy notes from his ma. Perhaps I have neglected to mention that each day, mothers lined up along the schoolyards during lunchtime with hot fish curry and rice tiffins to spoon-feed their progeny. Since my mother worked as a scientist for much of my childhood, my tiffins were cold butter sandwiches carried from home, and I was spared this maternal attention.

All those years of spoon-feeding and exams led up to the standardised tests in tenth, and then twelfth grade. Six hundred thousand tenth graders took the state's final exam in 2009. The boy who ranked first was featured on the front page of the newspaper, just under the article on the national parliamentary elections. On the inside pages each year are stories of kids hanging themselves because of a poor exam result. The preferred mode of suicide for spurned lovers is drinking acid. The preferred mode for exam victims is hanging.

The target of every Bengali family is to produce a doctor or an engineer. Both fields have rigorous entrance exams at the end of twelfth grade, known in Bengal as the joint entrance exam. By the time you reach twelfth grade, exams have provided the entire drama of your existence. These results are the measure of your self-worth. Each year, with each new report of suicide, there is talk of easing the stress, perhaps doing away with some tests altogether. Nothing much changes except that more shortcuts appear – more reference books, more coaching centres, more compilations of old exam papers – and more people pass.

May was the peak shopping season on College Street, because the new academic year was about to start. On College Row, the Chhaya Publishers' storefront was blocked by a collapsible metal gate, as you would find at a para liquor store, to avoid a stampede on the counter. Uniformed guards were temporarily on hire. A crowd of distributors from across the state had honeycombed around the gate. The men in the crowd were an instant community as such men often are, cracking jokes with one another. They came from Burdwan, Murshidabad, Nadia, each with several of the large woven bags you take to the fish market. They were waiting for their orders, to fill up those bags with books and take the evening trains home to the countryside.

Since the 1970s, the book business has increasingly become the notes business. Most of the books on sale in the stalls now are for Brilliant's, Competition Success, Manorama Yearbook – all preparation manuals for competitive exams. They comprise a publishing business that is like Princeton Review on steroids. Publishers have realised that what little money there is to be made comes from cashing in on the insecurities of the young. Chhaya is one of the biggest textbook publishers on College Street. Yet the bulk of its business is not textbooks but 'practice books', 'workbooks', 'companion books', 'reference books' – a whole set of euphemisms for made-easy test-preparation manuals. A book is a window into a world. These books are, first and foremost, tools with which to avoid reading other books, to crib for exams and pass through the next hoop.

The Chhaya offices were on the ground floor of a mansion on College Row. There I met T. Dey, a thirty-something with red highlights in his hair. This was go time. His phone kept ringing. For these few weeks, while guards were stationed outside the store, Dey was like a medic passing out first aid in a refugee camp.

In the past, there was no need for reference books, he explained, but now the notes business thrives because they are a necessity. During the school year, Chhaya's representatives fan out to educators across the state with their book samples. They aim to ensure their books are prescribed by teachers. 'The marketing works just like medical representatives,' said Dey. 'Teachers write out prescriptions of books for students. Students in turn demand the books from distributors. Then the distributor comes to us. We create demand.'

The first run for popular test-preparation books for the tenth-grade exams is 100,000 copies. Chhaya provides a whole bank of ready-made prose you can memorise and copy into the competitive exam. These books are usually written by teachers and professors, with their qualifications noted up front. *The Higher Secondary English Tutor*, a bestselling 'companion' book for eleventh and twelfth graders, is written by a retired professor whose degrees include 'MA (Double), M. Litt., PhD'. You never need to read 'The Rime of the Ancient Mariner', John Osborne's plays or Mark Antony's speech from *Julius Caesar*. The many-degreed professor will give you the answers, within the prescribed word-length, for every single question in the assigned readings for eleventh- and twelfth-grade English. Also provided are sample letters and formulated answers for each of the last fourteen years' higher secondary exams, to mentally copy and paste at exam time. Follow this, or the hundreds of less illustrious guides that are for sale on College Street, and you will be spared the pain of thinking. As the saying goes, 'Commit to memory, and vomit.'

'What subject did you study in college?' Dey asked.

'Political science,' I said.

'Well, then you must have read Prof. Nimai Pramanik's book.' Prof. Pramanik has written several books of notes in Bengali for BA, MA and M Phil courses in poli sci.

I had studied in America, I told him. I hadn't needed his drugs.

Dey didn't like that at all. 'I have told you all this based on trust,' he said. 'How do I know you are not a competitor?'

He advised me to get a business card.

***

Behind College Square, the lanes were narrower than my living room. Both sides were lined with those metal boxes that opened up to reveal books. A lane forked. I picked the narrower lane – they are always more interesting. It was dense with vendors and covered like an arcade by the canopies of trees and blue tarps that block the rains. In one of the stalls there, I found pocket 'Shaayari SMS' books. Romantic couplets from Urdu poetry, or *shaayari*, had been transliterated into English and packaged to send as text messages, or SMS's. On page 62, above a cartoon of a man on his cell phone, it read: *'Hamare dewanepan ki bhi koi dawa nahi, humne tow who bhi sun liya jo unhone kaha bhi nahin.'* There is no medicine to fix my love sickness. I have already heard the words which my beloved has not yet uttered.

The SMS books were an index of ready-made pickup lines for any man with a phone and a target. Thankfully, there were also 'Sorry SMS' books. Just like the essays on summer vacation and Mahatma Gandhi that you could find in the reference books without ever going on summer vacation or reading Gandhi, there was no need to read and memorise Mirza Ghalib's couplets or even write down Gulzar's film lyrics to impress your potential girlfriend. Even a love affair could be done by rote.

Around me, cycle vans and hand-pulled rickshaws carried binding, galleys and books, bound and unbound. A Tempo truck was trying to get out of the lane as an Ambassador car was trying to get in. In between them, the rickshaws had stopped to make deliveries. Everyone was yelling at everyone. No one was moving, except the nimble pedestrians trickling through, who made the snarl worse. Right there, squatting on the pavement, was a man with a sepia glass box, lit with an incandescent bulb and full of chicken patties, doing business as usual.

The big publishing houses control archipelagos around College Street. Aside from their offices and store fronts, they occupy islands of space – containing workshops, printing presses and bookbinders – in the lanes and gullies. Little is shipped out, offshored or outsourced. The brain and brawn work of making and selling books all happens here. Van rickshaws pulling goods, delivery men rushing with stacks of books on their shoulders – the hustle and bustle all around reveals a place where thousands of people make a living. Street into lane into gully into courtyard, these telescoping tunnels of bibliomania support a whole industry at work, inside stalls and one-room presses, on rickshaws and on foot.

Heading off College Street, I turned into an alley that was only a yard wide. Nabin Kundu Lane went past a sweet shop, an open garbage dump, a Kali temple with a fantastic sculpture glaring through a grill, and several offices of book publishers. Through all this, Nabin Kundu Lane never widened beyond a yard until it dropped me off on College Row. Two steps down and I was at Naren Sen Square, sipping tea at a stall with a few old timers while taking in the cricket match on the dirt-patch square. An old man in white pyjamas watched from the veranda above. These people were blessed, I thought to myself, to have such miniature perfection in the heart of the city.

From there I followed a rickshaw into a lane with bits of genteel slum on one side, middle-class solicitors' houses on the other. In the front rooms of both were workshops and presses. On a *roak* – a Calcutta stoop – a woman from the slum sat in a cotton sari with freshly oiled hair. She looked as if she should be sunning herself while chatting with neighbours. Instead a two-foot stack of sheets, fresh from the press, sat next to her. She was folding pamphlets that said 'University of Calcutta'.

Through the window of one house I saw a fringe of sari and yelled, 'Oh, sister!' The woman who appeared passed me a pack of

Filter Wills through the bars as if she was trafficking contraband in prison. The window was a cigarette shop – no storefront, no counter, no metal box. The lane ended and suddenly I was in front of Saint Paul's School, where my Boro Mama went to school, and morphed from Kiddo to Ashoke, on august Amherst Street.

I turned right again and on Sitaram Ghosh Street were more presses, and front rooms with squatting boys heating sheets of metal on stoves. A man cycled past with a rolled-up metal sheet as wide as a twin bed tied behind him. On the sheet were mathematical proofs and diagrams – the pages of a geometry book. Briefly I was back out among the wedding-card printers on Mahatma Gandhi Road, before again submerging into Beniatala Lane, where there were more workshops, publishers, little magazine offices, which led back to College Row. In the old houses, each courtyard led into a shop, a press, a warehouse, a cyber café, a coaching centre or some form of a place of business. In the lanes, scenes of domestic life unfolded. Courtyard, corridor, gully, lane, street, the publicness of private homes blended with the privateness of public spaces. The whole world of College Street, with its narrow lanes and tarps and tree-cover, felt unified, intimate and indoors. Sometimes the courtyards were wider than streets. Some streets had steps, like in a house. Was I inside or outside? I felt I had entered an Escher painting. For College Street was not just a street, but a labyrinth made of books.

***

Bankim Chatterjee Street, named after our first novelist, turns off from College Street at the Coffee House. A flock of sheep passed through Bankim Chatterjee Street each afternoon. Every day they marched through the book neighbourhood as if in a pasture, about forty poor bleating fellows headed to slaughter. An old man trailed them. He was a real-life shepherd, like those in the Bible. If one sheep tried to mount another for a last bit of fun, the old man beat both down with his switch.

Run! I silently screamed at them. Escape your death march with the flock. Each one of you take a separate gully, past the van rickshaws, the presses and the women folding pamphlets, and you shall be free! They were so docile.

Why blame the sheep? The fault is ours. For thousands of years, we have bred sheep to be this way. The courageous ones that sought to flee were slaughtered first, martyrs with no offspring to pass on their valour. The docile ones rushed to the centre of the flock, into captivity. They lived and reproduced more of their kind. This story has been repeated for countless generations.

We were bred to be clerks. The British gave us Western education so that we could do the busywork of their empire. We were trained to sit in offices at Writers' Building and a myriad other buildings, draw salaries and copy ledgers. It is said that if a dead fly fell onto the page of a ledger while it was being copied, a clerk would kill another fly and set it down in just the same spot in the ledger he was copying to, inspiring the Bengali phrase, 'a fly-swatting clerk'. Get notes, memorise, vomit them out onto exams. Copy, don't create. From the beginning this has been the mode of our modern education.

Colonial education made us clerks for the traders of that era just as the prized technical learning in computers today is making us clerks anew. Now, in Sector Five and elsewhere, instead of ledgers, we fill up screens with code, eagerly doing the 'back-office' busywork of America's global corporations.

We are perhaps as blameless as the sheep. To stay safe you have to pass the exams, then get a degree, then a job. The job will kill your spirit, but at least you won't starve to death. After two hundred years, is it a surprise that there is a fly-swatting clerk in all of us?

***

Joy had taken his parents away with him to Delhi. Two weeks later, my uncle called from exile: 'There is a problem. The insurance people have sent a letter to the university saying the release certificate has been tampered with.'

The work of the clerk who had changed the '4' to a '5' had come undone. It took me two full days of crisscrossing the city to get that one elusive digit altered.

Yet, for all this fastidious officiousness, it was possible to get fake documents for anything. A birth certificate, a business receipt or even a college degree could be cheaply acquired.

In New Jersey, my father still carries the business card of an old Calcutta colleague in his wallet, which he sometimes pulls out as a party trick. It reads:

Prof. Col. Dr Haridas Pal
FDS RCS (Edin.), PGTOS (London), DOS (Leiden), PhD,
    LL.B (Kol.), DA (Jad.), FAScT
Senior Consultant Head and Neck Surgeon and Oncologist
Prof. & Head, Head and Neck Surgery, Katihar Medical
College
Visiting Professor, Forensic Science, Kolkata University
Criminal Detection Training School, Govt of India
Included in the International Directory of Distinguished
    Leaderships, USA
Honoured by the Commonwealth, UK
Formerly Prof. & Head, Oral Surgery Unit, Kolkata Medical
College
Chittaranjan Cancer Hospital
Lecturer, University College Hospital, Eastman Dental
Hospital, Italian Hospital and Whipps Cross Hospital, London
Author of 11 Medical Books and 1 Law Book

When you have finished reading this astonishing list of accomplishments, my father always grins as he delivers the punchline: 'The man is a dentist'.

Along Mahatma Gandhi Road, a whole industry thrives to legitimise any claimed accomplishment. Among the stationers who sell bulk quantities of book wrappings, paper sheaves, dangling lines of metal clips and staplers are the lines of shops that make rubber stamps, print business cards, and engrave medals and trophies. As a child who won no trophies, I was tempted to now crown myself 'Captain' or 'Best Striker' of a football club of my imagining. More realistically, I wanted a business card. I could crown myself Professor, Reporter or Writer, but without a card I felt like a nobody.

'For to articulate sweet sounds together,' W. B. Yeats wrote,

Is to work harder than all these, and yet
Be thought an idler by the noisy set
Of bankers, schoolmasters, and clergymen
The martyrs call the world.

But sometimes we idlers have clerical fantasies. We, too, wish we could spend our days stamping things, pushing paper, feeling important.

From one of the printers' shops on Mahatma Gandhi Road, a shopkeeper led me into a gully, and then into a niche where I took off my shoes before entering as if it were a Hindu prayer room. A young man sat in front of a computer with the design motifs for wedding cards laid out before him. On the board above were samples of various visiting cards. One had a multi-coloured collage of Lamborghinis and zooming 747 jets.

'That's for a neighbourhood car-rental company,' the man said. 'Yours should be understated.'

In twenty-four hours, I had 200 cards printed, which began: 'Dr Kushanava Choudhury, Research Scholar.' And behold! I was somebody.

***

No one who came to the Budh-Bikel adda off Tamer Lane was famous. Well-known poets like Sunil Ganguly had their own addas. But here, an ordinary writer – even a first-time poet – could read his work in public, have an audience and, maybe, have it published in a little magazine. There is a lot of politics in the literary world, one of the writers warned me, patronage combined with clubbiness and deceit. Who will take my piece in their magazine? thinks the poet. Who will pay me a one hundred-rupee donation to keep my magazine going? thinks the publisher.

Many of those who came to the adda ran their own little magazines, like Jagabandhu Kundu's *Sahitya Setu* (*The Bridge of Literature*), a magazine on literary criticism that also features poems and short stories. Kundu has been publishing it since his college days – he had just done a special issue on the biographies of Rabindranath Tagore. He had retired from his job with the municipality in Hoogly, a town near Calcutta. Now he practised homeopathy and brought out the magazine.

One evening, Ranjan'da said: 'Listening to the poetry and short stories being read here, I feel that we're stuck in one place. I would like Jagabandhu to speak on this.'

Jagabandhu is tall, taciturn and bent like a palm. Recycling old ideas didn't work any more, he said. Readers want contemporary themes.

'This goes back to the old debate,' opined a retired professor of Bengali. 'Art for art's sake, or art for people's sake. You are saying the latter ...'

Jagabandhu was taken aback. His career had been spent pushing files in a municipal office, not in faculty rooms. 'Of course you have to think about readers! Many days I leave here and think, 'That was not a poem.' But I encourage everyone and keep it to myself. Just writing down your thoughts is not a poem.'

'Ah, well,' said Prof, 'now we are coming to structuralism versus deconstruction—'

'This isn't an academic debate,' Ranjan'da said.

'To write poetry, you need to know the evolution of poetry, beyond Tagore to Jibanananda Das to Benoy Majumdar and on down,' said Jagabandhu. 'Today's poets don't read.'

'Yes, reading is important,' said IBS, 'I have also said—'

'I think something is missing,' said Ranjan'da 'We don't know where world poetry is going. We need to know about that and write poetry based on it.'

As we left Budh-Bikel, Nilkashyap was cornered by a younger poet at the mouth of the gully. The other man's glasses had photochromatic lenses. Under the amber street light they had turned brown, making him look like a villainous spy from a B-movie. He was listing all the places where he had contacts: the Russian consulate, the American embassy, the Swedes, the Norwegians, the Danes – as if poetry were a cover for espionage. 'You should have seen my program on Doordarshan,' Spy said, of his appearance on the state-run TV channel. 'They gave me fifty minutes.'

Another poet passed by and requested Nilkashyap to buy her new book. 'Only fifty rupees,' she said.

'Fifteen?' asked Nilkashyap. 'No, fifty,' she said. He demurred. 'I can't sell any of my own books, and they're only twenty.'

Nilkashyap returned to Spy: 'You should have seen me at Nandan. I was on for five days. They couldn't stop praising my work.'

Spy promised to send Nilkashyap's work to Norway. 'Are you willing to pay?' Spy asked. 'How much? Five thousand?'

'No, no fifteen hundred, two thousand,' Nilkashyap said. They sounded as if they were conducting an arms deal in the gully off Tamer Lane.

***

Ranjan'da had a tidy two-storey house on the wrong side of the tracks in Dhakuria, an area in South Calcutta that was now being filled up by new construction. When he bought the property there was nothing around but slums. But it was something, a piece of land in the city. He had saved for years to build the house.

'They say poets are careless with money,' Ranjan'da said, when I went to meet him at home. 'Poets are the most careful. They have to be.'

He felt that most of the poetry read at Budh-Bikel did not count as such. 'I encourage everybody to keep writing, but poetry today is technical. You have to love the crafting of poetry to become a good poet.'

Writing poetry is always a fool's errand, he said. Even most good poets are not remembered a generation afterwards. The muse is fickle. 'It picked out Tagore, then Jibanananda Das, and then skipped over the rest to Shakti Chatterjee, and then to Joy Goswami. Even Sunil Ganguly won't be remembered as a poet.'

Sunil, who said he had the world at his feet when he was in America, but chose to return to Calcutta for poetry's sake. He may be read as a novelist, Ranjan'da suggested, but not as a poet.

Ranjan'da knew something of the fickleness of fate. His father had been an administrator for a wealthy landlord near Dhaka, the capital of today's Bangladesh. He had enjoyed hunting, fishing and leisurely evening teas on the estate. In 1943, the British created a famine by diverting rice away from rural Bengal for the war effort. Prices skyrocketed as colonial police seized grain in the villages. In Calcutta, prices were kept low by the colonial government because the city was a part of its war machine. But three million people died in the countryside during the Bengal Famine. Ranjan'da's father helplessly bore witness as hundreds of people starved to death on the estate. He had a heart attack and never worked again.

At the same time, sporadic riots and violence between Hindus and Muslims flared up in Bengal. They culminated in the Great Calcutta Killing in 1946, which made Partition inevitable. When the British left the next year, Bengal was divided into India and Pakistan. East Bengal, which had a Muslim majority, became East Pakistan (and eventually Bangladesh); the Hindu-majority areas in West Bengal, including Calcutta, went to India.

Ranjan'da's family, like my father's family, were Hindus from the east. They had to leave their homeland for ever and move to Calcutta. Becoming a refugee traumatised his mother, who sank into a depression from which she never recovered. For several years the family was split up, with each ailing parent living on the reluctant charity of a relative while the two teenage sons scrambled to make a living.

'We were all scattered and none of us had any income,' he said. 'Those were terrible years. My brother had to sell diaries outside the high court to make money.' Diaries like the one in which Ranjan'da now pens his poems.

Partition bludgeoned his literary ambitions. He took a government job in the public works department. He was posted to remote areas in central India where he installed tube wells and built roads. He didn't write anything for thirty years.

The great poet of the post-Tagore years, Jibanananda Das, was also a son of the east. His verses called upon an elusive dreamscape of haunting images of bucolic East Bengal, of a world he had permanently lost to Partition. Das lived a reclusive life in Calcutta and had an unlikely death, killed by a speeding tram. A half-century after his demise, his work continues to emerge – both literally and metaphorically – like a slowly developing photograph.

Ranjan'da began reading and writing poetry again when he was in his fifties. He had never published anywhere, didn't know any writers. 'I was already so old when I started. I had no self-confidence,' he said.

A chance encounter with a publisher led to a book of his poems being printed. Then came positive reviews, introductions to other writers and encouragement from various quarters. The same year, Ranjan'da retired and devoted himself to poetry full time. He has been coming to the adda ever since.

***

The rumour is that College Street was once awash in addas, and nowhere were there more addas than at Coffee House. By the time I arrived, the mythical poets with ruffled hair and cigarettes on lips, who recited Baudelaire and Buddhadeva Bose, had long left the building. The young writers of the

1950s graduated from coffee to country liquor by making the southward trek from College Street to Wellington. Khalasitola is a legendary bar in Wellington that serves only Bangla, or country liquor. Kamalkumar Majumdar was the figure who turned Khalasitola into a pilgrimage place for intellectuals. Kamalkumar was like Socrates, writes Sunil Ganguly, holding forth among the benches at the bar with a crowd of young poets around him. His knowledge of Bengali folk music, the theatre and French literature was unparalleled. Those addas in Khalasitola gave birth to the *Krittibas* generation – Sunil, Shakti, Sandipan and the other poets and writers who put out the little magazine, *Krittibas,* which was both a forum for their work and a vehicle for their unruly, chaotic form of Bengali literature, which defined the turbulent Calcutta of the late 1960s. Initiated into the glories of Rimbaud, Ginsberg and Bangla, the *Krittibas* generation would devote ink to their drunken hallucinatory visions of the city.

I was standing at Wellington crossing at dusk. The number 5 tram came down Lenin Sarani, turned left, climbing northward toward College Street and I latched on. As we rode through Bowbazar, I looked through the large open windows of the tram. Stray dogs ranged upon the dunes of garbage at the open public dump. *Parathas* were being made at the corner shop on white tiles and under bright lights. Each vista became a freeze frame in a motion picture of the city.

Nilkashyap was late. It had been a week of unrest. A transport strike, torrential rains and an opposition party *bandh* – literally a 'shutdown' of all businesses for one day – had hit Calcutta in succession. A hundred miles away, the villages of Lalgarh were at the front lines of India's civil war between the state and the Maoists. A generation ago, the Naxalite uprising had turned Calcutta into the epicentre of the first Maoist rebellion. Like those urban ancestors, the new Maoists sought a violent overthrow of the democratic state. They were operating in the jungles, organising in the forested areas in half of India's states. Beamed in through twenty-four-hour cable news, we now watched as Indian army commandos took on tribal people who subsisted in the forests as hunter-gatherers. They represented a mortal threat to the nation, we were told. But on TV, the commandos wielded automatic rifles while the indigenous people they called 'terrorists' had bows and arrows. A war waged with such asymmetrical weaponry made any sensitive viewer uneasy.

Nilkashyap started reading. He was wearing an orange panjabi. His poem was about Lalgarh: '*Aagun je andho, angun janena ki mondo.*' But fire is blind. It knows not right from wrong.

He finished and looked straight up at me: 'You liked it, yes?' He was impressed and delighted with himself as always. '*Aagun je andho, angun janena ki mondo*' he repeated. '*Chirag!*' he said, using the Urdu word for fire. Before I could follow what he meant, the next poet started reading.

Shyamal'da recited a poem called 'Belpahari's Sita'. Belpahari is an area where tribal people had starved to death in 2005 – something shocking in contemporary Bengal – a region beset by food shortages each year while the Communist government looked away. Now Belpahari was slowly seceding from the state and being 'liberated' by Maoist guerrillas. The poem described the first day after a long time when there was rice to eat. Heaps of white rice. It was cause for relief and celebration. But, the poet asks, 'Sita, what shall I eat this heap of rice with?' Sita replies: '*Khidey diye bhaat mekhe kha.*' Mix it with your hunger.

After Shyamal'da, Anirban, poet and publisher of a little magazine, read another Lalgarh poem.

'Political events are coming into poetry,' Ranjan'da said, 'That's fine. We are human beings too. But please, remember to honour poetry. Poetry should not be a "statement".'

Nilkashyap was nudging the lady next to him. She spoke up: 'Ranjan'da, Nilkashyap would like you to say something about his poem.'

Ranjan'da asked Nilkashyap to read it again. The poem had the subtlety of a telenovela. When he finished, Ranjan'da deftly turned to his left and said, 'Anirban, why don't you say something?'

'Your poem, it is almost a short story,' Anirban said. 'The line between poem and short story is getting blurred, but I will take it in my upcoming issue of short stories.' Nilkashyap, as ever, was pleased. Anirban said nothing about the quality of his poem.

Nilkashyap said: 'At Nandan, Anirban said, "Nilkashyap's poems are beyond criticism." That's my asset.'

On my way home, I ran into Nilkashyap in the gully of the phantom urinal. It was brighter at night than in the daytime. Under the amber street lights, Nilkashyap in his orange panjabi emerged like a flame. He looked lost.

'Do you go home this way?' he asked me.

We were standing in front of a house that opened into the gully. A beautiful girl entered through the gate as a rat exited and darted away. Under the lights the gully took on a charming new complexion.

'*Swatilekha eshob kotha tomae kokhono bola jabe na,*' he started quoting himself in verse, '*shob shotti ki bhag kora jae.*' '"Swatilekha, I can never say these words to you. All truths are not to be divulged."'

'There are some things you can't tell your wife. Or they will create domestic distress,' he said, 'I was always writing this poem away from her, keeping in mind the visions of that Rajasthani girl. That's why I've written, "Every night I seat her in my poems facing me."'

A few years back, Nilkashyap was flying to see his daughter in Bombay. There was a young woman who sat next to him. They exchanged a few pleasantries, nothing more. On the flight back, there she was again, sitting a few rows away. So when the plane was landing, 'I went to the bathroom. They told us to sit down, but I thought, this is my chance. I went up to her and I said, "Madam, I think we have met before." And she said, "Yes I think so also." And I said, "Are you a Parsi?" because there are many Parsis in Bombay, you see, and they are very beautiful.'

The woman turned out to be Marwari, from Calcutta, which was nothing as exotic as a Zoroastrian from Bombay.

But it was the start. 'I'm telling you the origins of this poem. Listen.'

At his local public library, where Nilkashyap is a member of the governing body, he encountered an English poem about an Irish girl's love for a bearded tour guide. 'It is midnight, and the girl says, "Take me to the tour guide, the man with the face full of beard." It's midnight, mind, and she is saying this.'

That was the second inspiration. The trifecta was achieved when he met the tour operator in Rajasthan. The Marwari girl's face, the Irishwoman's longing and the Rajasthani's body fused together. The poem, 'Festival of Melancholy', practically wrote itself.

'She only touched me once,' he said of the Rajasthani tour operator. 'She grabbed me to help me cross a puddle. So I've written: "When we crossed that slippery road, she once held my hand, an impish smile on her face. The deer left the forest and silently ran into her eyes."'

'I am forever in the thrall of poetry,' Nilkashyap said as we crossed Mahatma Gandhi Road, dodging taxis and autos. 'Poet Kalidas said, "Poetry is like a woman. You cannot force it. That is like rape. You have to let it come of its own will."'

A tram came at us. 'This is how we poets die!' Nilkashyap said, scampering across the road to avoid what fate had dealt to Jibanananda Das.

I walked him to the tram stop on College Street. Somehow, I did not care any more about the quality of his verse. I admired him, and the countless poets and writers attending addas, self-publishing books and filling up the pages of little magazines. They could have stopped long ago, caved in to the pressures of family and work. They could stay home and watch television like the rest of the world. But they persevered, because to craft verse, however unappreciated or inadequate, still brought satisfaction. After a lifetime of dodging trams and buses in a city like Calcutta, Nilkashyap could still be moved enough by a beautiful young woman to compose a poem. He would never woo her with it. It probably would not make him famous, no matter how many times Nilkashyap told me little mag editors were begging to publish his poems. But there it was, a retired assistant bank manager's bittersweet lament.

Nilkashyap got on the tram headed south towards Khalasitola. I helped him up and waited till the tram started moving, as if he were my own uncle. I felt responsible that he get home safe. I wanted him to keep writing.

Victoria

In primary school, we had read that India was the birthplace of one of the world's first civilisations. Along the Indus River over four thousand years ago rose the great cities of Mohenjo Daro and Harappa. Their written language has not yet been deciphered, but archeologists believe that the cities were commercial centres. We do know that the cities were laid out as grids. Their most impressive feature, which was always mentioned in our school books, was that the cities had extensive covered sewage systems.

And yet, four millennia later, to live in Calcutta is to perpetually stop, sniff and wonder, is it, can it be ... the smell of piss? But I'm entering a top-flight private hospital. But I am walking along a busy corridor in a government office. But I am standing at a bus stop in the middle of five thousand people. And yet there it is, that unmistakable bouquet. One day I saw a man urinating on the median of the Eastern Metropolitan Bypass, with his goods exposed to three lanes of heavy traffic. The woes of women are at an altogether different level, especially those who are up at dawn to work in houses as maids, where they are still not allowed to use the bathroom, long after we have ceased to speak publicly about untouchability and the violations of caste. For us men, the city is simply one big pisspot.

Men piss everywhere: on the streets, in alleys, on highways and, improbably, even in the dark corners of office corridors. There are no uncontaminated piss-free zones in Calcutta, no elite enclave without the stench. To combat the contagion, there are murals all across the city that look like para portrait galleries. This is how homeowners protect their turf from the ubiquitous urination. The portraits are of our pantheon of nationalists, poets and reformers. They are the faces you can't piss on.

There's Raja Rammohun Roy, turbaned and moustachioed. Rammohun was among the first generation of Bengalis to take to European education, the father of the so-called Bengal Renaissance. He knew several languages and many holy texts, campaigned against widow-burning, and started a kind of polite, Quaker version of Hinduism called Brahmoism, bereft of deities, with prayer meetings and progressive zeal.

Then you will find Iswarchandra Vidyasagar, the exemplary poor Brahmin's son. His life was chock-full of instructive anecdotes: young Iswarchandra used to study under street lights, we were told as kids. He learned English by reading milestones as he walked from his village to Calcutta. Young Iswarchandra once swam across the Ganga, we were told, to see his ailing mother in the village. When not making interesting commutes, Iswarchandra standardised the Bengali language and campaigned for social reforms. He produced elementary-school primers, which even I used, and mobilised in favour of widow remarriage, which still remains taboo.

His friend Michael Madhusudan Dutt, was a more colourful man. Madhusudan became Michael, a convert to Christianity, then went to Europe, turned Francophile and married a Frenchwoman, failed as a poet in English, then came home and reverted to writing in Bengali. As the father of Bengali free verse, he wrote revisionist Hindu epic poems, borrowed lumps of cash from the prudent Vidyasagar, and died an indebted and unrepentant drunk. On the wall murals, Michael always sports killer mutton chops.

Following Michael is Bankimchandra Chattopadhyay, clean-shaven, turbaned, looking austere. Bankim was the first Indian novelist. He, too, wrote initially in English, then reams upon reams in Bengali. He penned some of the earliest 'nationalist' novels, essays and songs. For his role in conceiving the nation, Bankim remains an icon not just to the Bengali bourgeoisie but to all Indian nationalists.

Rabindranath Tagore, of course, is omnipresent. His pensive bearded visage, looking like a Bengali version of Michelangelo's God, can deter even a piddle emergency. After all, he was Asia's first Nobel Laureate, our Shakespeare, our Homer, our Moses. The scion of a wealthy trading family, Tagore was a poet, playwright, novelist, painter, essayist, philosopher, lyricist, choreographer and interior designer who also founded a liberal-arts university in his spare time. He delivered us to our modern idiom, largely inventing the Bengali we speak today.

Alongside him is the bearded Ramakrishna, his eyes half shut in a trance. A village mystic and Kali devotee who travelled to the city, Ramakrishna became the patron saint to the nineteenth-century Bengali bourgeoisie. Venerated in life and deified in death, his image is on sweet-shop calendars and cab-drivers' dashboards across the city.

His best pupil, Swami Vivekananda, was an English-educated Calcutta boy who went native. On the murals, he is always painted in ochre robes and turban. Inspired by Ramakrishna, the city boy turned monk, and founded the Jesuit-style Ramakrishna Mission, whose celibate priests run some of the best schools and social service organisations in India.

Finally, there is always Netaji – literally 'the Great Leader' – Subhas Chandra Bose. In the murals he is an amalgam of chubby cheeks and glasses paired with military fatigues and cap. Netaji was Bengal's greatest freedom fighter, and Gandhi's political and ideological rival. Netaji believed his enemy's enemy to be his friend. He raised an army to fight the British by joining hands with the Nazis and the Japanese, and was hopelessly defeated near Burma, his army killed and captured by the British. His mysterious, untimely disappearance – in a plane crash en route to Japan – makes him a modern-day messiah. In Bengal some are still awaiting his return.

These are the Bengali all-stars. There are many others on the murals, among them scientists, bomb-throwers and saints. The only post-colonial faces you can't piss on belong to Satyajit Ray, Mother Teresa and Amartya Sen. The rest all lived during the two centuries of British rule, as if the colonial oppressors left, and Calcutta ceased to produce great men and women.

In street-corner busts and in parks, in street signs and on school gates, Rammohan, Bankim, Vidyasagar, Rabindranath, Netaji, Ramakrishna and Vivekananda are memorialised over and over. In Shyambazar, Netaji rides a horse over the five-point traffic snarl; in College Square Vidyasagar keeps watch over students rushing to tuition; in Gol Park Vivekananda stands tall, asking us to arise, awake to the new dawn. And Rabindranath Tagore peers down at us everywhere, at Rabindra Bharati University, or the concert hall at Rabindra Sadan, on a tram in Rabindra Sarani or while stealing a kiss along the lake at Rabindra Sarobar.

After the British left, most of the colonial statues were taken away and the colonial names changed. Dalhousie Square became Binoy-Badal-Dinesh Bagh, Amherst Street became Rammohan Sarani, Landsdowne Road became Sarat Bose Road, making a city in which the colonial past was reinscribed as an age when Bengali giants strode the earth.

In 1911 the Calcutta football club Mohun Bagan had defeated a visiting English military team at their own game, playing barefoot. Every kid in Bengal who had ever touched a football knew that story. Recently, a statue of that famed 1911 team had been erected on Mohun Bagan Row in Shyambazar. Yet Mohun Bagan today is routinely defeated by teams from the most obscure corners of Asia's steppes and deserts. Maybe that was the last great trick of the rulers, to leave us with a tropical variant of Stockholm syndrome, so that the time when we were ruled would also be the era we would remember as our most glorious. It echoed my Dadu's lament: our golden age was when Calcutta had been the capital of the empire, its port the conduit of the loot of Asia. With the sahibs gone, our best days were done.

***

'Nothing happens in Calcutta, *yaar*,' a Bengali émigré said to me at a farmhouse wedding in Delhi. 'It just sucks you up in its shit.'

Durba and I were in her hometown to attend the wedding of one of her school friends. Delhi was flush with a sense of sudden self-importance as it prepared for the upcoming Commonwealth Games, Delhi's answer to Beijing's recently completed Olympics. The newspapers kept calling it a 'world-class city', whatever that was. Delhi-ites began to see its renewal in millennial terms. After all, the planned city of 'New' Delhi had grown as a colonial tumor upon 'Old' Delhi, which had been the capital of successive kingdoms for a thousand years. In Delhi, Durba showed me the ruins of past empires, which were casually strewn in residential neighbourhoods like Khirki and Hauz Khas. She took me to Lodi Gardens and Humayun's Tomb, which were iconic heritage sites that drew international tourists.

What could I possibly show Durba in my city? Calcutta, by contrast, was yesterday's child. Born as an English trading post on the Ganga and only three hundred-odd years young, for the camera-lugging foreigner who has visited Delhi, Calcutta offers nothing to see, nothing to do, and no one famous. Say this to a Calcuttan and he will become immediately defensive and retort: Why? What about the Victoria Memorial?

In the centre of Calcutta is the Maidan, a great green that stretches from Esplanade to the river and is a favoured grazing ground for the city's flocks of sheep and unemployed men. In the middle of the Maidan is the Victoria Memorial, our deranged Taj Mahal.

In the days of Umbrella Park, like all lovers in the city, we had eventually ended up in Victoria Memorial. The lawns in front of the Memorial are for families with kids. It was the only place in Calcutta that had elbow room. The grounds behind it are unofficially reserved for couples. On the southern lawn, nestled behind shrubs, they get busy, Victorian-style.

In Calcutta, love is sitting two by two at Victoria Memorial, whispering moodily to one another. The manicured lawns, peanut vendors and bribable police offer an opportunity to take your beloved in your arms and sneak a quick peck. Along the benches, young couples solemnly sit two by two, waiting for just such an opportunity. The brazen bring umbrellas. Sitting on a park bench, umbrella open in one hand, lovers briskly and arduously make out.

Dowdy Victoria sits on her giant armchair, surveying the hanky-panky all around. Behind her stands the building that bears her name. Built in the early 1900s, it is a specimen of the so-called Indo-Saracenic style popular with British architects in India at the time. The idea was to blend colonial styles with medieval Indian aesthetics. It sounds appealing in theory, but the results often look like imperial hubris in stone. If the Taj Mahal is a paean to eternal love, then the Memorial is an elegy to Calcutta's Victorianism.

Victoria was the first English monarch to rule India. By the time she became Empress, the British had already been running the place for a hundred years through a corporation called the East India Company. Calcutta, its capital, had ballooned into the largest city in Asia and the continent's most important centre of global trade. But the Victorian era brought more polish to the colonial enterprise. It dressed up naked moneymaking with a higher mission. For the first time, large numbers of British women arrived in India, which produced British families and British neighbourhoods – a racially separate world of bridge at the European club, civil lines and white towns. Most importantly, it produced a white supremacist idea of 'Britishness' as an exemplar of culture, as a bearer of something beyond guns and hunger called 'civilisation'.

The British left India in 1947. The Europeans who had lived in the old White Town had died or left, leaving an entirely brown metropolis. Park Street, the heart of that caramelised White Town, was lined with the best restaurants of the city. Legend had it that cabarets, with chanteuses and high kicks, used to take place on Park Street until the 1960s. That was all long ago, before the Communist years, before I was born. When I worked in Calcutta, the scene was somnolent. The menus and prices of most of the relic restaurants were still pleasantly congealed in a time warp, much like their decor.

In the years after I left, the new Sector Five money had awoken Park Street. On weekends, crowds swelled on the footpath outside Peter Cat, everyone speaking English all at once to get in through the door. I once took Durba to legendary Mocambo in our Umbrella Park days, before we were married. We slid into a couple of low armchairs like characters in a Graham Greene novel. We ordered beef steak accompanied by boiled vegetables and bhetki Filipino. The fish was prepared just as Imelda Marcos liked it, the menu said. The red fabric lampshades dangling above each table spread a warm vibe across the dining room, as if it were the twilight of a golden age.

***

Jayanti, my neighbour, had lent me a tattered copy of one of her favourite novels, Doris Lessing's *The Grass is Singing*. It was a book about white society in colonial Rhodesia, which is modern-day Zimbabwe. Among white Rhodesians it was a taken as a matter of pride that each Englishman who arrived in the African colony armed with highfalutin liberal principles would soon succumb to the colonials' racist worldview. It provided them with justification for their way of life. There was no other way to treat the natives really. A white person simply had no choice.

I was telling Durba about the Lessing novel after we had ordered our food at the Punjabi Dhaba. The Dhaba was in Phoolbagan, where we had once waited for Toton the fishmonger and his motley crew of associates during our flat hunt. The naans there were hot and the chicken curries hearty. The head waiter was always happy to see us, a middle-class couple in a place frequented by cabbies and chauffeurs.

We had ordered chicken *dopiaza* and naans, and a Coke for Durba. By mistake, the busboy brought us two Cokes. He was truly a boy, prepubescent, ten at most. But the smiling head waiter noticed and the yelling commenced.

'Imagine if the Ethicist column in the *New York Times* were set in Calcutta,' said Durba. 'Instead of "Do I have to purchase a gift from an overpriced registry for my cousin's wedding even if I don't like her?" or whatever, it would be "Should I stop going to my favorite Dhaba because it employs child labour?"'

'Would we come here if they employed slaves?' I asked.

'No,' she said. 'I guess that's our answer.'

'Will you stop going to street-corner tea shops, which all employ kids? Would you stop going to the houses of people who have children working as live-in maids?'

'Child labour is illegal,' she said. 'We could report them.'

'Slavery is illegal too,' I said, 'but that doesn't stop people from keeping children in their homes whom they feed and clothe but do not pay.'

Durba knew a woman who had raised a child from the age of eight to do her household chores. The woman would always say of the child: 'She is a daughter to me.' But the 'daughter', Durba explained, was never to marry, never have children, never leave. Instead she was to be a captive to her 'mother', insurance for her employers' old age, to care for the woman when her own children had left for more lucrative shores in Europe and America.

'I thought that form of subjection was uniquely Indian,' I said, 'until I discovered it recently in Edward P. Jones's novel *The Known World*, among slave owners in the antebellum South.'

One of our first arguments in Calcutta had been over servants. Every middle-class family in Calcutta has servants who come twice a day, seven days a week to scrub floors, do dishes and wash clothes. We both disliked the awkward dealings between 'master' and 'servant', the everyday enactment of domination and exploitation. I did not want to hire a servant. I did not want someone sweeping my floors and washing my boxers. Durba believed I was being impractical. Worse, she accused me of being a misogynist, for when servants were scarce, the work typically fell to the woman of the house.

There is a scene that appears early in the film *Gandhi*, when young Mohandas is cleaning latrines. It is from his early days in South Africa, where Gandhi went from being an unpromising lawyer to an exceptional activist. At his utopian ashram, Phoenix Farms, Gandhi had insisted on cleaning toilets, a caste-bound task that was considered the chore of 'Untouchables'. His wife refused to follow him, to which Gandhi reacted with righteous outrage. In the movie, we see a leader who is in turns idealistic and tyrannical, and ultimately contrite.

I struck a deal with Durba that I would sweep the floors and wipe them clean each day, and that she need not help. For a while, I squatted down with broom, rag and bucket. The idea of a middle-class man getting down on his haunches and scrubbing the kitchen floor was unthinkable. None would literally stoop to do such work.

My floor-washing embarrassed Durba, made her feel guilty, as if my sweeping and scrubbing were part of a strategy to show her up. I had not asked her to take on any household chores, but even while I cleaned the house, the arguments escalated.

Eventually I gave in; I wanted our fights to end. Durba hired Babita, a reed-thin woman who scrubbed our floors, cleaned our clothes and washed our dishes seven days a week for less than $20 a month.

When I read Lessing's descriptions of colonials in Rhodesia, I said to Durba that I felt I was reading about my society. I knew the mentalities of those colonists. Nothing about them shocked me or felt alien. Nor was I surprised by the ease with which outsiders fell into the local ways of being, of determining who is human and who is not. I could see it happening to myself.

'If we had been the whites there, we would have left.' Durba said. 'Why have you voluntarily come back?'

***

Moving to Calcutta was not like buying a summer house in Provence. It was not one of those fantasies that couples in America nurture together while folding the week's laundry or watching Netflix. In fact, only one half of our couple had wanted to move at all. Durba had arrived reluctantly and, as time wore on, her frustration with the city, and with me, only grew.

Bipedal movement, which can be optional when dating a woman in America, becomes essential in a city where there is ostensibly nowhere to go and nothing to do. You have to keep moving. In the mornings, Durba and I began to walk.

A *bhaar* of tea from the para shop, and we were off. Maniktala, Beadon Street, Hatibagan, Sovabazar – the North was all our own. One morning we stopped where Gray Street meets Central Avenue in Sovabazar to have breakfast at Mitra Café. Like the Coffee House or Basanta Cabin, Mitra Café was an institution, famed equally for its cutlets and its adda. The place was tight, about five wooden tables forged together. We sat on two chairs facing the road with a view of the open gutter and ordered toast, omelettes and tea, the traditional Bengali café breakfast.

Baskets of potatoes arrived from the morning bazaar and squatting workers began to peel them right in front of the gutter.

The man who sat across from us fished a hair out of his omelette. 'For the second day in a row,' he said, observing the specimen.

We ate quickly and left.

'That place was disgusting,' Durba said, as we walked through the morning bazaar.

I mumbled reluctantly that the tea was tepid, and the omelette could have been better.

'How is it,' Durba said, 'that back at Yale there were places where you refused to eat because the waiters didn't wear clean shirts. But here, you will happily dine on hair-stuffed omelettes in front of an open gutter?'

We turned right onto Chitpur Road. Hillocks of garbage lined the lanes. In gully after gully, we saw street dogs, public taps and one-bench tea shops with old men in thick glasses. Durba had spent a summer in Dar es Salaam, Tanzania, and these neighbourhoods, she said, looked worse than a Dar slum.

'You can understand at some level the desire of elites to secede,' she said. 'They are surrounded by this.'

Through one lane and another, following my intuition, we reached the railroad tracks. I found a breach in the fence and slipped across to the river. The Ganga was the colour of milky tea. There was no promenade but a few concrete benches. Down below, the morning bathers were washing themselves in peace. It was still early, and while we walked, street cleaners arrived with their wheelbarrows and brooms to sweep the garbage away.

***

A stack of parked rickshaws greeted us as we turned into a side street from broad Central Avenue. Muktaram Babu Street was narrow, lined with paan shops, sari shops, sweet shops, and a warehouse. None of these precursors prepared Durba for the first sight of Marble Palace. From the gate, you saw a garden, white columns among palm trees, a fountain, alabaster lions, wrought-iron verandas and statues of Europeans. The Palladian facade of Marble Palace was set back from the street so you could enjoy a panoramic view. It was a sight unlike any other in Calcutta.

'We would like to go inside,' I said to the guard at the gate.

'You need a permit,' the guard said.

'We haven't got it.'

'Then you can't get in.'

'Surely there is another way,' I suggested. 'I've been here before.'

The guard became suddenly bashful, as if I had asked him to belt out his favourite Bollywood tune. 'OK. Have a look inside,' he said, 'but don't forget us afterwards.'

There was a time when you could buy tickets at a counter outside. The counter is gone. Now you needed to acquire a permit twenty-four hours in advance from a government office in Dalhousie. The first time I bribed the guard, I did my best imitation of a drug buy on American TV, surreptitiously sliding the folded note into the guard's palm as I looked away and walked off. I had seen motorists bribe Calcutta traffic police my entire life. But I had never done it myself. Much like the first time I scalped tickets outside a ball game in America, I vastly overstated the gravity of my actions. The second time I bribed the guard at Marble Palace, I was more relaxed. I felt more guilty too but also strangely proud that I now knew how to work the system. By the third time, I felt more resentful than guilty. Had I been paying the guard more than the going rate? Why did these lazy fellows deserve a bribe anyway?

Bribing the guard was one small ethical compromise among a dozen others we made each day. Who wants to stand in line in a government office in God knows where, that, too, the day beforehand? The crooked path was easier and more efficient. After the third time around, it hardly felt wrong at all.

A portion of the Mullick family, who own the palace, still lives in the rear quarters of the compound, but the Marble Palace was never intended for habitation. It was built for show. When Rajendralal Mullick built it in 1835, he wanted to create a spectacle, a mini-Versailles on Muktaram Babu Street. At the side entrance to the palace, another guard was appointed as a guide. We took off our shoes as we would to enter a private house as he led us past the moose heads and the billiards tables with cue sticks as long as javelins, to start the tour in the corner room. The central attraction of the corner room was a wooden statue of the young Victoria, at least 12 feet high and made of a single piece of wood, with a face so pointy that she might have been Pinocchio's sister.

Mullick was roughly a contemporary of Queen Victoria. In the late 1700s, a group of villages were consolidated by the new rulers, the British, and transformed into a metropolis, forged by the forces of colonial power and global capital. In the 1770s, a third of the population of Bengal was wiped out by famine soon after the British began their rule. Farmland turned into jungle, as a society was decimated and turned upside down. Our experience of colonial contact was comparable to what had happened in the New World, in Hispaniola and Tenochtitlan. But those who were well poised for this transformation became rich beyond compare. The Mullicks have been in Calcutta since before the British. Like the Tagores, the Mullicks had owned a lot of the land that became Calcutta. They became one of the key trading families in the Company days. In his nineteenth-century life, Rajendralal Mullick amassed a collection of the bric-a-brac of Europe. The Music Room features Italian marble flooring that looks like a Persian rug, and marble statues of various sizes of Juno, Jupiter and Napoleon, as well as a Chinese incense holder the size of a wood stove. In the courtyard are alabaster statues representing each continent, and live tropical birds. The courtyard altar is used for prayers to Hindu goddesses, but the background panel features Diana the huntress, flanked by a plaster of Paris pantheon of Apollo, Sita and Ram. The guide led us across the courtyard and up the staircase. Every inch of wall space was covered with paintings from Europe, save the portrait of the palace's creator, Rajendralal Mullick, portly and moustached and wearing Indian clothes, at the top of the stairs.

On the second floor, 20-foot high Belgian glass mirrors bracketed both ends of the Ballroom. Beneath thirteen chandeliers were statues of Jesus, Mary, Galileo and Christopher Columbus. Around the balcony overlooking the courtyard were more statues, of Venus, gorillas, Autumn, an Orphan, 'Early Sorrow' and a four-person hookah larger than myself. Everything there had once been shipped, the guide said, piece by piece from Europe.

'Her eyes follow you,' he said as he switched on the lights of the Painting Room, and pointed to a life-size painting of a gypsy girl. Among the more valuable pieces in that room was a Murillo and also an original Rubens, *The Marriage of Saint Catherine*. The last Rubens on auction at Sotheby's in London had sold for $76.7 million.

Outside, pelicans strode the grounds, occasionally dipping into the giant fountains or fluttering their massive wings ominously to ward off international art thieves. The grounds included an aviary and what became the first zoo in India. Not much was left of it now, save the pelicans, some peacocks, monkeys and deer, surrounded by concrete buildings and old mansions, unpainted for several monsoons and now the colour of muck. These were the houses of traders allied with what was once the world's most powerful corporation.

At the corner of the Mullicks' property was the family temple to the god Jagannath, the reigning deity of the Rath chariot festival. The temple predates the palace and the aviary. Rumour has it that once 4,000 people were fed at the temple daily. Rajendralal's will stipulated that the daily feeding of the poor must go on. Even today, 400 destitutes are fed each afternoon. Among Hindus, feeding the destitute is a part of various religious events, a way for those blessed with wealth to rack up good karma.

'Whenever anyone needs paupers they come here,' said the guard, as I bribed him on the way out.

When I worked at the *Statesman*, I had visited the palace grounds with Sumitro during Rath, when the gardens and aviary were opened to the public and turned into a fairground. The para's rickshaw-pullers and street vendors milled about with their families, bought wind-up toys, rode ferris wheels and took aim with BB guns at balloons. As in the villages, a big man's power counted in feudal and not capitalist terms. Money was not the main measure. When traders and landlords moved from villages to Calcutta to form the Bengali elite, they had brought with them entire entourages of servants, guards, *punkah*-pullers, cooks, nurses, weavers, potters, shoemakers, jewellers, and so on. The retainers settled around the big man's house, in mini urban villages which today we call 'slums'. The more people you had around at your behest, the more servants, peons and underlings, the more prosperous you were considered to be. Power was defined by the capricious use of kindness and cruelty upon the many.

How different it was from Paris or Versailles, where the Marble Palace would otherwise not be out of place.

Rajendralal's wondrous collection may have seemed a shameless exercise in mimicry of Europe. Yet this motherlode of all things European resembled no place in Europe. It was a phenomenon possible only in nineteenth-century Calcutta. When Baron Haussmann redesigned Paris in the mid nineteenth century, and in so doing producing the template of the modern city, he widened the boulevards and opened up vistas to the grand monuments, and moved the slums to the urban fringe, out of sight. To create a picturesque city, the rich were sifted from the poor, the filth removed from the gates of mansions. In Paris, even today, the housing projects on its urban fringe are full of immigrants from the former colonies, unseen and unvisited by other Parisians unless they riot and appear on television screens.

For Calcutta's rich, the poor were an asset, not a problem. The aristocrats needed to live among their gophers, underlings and retinues of servants. Mullick's Patronage was the basis of the big man's bigness, as it still is today for the political bosses in Calcutta's paras. The city's design follows a logic entirely at odds with what we expect modern cities to be. All those forces and peoples that other cities have struggled to segregate and sequester have been here together from the start.

The Epic City

The harsh afternoon sun turned sepia. The panwalla rushed for cover, taking his pans, moist and wrapped in burlap, to stow away somewhere dry. The panwalla's 'boy' huddled underneath the stall next to the crates of supplies. Two medical representatives had been waiting at the stall, talking shop, periodically interrupting each other to speak into their cell phones. They were going to Convent Road, then Deshapriya Park in South Calcutta. They grabbed their order quickly and rushed off. The ominous line of darkness was advancing from that side of the city.

The winds came first. They arrived suddenly. What was the English word for these winds? Gusts? Gale forces? A tempest? In Bengali we call it *jhor*, aspirated, onomatopoeic. *Jhawwwwr*.

The jhor upturned the tenuous lives of tarps and tenterhooks. The tarpaulin roofs of pavement eateries began writhing, then flying open like giant capes. The jhor propelled the darkness. I heard the whoosh of the wind, the gurgling *gorjon* of clouds, then the beating of rain. The monsoons had arrived.

I took shelter under a shop's tarp. The ferocity of those drops drew lakes on the pockmarked pavement. The lid of a jar floated by like a little round tugboat. Two teenage boys in vests and sandals rode up on a motorbike, drenched, looking to buy cigarettes, and rode off. A taxi with arthritic wipers passed by, all its windows rolled up, the passengers squished together exchanging their warm breath.

A crowd of us had sought refuge under the tarp. It was pouring from above, from the side, from every direction. We teetered on ever-shrinking islands of dry earth. The tarp was now heaving with water. It sagged and water tapered though a furrow and poured down like from an open tap. Soon we would be soaked.

Moments like these had seemed so thrilling were when we were small: rainy days off from school and paper boats to sail as streets turned to rivers, a Bengali boy's vision of Venice. Now, I worried about all the trash piled in the streets, all that dog shit flowing together in those streams, ferrying disease and calamity.

Our fights came like the jhor. It was a blessing that there were so many rooms in our flat – all the more doors for Durba and I to bang. This time it was about Barista, an upscale coffee chain that had come up in our para. Barista was air conditioned, set off from the road. What a difference air conditioning made in keeping all the elements out, not just the heat but dust, smells, and most of all, noise. The city is a soundscape – politicians' street-corner speeches, loudspeakers belching Bollywood music, promoters yelling business deals into their cell phones, the cadences of passing hawkers, the *tung-tung* of trams, the calls of bus conductors from footholds. You could listen to a tea shop, a para, a city as if it were a symphony. Peering out from Barista, the city seemed set on mute.

For Durba, the café was a place where she went to work, to relax, a refuge among the detritus. One morning, we were quibbling and I said, 'You want to live and die in a Barista.'

The jhor arrived. The whoosh and bang, *sturm und drang,* the maelstrom.

'Who are you here?' Durba asked. 'You wouldn't think twice about going to Starbucks in America, but here, oh no, you're a Bengali bhodrolok. You must drink tea from a tea shop served by a ten-year-old boy while you discuss Marxism with your bhodrolok friends.'

'All you want is to escape to a mini America,' I said.

'The person you are here has nothing to do with what you are like in America.'

'What is so horrible about Calcutta that it needs to be escaped?'

It was a way some people tried to live in Calcutta, pretending to belong to a world that is perpetually not only climate-controlled but socially controlled. From their little glass chambers, they had nothing but shame and disdain for the world in which they lived. 'Ooof!' they said when they stepped outside of their air-conditioned glass chambers and walked two steps to their air-conditioned, chauffeured cars. 'Ooof!' they said when they had to deign to interact with a guard, a shopkeeper, a clerk. Their haughtiness comprised entirely of surfaces, the way they intoned Bengali words with an odd inflection, the way they mixed in English words unnecessarily in their speech, not to express their thoughts but to make distinct their difference. Their city shamed them. They were only Calcuttan accidentally, they thought, born there by mistake when they really belonged in Paris, London or New York. But like Rajendralal's Marble Palace, these creatures could exist only in Calcutta. Their Ooofs and sighs and Beng-lish intonations made no sense anywhere else.

'What a world there is around you!' I wanted to grab them and say, this city of such curiosities and possibilities, this amalgam of all that we modern humans have been, in all our glory and callousness, and all that we can yet become.

'You are an American from New Jersey,' Durba said. 'You were born in Buffalo. You want to make me feel guilty about going to Barista, you American hypocrite? Who do you think you would marry who would be happy here? Except a little *bou* you can get from an arranged marriage who will cook you *shukto* and *bhaat*. Which of your friends from Yale or Princeton would last out here?'

Then she would list a series of women as potential alternatives for the position of spouse, as if to say, 'None of them is as tough as me. I am the best option around.'

Durba's way of thinking – as if I had gone comparison-shopping when falling in love – made no sense to me at all. When the feuds ended badly, she would say that I was 'a fake Gandhian fraud', that my return carried with it some bogus idea of salvation. Hypocrite. Fake. Fraud.

In the end it always came back to themes we had debated from our earliest days together, between the Indian who did not want to live in India – amid its mediocrity and moral compromises – and the American who insisted on returning for reasons he could not yet fully articulate, for reasons that were sentiments and intuitions, not really reasons at all. In Calcutta those pitter-patter April-shower arguments became full-blown monsoons.

How could a marriage be built in this climate? The city seemed to conspire against us.

At night I lay alone, unable to sleep. The insomnia of earlier years returned, new miseries triggering familiar symptoms.

'The neighbourhood lies in sleep with doors closed/But I keep hearing the night knocking at my door,' the poet Shakti wrote, 'In my heart, half-dissolved, long-travelled/I fall asleep within pain/Suddenly I hear the night knocking at my door.'

Day after day, I lingered in bed till after noon, the hangover of dreams still clinging to me. I had a recurring dream of Calcutta covered in snow. Durba said it was my subconscious telling me I wanted to be back home in New Jersey. Was it her interpretation, or was it her twist of the knife?

'Aha, you phoney, you would rather not be here yourself.'

When we fall in love, we each feel our story is unique. But when we fight, we learn how pitifully common we are, how like every other warring couple everywhere. None of our education and upbringing has protected us from this banal fate. I could hear myself acting like my feuding uncles and aunts, shouting, 'Bullshit-No Bullshit,' playing insult ping-pong over the dinner table while the rice grew cold. Each time, I saw the jhor coming and I stood there, waiting helplessly for the torrent. It would be smooth sailing, they all said. The first year of marriage was supposed to be bliss. In those dreams of a tranquil snowcapped city perhaps it was not Calcutta I sought to escape, but our private hell.

In Dida's house my grandparents had had separate bedrooms, serving and volleying their invectives across the open air of the long dalan. In that game of long-distance disputes, there was an aspect of sport. The capacious venue and our spectatorship provided each quarrel its due and then let it dissipate. That older order of living in a crowd with so many nosy mothers, brothers, nephews and aunts, seemed to buffer the blows between two people. I knew, too, from my own childhood that that older order was thick with politicking and intrigue. Better to go off and live apart, in separate rooms, separate flats. But in those truncated lives jammed into little boxes, those flats for a husband, wife and child, with 600 square feet and a cage called a veranda, where was the space to air discontent, and the people to serve as buffers and blunt the blows?

Others in our position might have sought the services of an astrologer, made offerings at Moulali's mazar or at Kalighat temple. Durba held fast to American dogmas. She had determined that we needed couples counselling. From somewhere she found a German marriage counsellor. I had never met a German in Calcutta – white people of any nationality were so rare that they acquired the status of local celebrity. We met the counsellor in her home in a high-rise flat. She had her blonde hair in two braids done up into a crown, and wore a maxi, the shapeless printed kaftans that some Bengali women wear at home when they are not expecting visitors. We spent forty minutes fielding sharp questions that felt like a police interrogation. When we left her office, for the first time in a long time, Durba and I were united about something. Better to risk divorce, we agreed, than to sit through that again.

***

It had taken me a few tries before I found Allen Kitchen Restaurant in Sovabazar. For one thing, they are only open four hours a day, less if the food runs out. For another, they are more kitchen than restaurant. Allen is a throwback to the old-style Bengali 'cabin', with bare wooden tables and benches in the back, a tiny sink, and bulbs that are hardly more candescent than the kerosene lamps we used during power cuts in my childhood.

Shrimp sells at astronomical prices in Maniktala Market, because the best stuff is exported to Europe or America. The coveted delicacy can still be found on plates during special occasions, like Jamai Shosti (the festival of the son-in-law) or a championship win of the Mohun Bagan football team. But the shrimp cutlet, the prince of street-food during my childhood, has morphed beyond recognition. What has replaced it in most Calcutta establishments is a mound of batter packed with filling of questionable provenance, deep fried in shortening with a fantail sticking out. The tail may be the only part of the cutlet that originates from a shrimp.

Not at Allen. Each evening, the Saha brothers, who run Allen, make sixty-five shrimp cutlets and not one more. The shrimp sits in an icebox. Upon ordering, they are butterflied and then gently hammered into a flat cutlet shape, then battered and fried. No shortening, nor even vegetable oil, is used. At Allen, the shrimp cutlets are fried in pure ghee.

Nostalgia is the feeling that always disappoints. The taste of something you remember from your childhood can almost never be recovered as an adult. The flavour is gone. The shrimp cutlets at Allen tasted like my childhood, only better. They were so delicious I could simply eat the batter alone. No filler, no skimping, no corners cut. It was a thing of beauty.

The man who worked the fryer wore a white T-shirt stretched taut over a substantial belly. He looked like he could have been grilling burgers at White Rose System back home in Jersey. Allen was run almost like a speakeasy, known only by worth of mouth. There was a mention of the place in an article in the weekend section of *Anandabazar*, the Bengali daily, which was how I had heard of it, I said to him.

He shrugged. Many such write-ups had come out, he said.

Why didn't they have them framed and adorning the turmeric walls? I asked, as was the norm in most eateries.

'We're not into that,' he said.

'Why don't you fry more than sixty-five a night?' I asked.

'This is enough for us.'

I felt like a philistine for suggesting they prostitute their God-given talent at making a shrimp cutlet into an enriching scheme. It was as if my logic, which demanded that a business seek to maximise profit, advertise and accumulate, was flawed. Frying shrimp cutlets was less an enterprise than a pastime, something to do between tea and dinner time, in a shack, with sixty-five shrimp. There was a momentary pleasure in a job done well. His logic was unimpeachable: This is enough for us.

***

Durba and I kept walking, always river-bound. In the mornings we would stop for tea at the corner stall, pass the morning walkers in adda repose at Niranjan's, and walk onward through Maniktala, towards the river. Along the Ganga, waterfront property comprised warehouses and old mansions. Residents peeked through the windows of the subdivided warrens. Others had become places to stack and store merchandise. In one old mansion, we spotted a roaring lion.

We doubled back over the train tracks for a closer view. A row of lions, fangs bared, tongues precisely sculpted inside their gaping mouths, led from the entrance of the mansion down to the narrow corridor inside. They almost made me flinch. Accompanying each was a statue of Durga, the mother goddess, bearing weapons in each of her ten hands. At her feet lay Mahishashur, the demon with eight-pack abs like a Bollywood villain, being speared to death. Ten of these tableaus were lined up along the passage that led into the courtyard. In that narrow space, a divine drama was being readied.

Under a naked bulb, a sculptor stood on a chair, daubing a clay and water mixture on the torso of the last Durga statue, preparing it for painting. Past him, inside the courtyard, were more statues. At one time, mansions like this one hired sculptors to construct the family's Durga in the courtyard, where she would later be worshipped. But these deities, the sculptor said, had been commissioned for various neighbourhood *pujos* across the city. The mansion had become a workshop. It now belonged to that archipelago that was Kumortuli, literally, the neighbourhood of *kumors*, who are clay sculptors by caste. This was the time of year when the sculptors of Kumortuli transmuted Gangetic clay into divinity. The monsoons and their maelstroms would soon be a thing of the past. Everywhere scaffoldings of *pandals* would arise, bamboo lattices built several storeys high, blocking streets, houses for the goddess.

***

On the first morning of *pujo*, we took a taxi to Sovabazar. A stone's throw from Allen was the Sovabazar Palace of Nabakrishna Deb. The first ever major Durga Pujo in Calcutta was hosted by Deb. It was a victory party for the East India Company to celebrate the beginning of British rule.

Wedged between a river and a swamp, the great Bay of Bengal a few miles below, Calcutta's unsuitability for urban habitation can be matched only by New Orleans, that other tropical port city built by colonial capital. By the late 1600s, the Ganga was full of traders – the Danes, the Dutch, the French – who had set up trading towns under the protection of the local king. The British needed a base too and so the East India Company set up a trading post on these banks in 1690, the official year of Calcutta's founding. Rivalries between European traders would cause the British to build fortifications in Calcutta, causing tensions with the host Nawabs. In 1757, the Company decided to pursue a hostile takeover. Fifty thousand of the Nawab's troops faced about 3,000 troops of Lord Clive of the East India Company in a village north of Calcutta called Plassey. As the battle commenced, a flank of the Nawab's troops, led by his traitorous general Mir Jafar, abandoned him and refused to fight, having been paid off by Clive and his Indian financiers beforehand. It rained a bit and by sundown, like a good day's cricket, it was done. A corporation had won the wealthiest province in India in an afternoon, losing about twenty men in the process. It was the birth of British colonialism in India.

What happened at Plassey was the final formality to a business deal. Clive walked away with Bengal's treasury. The Company loaded the province's gold and silver – equal to £2.5 million British Pounds (or about £200 million British Pounds today) – in a fleet of more than a hundred boats and sent it to Calcutta. Clive kept about 10 per cent of the booty for himself. When Clive came back to Calcutta, he was feted by the local merchant class that had bankrolled his intrigue, most notably Nabakrishna Deb of Sovabazar. Deb's Durga Pujo was a victory party for Lord Clive and his men. A thousand and one animals were sacrificed, food and clothes were distributed among the poor, and dancing girls and Madeira wine were enjoyed by the British guests. To this day, the annual festivities at the Deb palace are called the 'Company Pujo'.

As per tradition, rifles are still fired to kick off the festivities. The dancing girls are gone, but the spectacle remains. The courtyard of the mansion is full of guests dressed in their finery to see Durga at her altar, as it has been for over 250 years.

From Sovabazar, we walked northward to Bagbazar. Bagbazar's Durga was housed in a temple-style pandal in a public park, just as I remembered from my childhood. Bagbazar was one of the first *sarbajanin* – literally 'for everyone' – pujos in Calcutta. It was founded about a hundred years ago, when pujos were democratised, moving from the courtyard altars of aristocrats into the streets. Among para pujos, Bagbazar was also the standard-bearer of tradition. It did not deviate according to the aesthetic whims of the moment: its deities and demons did not look like Bollywood icons; they did not levitate or wear sarongs. Durga's skin was yellow, her eyes elongated, her face broad and flat and not naturalistic. Each year, they reliably presented the iconic traditional image of the goddess.

The *anjali*, or serenading of the deity, had just started when we entered the pandal. The venue was packed, and in our midst were the drummers with *dhols*, or drums the size of barrels. The drummers built up a frenetic, deafening beat as they moved around in a circle. Around them danced men and women with lit bowls of incense, smoky and strong. The smoke entered us, obscured our vision. The deafening thump of the drums roared faster and faster. The beat resonated in our bones. We were in a pulsating cloud that demanded trancelike submission of mind, of thought. It was not something to think about, or observe. There was nothing to do but feel.

***

When we were kids, pujo meant closed books, new clothes and cap guns. The guns were made of rough-hewn metal that scraped your fingers. Each pop set off an igniting flash, then smoke. Pop, pop, pop! Everywhere on D. L. Roy Street, where we spent most of our pujo holidays, boys with guns fired all day long. The loudspeakers in the background played Bollywood tunes, songs forbidden in my house, as in many bhodrolok Bengali homes where Tagore still reigned.

'Ek do tin, char panch chhae saath aath now daas egaaara, bara tera' – 'One two three, four five six seven eight nine, ten eleven, twelve thirteen. I count while I wait for you ...' I learned most of the Hindi I later used as a journalist from those loudspeakers. Of course, sometimes the lyrics were pre-linguistic yelps ripped from Gloria Estefan, like: *'Oye Oye, Oye Oye Aaaah.'* (Translation: Oye Oye, Oye Oye Aaaah.)

In my childhood the neighbourhood pujo was still funded by local collections. Young men from the local club came around to each house with receipt books to take up contributions to fund the para pujo. Now the para boys went instead to the big fish, the businesses and large corporations who viewed pujos as an advertising vehicle, paying for banner ads around the pandal. But the way pujo was organised was still the same. From the running lights to the drummers, everything was arranged and coordinated by the para *dadas*, the men who sat on benches drinking tea, smoking Filter Wills and playing carrom at the one-room para clubs, people like my Mejo Mama and his Congress cronies.

A club down the street from our flat had built Kerala's Padmanabhan Palace, with an ornate spire covered with sculpted gods and dancers. Around the corner, on a two-bit patch of grass grandiosely called 'Triangle Park' – a pocket too small even for an ordinary sized pandal – the organisers had installed a Megatronesque Mahishashur being vanquished by a Robot Durga who looked as if she had emerged from Fritz Lang's *Metropolis*. There were over 500 pandals across the city. Each was made of bamboo lattices built several storeys high, covered with cloth and a great deal else, to morph into the sinking Titanic, Hogwarts School, Machu Picchu, the White House, the Trevi Fountain or the ruins of Angkor Wat. In style, the deities were as varied as the pandals, but the story was everywhere the same: a duel between good and evil. Durga, the mother goddess, weapons in each of her ten arms, astride a lion, vanquishing Mahishashur. For one week, the city was taken over as the scene of the celestial battle. Calcutta was rebuilt and redrawn for gods and demons to stride upon.

During pujo, we went from spectacle to spectacle, 'pandal hopping'. Among us kids, pandal hopping was a competitive sport. How many deities had you seen, how many pandals? How about running lights at night? Each stop could take a couple of hours of waiting, in snaking lines through mazes built from bamboo poles, all to go inside the pandal for a quick viewing of the goddess in full regalia. The devout raised clasped hands to *pranam* the deity, but for us pujo had nothing to do with devotion. It was about racking up the digits. Did you catch the big attractions: Bagbazar, Ahiritola, Mohammad

Ali Park, College Square, Shimla Bayam Samiti, Vivekananda Sporting, all in the North? Well then, did you do the South – Park Circus, Ekdalia, Jodhpur Park, Mudiali, Behala? During pujo, a whole new geography emerged, subverting Dalhousie and Esplanade, Victoria and Park Street. The centre of Calcutta lost prominence as an epic city arose, inscribed by a new architecture.

***

In New Jersey, pujos are held pragmatically on weekends, in high-school cafeterias. Food is served on styrofoam plates. In high-school auditoriums, musicians from Calcutta are brought in for evening programmes. Pujo is an indoor affair, perhaps more intimate, perhaps even more devout, full of the good intentions of organisers who want their children, raised in America playing travelling soccer and Xbox, to learn something of their 'culture'. But there are no loudspeakers, no pandals, no street crowds. At those pujos, I feel that Calcutta is mocking us – for leaving, for the hubris to think that something like a city and a culture can be packaged and plopped down anywhere. Can there be jazz, Second Line, Mardi Gras, without New Orleans? Can it exist without the overgrown cemeteries from which it arose, without the streets, narrow and crowded by houses packed close together so that the sound of funeral marches reverberate, beckoning all to empty out into the streets to join? Can it exist without the people who marched while playing their dirges? Can you put all that into an iPod and press play? The architecture of a city is not just big buildings, but corners and clubs and pandals, sounds and bodies and moments. Its social fabric is held together like bones and tendon and muscle and skin, to form a whole. You cannot carve one piece out and plop it in the middle of suburban New Jersey, served on styrofoam plates in a high-school cafeteria.

Another city rises during Durga Pujo, an epic city full of possibilities and visions, heroically redrawn. From the profane Company days, pujo was never about private piety. It was about strangers coming together for spectacle. That is why even a non-believer like me believes in pujo, believes in its epic narrative power to rewrite the destiny of a place. There is nowhere else in the world where such a spectacle exists, no other city where hundreds of para clubs put on a pageant that transforms a metropolis into an epic stage. It makes you believe in the endless possibilities of which human beings are capable when they choose to come together in millions to form a unique cosmopolis. It is only when the pujos arrive that we realise that our way of being is not finished yet.

PART III

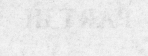

Crossing the Canal

'Work hard, play hard.' That had been the mantra when I was at Princeton, which really meant 'work work work' until you forget what 'play' even means.

When I first came back to write for the *Statesman,* no one was working hard or playing hard. I used to wonder how a daily newspaper could be produced in this climate. After decades, telephones finally worked, but no one wanted to do an interview over the phone. 'Come over,' they always said, and then, when you arrived, they would be 'not in their seat'. Waiting in the corridors of government offices soon became my favourite pastime, at Medical College, in Lal Bazar, at the Writers' Building, waiting and drinking tea.

For one of my first assignments, I had to speak with an official in the health department. After a week and a half of postponed interviews, the official finally granted me a hearing on a monsoon afternoon. I arrived drenched, with a photographer in tow, only to hear that the big babus at the Writers' Building had not given him authorisation to comment on the story. 'I'm very sorry. If there's anything I can do. Perhaps you would like some tea?'

Sit, have tea, and roll with the punches. There is no place you have to go that you are not late to anyway. So drink up.

The *Statesman* employed an army of men to serve tea at regular intervals. There were the liveried waiters in all-white uniforms, like Moulvi and Ashraf, who served tea in cups and saucers to the editorial department – the newspaper's bourgeoisie – at our desks four times a day. The office handed out little coupon books for two rupees, which contained seventeen coupons. In exchange for a coupon, Moulvi would serve you your morning cup of tea.

By late afternoon when the proletariat who operated the presses arrived for duty, a second battalion of tea-servers appeared, dressed in shorts. The 'half-pant' tea was intended to fortify the muscle power of the workers. It was strong and syrupy-sweet, and served in chipped cups without saucers. Officially, there was to be no fraternising between half-pant and full-pant tea; each class was to remain confined to its own cuppa. A press man would never dream of ascending to the cup-and-saucer elysium of editorial, just as a subeditor from the newsroom could be reprimanded for rubbing shoulders with the proles below. Yet every evening, the shorts-clad servers of half-pant tea did a surreptitious round of the newsroom. For half a rupee, I soon learned, you could score a cup of the contraband.

The Statesman House contained a whole society frozen in a time warp. Inside that stately edifice were hallways with hillocks of discarded files, patrolled by cats. They led to labyrinthine narrow corridors and secret stairs and mezzanine floors, to departments carved out by partitions and sub-partitions. In those back alleys of the building worked hundreds of peons, liftmen, waiters, cooks, typists, chauffeurs and clerks, and only about a dozen reporters.

I had just started working there when I met the bard of the peons, Nanhe Singh.

'What's your name?' he whispered, beckoning me like a bookseller on College Street as I passed him in the corridor. 'I shall make a poem from it. I have written poems about hundreds of people at the *Statesman*.'

Then he ratted them off one after the next. Over cups of half-pant tea, he would recite poems on Netaji Subhas Chandra Bose, the Mughal emperor Akbar, or Indrani in the classified department. Nanhe wrote epic verse about Ram and Krishna, and he penned rib-tickling satires of local political leaders.

Aside from poetry, Nanhe's other passion was politics, and he was a vocal union man. After decades, management had connived to chuck out the Communist labour union, CITU, from the premises, along with the life-size cutouts of Marx and Lenin, and replaced them with a docile company union. But Nanhe remained loyal to the CITU union, writing couplets mocking the management that he spread like samizdat.

When not penning revolutionary rhymes or writing epic verse, he perched on a backless wooden bench outside the newsroom, smoking bidis and watching a board of little red lights. A light went on when someone in editorial pressed the buttons we each had fitted below our desks. It meant that Nanhe was being summoned to carry a memo from editorial to the sea of clerks in accounts, or fetch takeout from Saina across the street. He was a gopher. Some peons brought lunches, some deposited their bosses' electric bills, some sold ganja to the reporters, and all peddled in gossip. There were more peons at the paper than reporters. Many were second- or third-generation *Statesman* employees. Among them, one peon was dedicated to polishing the walking stick of the editor in chief, C.R. Irani, a.k.a 'the Boss', a.k.a. 'the Old Man'. Our relationship to the Old Man was that of serfs to a feudal lord. We never saw the Old Man. We felt his aura from time to time, like while being apologetically shooed out of the elevator by Topiwala, the lift-man, because, 'the Boss is coming'. The Old Man rode the lift solo.

The Old Man was only known to us by his symbols: his car, his cane and his column. He wrote a 'Caveat' column, which appeared with alarming regularity on the *Statesman's* front page, typically hectoring some government official to 'sit down' or 'stand up', as if it were written by the headmaster in a primary school.

The Old Man was a member of the Bengal Club, which in British times had a policy of 'no dogs and Indians'. For a time, one of the officers at the club had run afoul of the Old Man. The Old Man unleashed a barrage of Caveat columns asking sundry club members to sit down and stand up.

The last British editors at the *Statesman* had left in the 1970s but even when I arrived almost thirty years later, the trappings of empire were intact. Bengali old-timers still ate fish curry and rice lunches with knives and forks, deboning *rohus* with surgical skill gleaned from the sahibs, who were long gone. Willie, the operator still announced, 'Staytes-mun', when you called the main telephone line, his stentorian voice carrying the gravitas of its century-old colonial tradition.

At one time the *Statesman* had been the largest paper in Asia, back when Calcutta was the capital of British India. It had exposed the famines of the late 1800s, which had been engineered by the British, sending reporters into famine-stricken districts for months on end, just as it was the first paper to report on the British-manufactured famine of 1943, when three million Bengalis had died. At a time of war, it had defied the embargo on the news by printing photos of dead bodies on the footpaths of Calcutta. In my childhood, it had exposed an international arms scandal which had implicated a sitting prime minister. The *Statesman* had a reputation for reporting the news impartially. For a hundred years, it had been the standard-bearer of Indian journalism. So, even though the paper's ageing readers were dying daily by the dozens, and even though the Old Man was doing nothing to compete with the newer newspapers to attract young readers, in Calcutta, the *Statesman* was still tenuously the king.

***

One morning, Mike called Imran and I to his office. Topiwala's son had gone missing. The boy was three and had wandered out of his mother's sight sometime that morning. Topiwala – 'the Hat Man', so called because he wore a golf cap at all times – was a lift-man, one of the legions of men from the downstairs world who were to remain unseen and unheard. Topiwala had come to Mike knowing he would be the most likely man upstairs to help. Mike turned to us.

In the afternoon, Imran and I took a trip across the Ganga to the city of Howrah, a cemetery of factories whose chimneys stood like tombstones. Topiwala stayed in a couple of rooms around a courtyard in a tenement. Less than a mile away was Howrah Station, where you could take a train to any destination from Kashmir to Kanyakumari. If the boy had been kidnapped, he could be anywhere in the country. But why kidnap a lift-man's son?

There were other more likely possibilities. Perhaps Topiwala had a feud with a neighbour who wanted to teach him a lesson, or had become a target of local toughs out to extort cash. But Topiwala had just moved into the area. He hadn't had time to make enemies. His wife stayed home alone all day with their children, without any family or friends to keep a watchful eye. Imran and I trawled the lanes and main roads. We spoke to the neighbours, the landlord, the local political *dadas*, the boys at the para club. We chatted with the paan and cigarette sellers. The boy had last been seen at around 11 a.m. There were a couple of Bihari women in the para who begged professionally at Howrah Station every morning. Imran bantered so well in Bhojpuri that the beggar women offered to buy us tea. But they had seen nothing. No one had any leads. But we made our presence felt: we were from the biggest English paper in Calcutta, and we were watching. Topiwala was not a man to be pushed around.

Over the next couple of days, we kept making calls to the local police station so that they would actually look for the boy. Two days later, the police found Topiwala's son not far from where he had disappeared. He appeared to have been fed, and was unharmed. Whoever had picked him up realised he had to be let go. That was the only time in my life I have been bear-hugged by a battalion of lift-men. To this day, Topiwala maintains that we found his son. Imran and I had done no such thing, really. We had only tried our best to help. We had exerted our influence. For anyone who was not in a position of power, who did not sit in an air-conditioned office, that was more than you could hope for.

That was the best part of being a reporter. You could be looking out the window while your bus was stuck in traffic, and see something that might lead to a story, or go to the hospital to visit a recovering relative and discover a man at the next bed who had a story worth writing about. A story could come from anywhere, at any time, if you kept your eyes open. Being a reporter meant having a blanket licence to go anywhere and ask anyone anything. There was no other line of work that would allow such latitude, the chance to go so many places and meet so many people. No other job gave you such a chance to understand the city.

Imran and I thought like reporters twenty-four hours a day, seven days a week. We talked about stories constantly, at the tea shop around the corner, or at Islam saab's stall in the gully that ran along Tipu Sultan Mosque, wolfing down samosas with fillings that were never clearly classifiable as meat or vegetable. All along the gully were cheap restaurants selling biryani, parathas and mutton. By day the editors sent off their favorite peons to fetch the slow-cooked savouries. Night after night, Saina restaurant sent clay containers soaked in oil, mutton *chaanp* – 'mutton chops' braised in spicy juices all day long – to the newsroom. They went perfectly with a bowl of biryani or a greasy paratha in a combination that today makes me salivate and feel ill at the same time. At the mouth of the gully, at six every evening a man arrived with a vat of raw beef and cow innards, squatted on the pavement and began skewering. The skewered mysteries were then stuffed into parathas with some onions, cut chillies and a squeeze of lemon, and wrapped into a roll with notebook paper. Within an hour, all the five-rupee beef rolls would be sold out. It was no Nizam's for sure, but it kept you going just like the half-pant tea and the endless cigarettes that fuelled our prose.

Imran lived in Kidderpur, a vast Muslim area around the port. His coordinates in the city were thoroughly different from mine, and that difference was coded by religion. Hindus lived among Hindus. Muslims lived with Muslims. Calcutta was a segregated city, and at least the Hindu side, the side that ruled, had long ago decided not to see this fact. One in four people in the state of Bengal was Muslim. At least one in five people in the city was Muslim. But you rarely found Muslims in newspapers, on television channels, on university faculties or even in government offices. A generation of Communist rule had stopped the riots and killings that happened elsewhere in India. The Hindu right couldn't spew its ideology here. It was considered odious 'cowbelt politics', the madness of people from the North, with their backward, fanatical ways. When Bengali Hindus, whether Congress or Communist, spoke, they sounded like Frenchmen, parroting abstract universals. But like Frenchmen, they protected their bounded society with wordless codes.

The *Statesman* staff was full of Muslims. They worked in the kitchen, delivered tea, ran the presses. There were no Muslims in the newsroom until Imran arrived. There were no Americans either, until I did. But somehow I could slide back uneasily into a former self, Bengali, Hindu, bhodrolok. Imran had no such fallback. Our friendship, in turn, was often suspect. Was I a CIA agent sent by the Americans to uncover terrorist plots, recruiting a young Muslim to help me penetrate clandestine worlds? Such were the divisions in Calcutta that this sort of theorising seemed more plausible than the friendship of young reporters.

The city to which I returned as a reporter was caught in a conspiracy of silence. The lines drawn by Partition went right through the city, pulling some people in and cutting others out. But everyone pretended not to see those lines at all. In the paper, there was no coverage of the Muslim parts of the city, unless there was a 'communal' issue, meaning when Muslims complained that their religion had been offended and took to the loudspeakers and the streets. What was the need? Everyone knew all there was to know.

Ask for directions and a man might get to talking about how you have to be careful these days who you ask – 'Muslims are everywhere, you know, not that they're all bad, but as a community they are full of criminals and pickpockets.' For me, it became like a game to see how it would pop up, how the communal angle would be worked into the most unlikely conversation. I once did a feature article on one of the oldest neighbourhood Durga pujos in North Calcutta, a feel-good story that papers run during the holidays. One day, when I went to interview the elderly doctor who headed the pujo committee, apropos of nothing, he began ranting that there were too many Muslims in the next neighbourhood. For a time, Imran was part of a team of reporters who reported on civic problems in each municipal ward. The problems were always the same: power cuts, water shortages, and so on. One day, Imran was in a Hindu neighbourhood abutting Muslim-majority Rajabazar, interviewing residents about civic problems. He asked one local if he had any complaints and the man responded: 'Our civic problem is Mohammedans.'

Of course, had the interviewee asked the reporter's name first, his response would surely have been, 'Lack of drinking water.' Quickly I learned the code of the street. What is your name? Where do you live? Those two questions unmasked your identity. Rajabazar, Taltala, Zakaria Street, Eliot Road, Park Circus, Topsia, Tiljala, Iqbalpur, Metiabruz, Watgunj, Garden Reach, Kidderpur. In these neighbourhoods, you would find the Muslim fifth of the city.

One's name and one's neighbourhood are the dead giveaways. I was read as Bengali and Hindu. Doors opened and closed based on those two signifiers. Trust was given and taken away based on them. There were many times when a man would begin talking and then change his tune once he had found out your name and your neighbourhood. When I reported on problems at the Calcutta madrasa, Muslim students would complain about Hindus until they discovered I was not Muslim, at which point the mask would come on. They would mouth the rhetoric learned from political speeches and schoolbooks about how all of us were brothers.

What was unsayable politically was enacted everywhere else. In Hindu paras, a Muslim couldn't rent a house. In many Hindu firms, a Muslim couldn't get a job any more. In many Hindu homes, a Muslim couldn't even work as a cook or a driver without taking on a fake Hindu name. There were no Muslim quotas for government jobs or college admission as there were for lower-caste Hindus, and little legal recourse for the daily discrimination, which was quite straightforward.

In the years when Imran and I reported for the *Statesman*, every day was an exercise in masking and unmasking. Nowhere was this more the case than when we reported on issues that might have a communal component. Hindus and Muslims look alike but yet wear entirely different masks around one another. You can't always tell a man's community by his comportment. While working on an article about a banned Islamist student organisation, Imran and I were once caught in a jam together, surrounded by a mob of Muslim students at the university's Muslim hostel (a relic of the colonial past when Hindus and Muslims ate and boarded separately). The local student-union dadas were leading the pack, accusing us of inflaming communal sentiments, threatening to call the police and their local political patron. They did not dare to pummel us – we were *Statesman* journalists after all – but they were scared, and their fear led them to swaggering bluster.

The daily activity of a reporter is mostly banter, employing the gift of the gab to get behind the mask to the man, flattering his ego, assuaging his fears, inflaming his jealousies, all to get the story. Imran and I had sufficiently diffused their fears to quell the mob, and left unscathed that day. A few days later, one of the union leaders ran into Imran on College Street. 'Hey, aren't you that Imran Siddiqui?' he said.

Ever the artful dodger, Imran said, 'Who me? No I'm Kushanava Choudhury. You must have confused me with the other guy.'

Perhaps as telling are those times when a Muslim source has turned to Imran, in confidence, and said of me, 'He is a Hindu, but he is all right,' or when a Hindu has said the obverse to me in appreciation of my friend, 'the good Muslim'.

Partition made two countries, a Pakistan for Muslims, and an India for ... whom? Hindus alone, or everyone who lived in it? That question was being asked long before the British left, and long after. In the monsoon of 1946, that question had been asked with daggers and bombs in the paras of Calcutta, when thousands of dead bodies rotted in the streets. Out of those carcasses had oozed Partition. A year later, on 15 August, the British divided their colony into two new nation states and left. For the next half a century, the city had been recovering. But that tearing apart, in our paras and in our hearts and minds, has never ended. Partition is still going on.

***

When I worked at the *Statesman*, every day I crossed the Beleghata Canal on the way to work and back. The stench of the canal brought back childhood memories of dead pigs floating in its black waters. My father was old enough to have seen cargo boats on the canal, ferrying timber and fish from the Sundarbans to the sawmills and cold-storage units along the banks. In Bagmari, I had grown up hearing the sawmill's siren and seeing lines of overloaded lorries being stopped by the traffic policemen to siphon bribes. By then, the boats had ceased, the waters stagnated and thousands of people had begun living on the canal banks. They were some of the poorest people in the city, below the ranks of the millions who lived in slums. Pushed out of the countryside by debts, hunger or feuds, they had failed to be accommodated anywhere in the city, and ended up at the canal of last resort.

The canals were part of Calcutta's drainage system. When they got blocked, each monsoon the streets flooded. Since my childhood, the Beleghata Canal had become progressively more constricted. Now it resembled a sewer. One day an item appeared in the paper stating that the state government would dredge the canal. I wondered what would happen to the people living there. It was a story worth following.

When I called the urban development minister, he informed me that the land belonged to the government and the people living there were squatters. They would be evicted without any kind of compensation or resettlement, because they were breaking the law. To give compensation here, the minister explained, would only reward the law-breaking and encourage more people to squat on government land.

The minister's argument sounded familiar. When I was a student at Calcutta Boys' School, it was this same argument that certain teachers would use to refuse to let us go to the bathroom. If you let one boy go, they reasoned, it would only encourage the others to go as well, producing a shitting outbreak of epidemic proportions. Those teachers had been sadists and tyrants, holdovers from a colonial form of schooling whose whole ideology could be boiled down to one dictum: spare the rod, spoil the child. I could not understand how a democratic government, a democratic Communist government, could render thousands of its poorest citizens homeless without even giving them a check.

I had seen the squatters' shacks a hundred times from my bus window. One day, I got off the bus to meet the people there and see their world up close.

The whole area stank. The canal bank was lined with huts several rows deep. Each hut was made of corrugated metal and plastic sheets to make a windowless room with a stove in one dark corner. Each room had a bed raised up with bricks to make two levels. The parents would sleep on one level, separate from the children for a little privacy, a semblance of a normal life.

From the road, I walked down muddy paths toward the stench of the canal. Along the water's edge, rising up from the muck were little bamboo towers that looked like birdwatching stations in a sanctuary. Each tower was covered on all sides by discarded plastic tarps. In the middle was a hole through which to shit right into the canal. They were the communal toilets.

I met Gora Ghosh, who ran a school along the canal, which was full of kids who lived in the shacks. He used to work in a government job, but there all he did was sit in a chair year after year. Nothing changed except the bedbugs, he told me. He left and started the one-room school. The municipal schools were a disgrace, but these children had no birth certificates and no addresses, so they could not even go to those schools. Of late, the government had started running mass-education camps, where they would swoop in on a poor area for a few days as if they were running a blood drive. By the end of it, they made sure the children who attended knew how to sign their name. Then everyone was declared 'literate'. In this way, every decade the government's literacy statistics miraculously shot up, much to the delight of economists and development experts worldwide.

Most of the kids in Gora's one-room school worked in workshops along the canal in the battery-recycling business. They sat on the roadside sifting through piles of garbage looking for used batteries. Their job was to extract the carbon sticks in the batteries. In the workshops between the shacks and the toilets were vats of chemicals in which the sticks were dunked, without any gloves, and treated before they could be reused by local battery manufacturers. It was toxic, but it was work.

Most of the men did not have any work. Some did odd jobs hauling goods from place to place in cycle vans. Others did seasonal work in construction, building pandals in the pujo season or showing up near Ultadanga station in the early morning, hoping to be picked for a day's work as a labourer on a building site. They were men with irregular wages and irregular habits. There was a liquor store at one end of the road that stayed busy from morning. By 11 a.m. there were already men gathered in groups lounging on cycle vans, betting on cards and drinking. By mid-afternoon, little parties were underway on the flat-beds.

The only people with steady work in the area were the women. They worked as domestics in houses around the canal, sweeping floors, scrubbing dishes and doing laundry, twice a day, seven days a week. There was always housework in Calcutta, always jobs for women to do. If you could scrabble together jobs in four houses, you could at least survive.

In the villages the men had worked the land. But there was no land in the city for them to work, no job that felt like a man's job for them to do. In the city, it was as if everything was turned upside down. The women became the breadwinners and the men became superfluous.

One day I asked a group of card players what they thought about the evictions. They will never evict us, they said, and kept right on dealing.

Gora, the teacher, was worried about what would happen to the children if the shacks and workshops were demolished. He feared their families would scatter all over the city, putting an end to their schooling. He was looking for powerful people who could stop the demolition. One morning, he introduced me to a political worker from SUCI, one of the smaller opposition parties in the state assembly. His party was going to launch protests again the demolition, the man said. They were going to have demonstrations. There was no way there would be any evictions on their watch, he said, his bluster buoyed by a breakfast of booze that I could smell on his breath.

Slowly, I realised something about the squatters. Unlike the millions who lived in slums, these were people who had not been organised by any political party. No one had arranged their birth certificates or ration cards. No one had got them voter cards. The census-takers did not come to their door. Along the canal, on the Maniktala side, the squatters were Hindu. On the Rajabazar side they were Muslim. But otherwise they were precariously the same. No one knew how many people were going to be evicted because no one had bothered to count how many people lived there in the first place. They were people unaccounted for, people who were not people at all.

The settlements along the canal stretched several miles. Taken together, they were as many as 50,000 people. If they had lived in one dense patch and formed a great slum, some leader would surely have come along and got them fake birth certificates and arranged their voter cards, turned them into a constituency and championed their cause. But they were stretched thin across several city wards, and so they did not count as a voting bloc, and hence did not count at all.

All the politicians I called, the ministers, municipality officials and Members of the Legislative Assembly (MLA), said something had to be done, of course. A local MLA met me at Flury's, the gaudy bakery on Park Street, to discuss his grand vision for the canal. Over pastries and tea, he showed me plans that looked like a fantasy from a children's colouring book. In his plan, an elevated highway would rise above what was now a row of toilets upon a river of shit. In the drawings, there were of course no shacks nor workshops, and no plans for the people who lived and worked there. They had been wiped out of the picture.

What I saw was this: a democratically elected Communist government was following a colonial law that denied its people a basic foothold in the city. The Communists had even stopped working with the World Bank, because it had a policy of providing resettlement to all affected squatters on its projects while the government did not. In my Princeton days, I had supported the anti-globalisation protests, which targeted the World Bank as the very symbol of capitalist exploitation in the Third World. Now 'capitalism' and 'Communism', 'democracy' and 'development' all seemed like terms whose meanings had been unmoored from their original forms. They were just empty words used by politicians with which we filled the pages of our newspapers and stuffed our brains.

What mattered was power, the power of having bodies you could put in the street to block traffic and votes you could stuff in a ballot box. Who got what was determined by who could make the most noise, who could block the most roads, who could show the most power. Each would be compensated according to their nuisance value. The meek would lose their hearths.

I wrote the stories; the evictions were delayed. But I was just skimming the surface. I was playing my part in a pantomime made of up minister's statements and government press releases, of 5 p.m. briefings and committee reports, of paper upon paper upon paper, of that typhoon of paper that governments produce and newspapers reproduce that in a city like Calcutta didn't mean a thing. There was so much below the surface that structured how things worked, that determined how power was organised and that I did not know how to write about. I only knew that it had little to do with what we wrote, or the big words we used, when we filed our 400 words each night.

After the Factory

Durba and I were riding home in an auto rickshaw from Maniktala one evening. The auto ascended the hump of the Beleghata Canal and stopped. On the bridge, a drunk was pantomiming a policeman, standing in the middle of the line of cars, buses and autos, directing traffic that was going nowhere. The road ahead was blocked. There was an *aborodh* – a barricade – in Bagmari.

The auto idled on the bridge. The driver in the next auto started telling his passengers how the drunk on the bridge used to be a dada, a local Party boss. 'Who knows how many murders he has committed?' To kill time, the driver began to narrate the drunk's former exploits. We waited a while and then followed the passengers in the nearby autos as they alighted and crossed the bridge on foot. On the other side, the dadas of the opposition party, the Trinamul Congress, had placed a line of cycle vans across the road. Behind the barricades, rows of trucks were idling almost as far back as the rail bridge. Police vans had arrived. In the sea of faces at the barricades, we saw clumps of men in white uniforms negotiating with the public. It turned out that there had been power cuts all day in Bagmari. The power had not been back long enough to run the water pumps, so now residents had neither water nor electricity. Hence the dadas had corralled a few van rickshaws and gathered their flock, and a barricade had been erected on one of the main arteries in North Calcutta at rush hour.

A few weeks earlier, in Maniktala, there had been another *aborodh*. Then, the public had pelted stones. The autos adjusted, shifting their route and avoiding the main road. At other times, these productions of street theatre required more fireworks, like after the killings in Nandigram, when a couple of buses on this road were set ablaze. Then there were the *bandhs*, or shutdowns, when all offices, shops and public transport were shut down for a day. The practice had come down from colonial times, when it was used against the British. In Bengal, the Communists had invented a new form of protest in the 1960s called the *gherao*, or encirclement, where a boss in an office was encircled by his protesting staff, and held captive for hours at a time, until labour demands were met. *Aborodh, bandh, gherao* – these words had become as much a part of our vocabulary as bus, tram and traffic. They were such commonplace events that everyone knew how to act. Are they blocking traffic, pelting stones, burning buses? We can grumble and adjust. Durba and I wriggled around the barricade and walked home.

Durga Pujo was over, that burst of creative genius had blazed and burned out. Now it was back to the same sourpuss city. Sometimes I sat in the front seat of an auto with half my ass hanging off the driver's seat, which I had to share with three other people, and scanned the faces at the crossing, looking for 'one of us'. I wanted to find a face without the creases of disappointment, without the contortions borne of petty deceptions, without the cloud of gloom. Just a normal fresh face. How rare they were in those days in Calcutta.

The sea of glum faces was most overwhelming on the Metro. On a bus, there was the regular hustle and circulation of conductor and passengers, the ruckus of the tickets rustling and change jangling in the conductors' bag, the helper belting out the names of the stops like a chorus. But underground, without that ensemble of noise, the typical Metro compartment felt like a morgue. Each face was covered by a dour mask unique to itself. There were *pancha* faces and *bhoot* faces, *pocha* faces and *alu-bhatey* faces.

The sheer range of their sullen *gomra* faces exhausted my vocabulary. It was just like Sukumar Ray had rhymed:

> *Ramgorurer chhana*
> *hashte tader mana*
> *hashir kotha shunle bole*
> *hashbo na na na na.*

The city was made up of fifteen million such faces, each unhappy in its own unique way. They drove Durba wild.

***

The therapist Durba and I settled on was a Freudian psychoanalyst who had been trained in America. She was an old-school dream interpreter. She saw patients in one room of her tidy two-bedroom flat near the Tollygunge Metro stop. Her flat was in a housing cooperative like the one where I had lived in Bagmari as a child. There was a patch of dimly lit garden ringed by low-rise apartment blocks. Who would suspect that in one of those little flats a respectable woman in a sari was exposing the Oedipal desires lurking in the bedrooms of an Indian metropolis?

On our first visit the Freudian seated us together across from her and asked us to introduce ourselves. Then she told one of us to leave and wait outside. 'If I have you here together you will only argue,' she said.

And so it started, our couples therapy, one flawed patient at a time. Different times, different days, in different languages – with Durba in English, with me in Bengali, though the Freudian herself spoke Hindi as her mother tongue.

The Freudian asked me if I was worried about getting divorced. Divorce was becoming increasingly common in Calcutta. Its number-one cause, she explained, was mothers-in-law.

In the 1970s, as Calcutta's middle-class horizons shrank, our family sizes shrank with it. The arrival of birth control at this time dramatically reduced the norm of bhodrolok procreation from four or five to one. Those little mama's boys, hand-fed fish curry and rice by their mothers during lunch break at school, were now getting married, and divorced.

'Do you know that the more patients I see, the more I realise how right Freud was?'

She told me of the case of a couple who had come to see her with marital woes. Both were professionals who had met and fallen in love. Their marriage was not arranged. The only problem was, the boy's mother slept between them in their bed.

Our case presented a conundrum: our mothers-in-law were on another continent. What she couldn't work out, she told me repeatedly, was why we had a problem at all.

***

A three-storey department store called Pantaloons had opened in our para, fully air conditioned, with salesmen who popped out of every aisle like whack-a-moles and blurted random English phrases. In a city where just about everything was sold by a moustachioed man standing behind a counter, Pantaloons seemed from another world. It stocked aisles of perfume, clothes, appliances, groceries, books and beer, in an obstacle course filled with salesmen chanting, 'Yes, sir,' and, 'No, ma'am.' On its top floor was a food court like Hangout. Above the store, the building rose over a dozen floors into a high-rise with 'luxury' flats. The whole edifice was so foreign to the existing architecture of the para that it looked as if an alien armada had docked at the CIT Market bus stop. As you passed Pantaloons on CIT Road, two-storey-high hoardings of women in bras hung from the display windows. Each time I rode shotgun past them in an auto, those giantesses looked like the totems of another civilisation.

There used to be a Small Tools factory where Pantaloons now stood. Big noisy machines used to chug behind high walls. During our cricket matches, if a ball somehow sailed over into that compound, we would have to take up a collection to raise a rupee and a half. There was no prayer of getting that ball back. During shift changes, lines of men would enter it. Otherwise the walls were impregnable. The Small Tools factory closed down a few years ago; the machines went silent, the men disappeared, but the building remained. Then, when Durba and I moved back, all signs of its existence had vanished.

I sometimes went to Pantaloons to buy beer. Each time, I felt like grabbing one of the associates who parroted American salutations and saying: 'Are you kidding me? Do you know how many balls I have lost here, in this vortex of roaring machines behind forbidding walls? There was a factory here!' That past was so neatly erased that sometimes I felt as if I was the only person who remembered it.

From the rooftop of our building, you could see the sprouting of a new city. Like the Pantaloons high-rise, in Beleghata luxury apartment complexes were coming up where the Phillips factory had once stood. In Sealdah, another high-rise arose from the Raja of Cassimbazar's compound. Then all along the Eastern Metropolitan Bypass, the eastern fringe of the city, out of wetlands and fishing ponds arose more towers. Once one high-rise arose, it effaced any sign of what had existed before – a factory, a fishery, a slum – not only on the space but also in our memories. Each deserved an epitaph, like the marble plaque outside the Armenian College on Free School Street that declared that the writer William Makepeace Thackeray had been born there on 18 July 1811. But outside the high-rises, there were no marble plaques, not even any commemorative faces you were forbidden to piss on. There was no memory of the industrial past. Soon the names of those past avatars would only remain as bus stops: Astabol, Phillips, Usha. Their memorials would be heard in the bus conductors' calls.

* * *

From our rooftop you could see the smoggy outlines of a behemoth upon the southern horizon. South City was one of the largest housing complexes in India, with 1,600 apartments in four thirty-three-storey high-rise towers. The front part of the compound is South City Mall, the granddaddy of Calcutta's malls, which would not have been out of place in Singapore or Dubai. On weekends, I had heard, visitors thronged the mall just to ride the escalators.

Durba's college roommate had moved to Calcutta to work in a market research firm. She and her boyfriend invited us to lunch at a new Thai restaurant in South City Mall. One Sunday afternoon we hopped onto an empty Jadavpur Airport minibus headed south. The Jadavpur mini has always been my favourite bus route. When I was a kid it would take me from my house in Kankurgachi in the North to Joy's house in Ballygunge in the South in half an hour. While the 45 bus was snarled up for an hour in central Calcutta's twin snake pits of Sealdah and Moulali, the Jadavpur mini would carom through the wormhole of Convent Road, and reach South Calcutta in minutes.

In the season of 'don't touch', Durba and I had once ridden the Jadavpur Airport bus together to go to Gariahat. Somewhere around Anandapalit, by Fortune's grace, we got seats next to each other. Squeezed together on the narrow seat, our bodies made contact at multiple points. Our hands, our feet, our hips all touched, and stayed touched. As we passed Linton Street and Park Circus, Skating Rink and Bondel Road, electric currents seemed to traverse between us on that narrow seat. I had understood then the Victorians' thrill at seeing a lover's ankle.

Durba and I both remembered that thrill as we rode the minibus to South City. At lunch we exchanged good-natured banter in English over pad thai, spring rolls and beer. Afterward we explored the mall's bookstore, which looked bigger than a hundred book stalls on College Street put together, all neatly arranged by category and in alphabetical order. You could wander and peruse and buy nothing for hours. Our companions departed; we made plans to meet again. South

City's escalators seemed to ascend to the heavens, its shops were full of svelte mannequins, everything was shiny and new, and bathed in air conditioning. It was a vast cathedral of comfort. On a hot day, one would be a fool to not escape there and ride the escalators all day. When we came out, it was the dirty, disorderly, teeming world outside that looked wrong.

***

Where South City Mall now stands, I remembered, there used to be an Usha factory, which made the sewing machines that were ubiquitous in my childhood.

The factory had vanished but the union office was still across the street from the new mall. 'It used to be a parade here every day at quitting time,' Manoj Roy Choudhury said when I met him at the union office. Manoj was the vice-president of the local unit of CITU, the Communist trade union. CITU offices were typically one-room affairs with functional wooden tables, red plastic chairs and portraits of Marx, Lenin and Stalin. A few men would be reading the paper or watching TV. CITU's room inside the *Statesman* had been like that, just like hundreds of other little union rooms across the city. The CITU office of Jay Engineering – the company that manufactured the Usha-brand sewing machines and ceiling fans – looked nothing like those rooms. It had desktop computers and conference tables like a research institute, and was fully air conditioned. It looked more luxurious, for that matter, than CITU's spartan headquarters in Sealdah. The only thing missing was workers.

Manoj had been retired for seventeen years; the factory had been closed for eleven. Most of the men in the office were about Manoj's age. As we spoke, they periodically looked up from their newspapers to peer through their big plastic glasses and eye me with suspicion. The union office was their social club, a gathering of retirees like you might find among the morning walkers at nearby Dhakuria Lake. It was hard to imagine that these men reading the newspaper were once militants on the front lines of the epic war between labour and capital.

In his lifetime, Manoj has seen the rise and fall of Calcutta's industries, and its organised labour power. Manoj started working at Usha in the 1950s. Over the next decade, the factory grew, hiring hundreds more workers. The British were gone, but Calcutta was still India's industrial powerhouse. The structure of the economy, though, was colonial, the wealth it produced undistributed. And so Calcutta also became the base of the Communist labour movement.

In 1977, a Left Front coalition headed by the Communist Party of India (Marxist) or CPM, was elected to power in the state. When the protesters became the rulers, CITU, its umbrella union, went from being the warriors for the revolution to the foot soldiers of the state. The techniques of agitprop, which had brought them to power, remained but without the rationale.

In the 1960s there were 5,000 people working in the factory, Manoj told me, and 2,000 more in another Usha factory nearby in Bansdroni. The Bansdroni unit still had about sixty union members. 'The workers at Bansdroni are like terminal cancer patients,' Manoj said. 'They are still taking their medicine, but they know there are going to die.'

Soon, he predicted, that factory, too, would be closed, and the land sold to developers and turned into flats. Then the air conditioners at the union office would be turned on each morning for the benefit of exactly zero members of the working class.

The factory where Manoj and his comrades worked and agitated and struck has long ceased to exist. In the lanes nearby was the new working class, made up of security guards and sales reps from the mall that had replaced the factory, eating chow mein at the roadside stalls while standing, always in a hurry, their ID cards proudly dangling from their necks. Manoj's union had as little to do with them as his parents' village world had to do with him now.

As he walked me out, Manoj suggested I go to Taratala, the area around the Calcutta Port. 'Here, some places are closed. There, the whole area is a crematorium.'

***

During the colonial era, Taratala was a hub of engineering companies, mostly British-owned. Many of them made heavy machinery for defence or railways, as well as machines that were used in other industries. Pranab Ray Gupta operated at the Kidderpur and Taratala branch of CITU. Pranab looked like your typical Party man, bush shirt partly unbuttoned, cloth bag on shoulder, white oiled hair. He once worked in a factory called MMC, owned by Mahindra and Mahindra, the jeep manufacturers, in Taratala. The factory made diesel engines and machines to manufacture textiles. This sort of high-end industrial production was fairly typical in Taratala. There were once 3,200 workers in his factory, Pranab told me. The factory declared 'work suspension' in 1988, because factory 'closures' require that a company follow numerous government regulations, like paying workers their outstanding dues. So factories delay the official 'closure' and merely maintain an existential limbo under terms like 'work suspension' when wages and production cease but the firm still exists on the books.

We were in a taxi on Garden Reach Road, driving south along the Ganga. Walled off on both sides are rail properties, port properties, places with names like Hastings, Napier and Belvedere. For over a century, the wealth of Asia passed through here en route to London.

Kidderpur dock. The Ganga to the right, docked ships on the left, an inlet of broad, still water with gleaming ships and godowns. Giant cranes loaded and unloaded goods. Mercedes-Benzes with rolled-up windows glided by, carrying foreigners. Containers were stacked like Lego blocks in a yard, to be plunked onto tractor-trailers and driven away. The dock was an impressive sight. The scale was imperial. Gigantism reigned.

Up to the 1970s, a generation after the British left, Bengal was the wealthiest and most industrialised state in India. Calcutta was the nation's manufacturing hub, the largest city in India and the fourth largest in the world. In the next four decades, the city de-industrialised, leaving a rust belt on the Ganga.

During the colonial period, waves of men migrated from northern India and settled in Kidderpur to work in the docks.

There were once over 200,000 workers in the Kidderpur area, Pranab said, 60,000 in the port and dock alone. Now there are 18,000, and most of them are temporary or contract workers. Thousands had once worked on the docks, loading and unloading ships. What remained of that work was done by machines. Besides, there was so little that Calcutta made any more that needed to be shipped around the world.

There are now almost no factories left. The hundreds of thousands of men and women who laboured there had lost their livelihoods. How had it happened? The story was that the dock was dead, killed by the recalcitrant river with silt piles so high that few ships can pass, killed by other ports elsewhere in India that are easier and cheaper to ply to, killed by the death of manufacturing, killed by the unions.

When the docks died, the next generation lost the opportunity to find jobs there, as their fathers and grandfathers had before them. Some moved away, to other neighbourhoods, other occupations. Those who could not, stayed. The leavers were mostly Hindus, the stayers Muslims. It was not unlike what I knew from going to graduate school in New Haven, where the skeletons of factories that gave the world Winchester Rifles and other armaments stood surrounded by neighbourhoods that were predominantly black and poor, and where drug dealing was a profession that let a young man feel he was doing a man's job. The profession that opened up in Kidderpur was smuggling. Somewhere down those alleys, in my reporting days, Imran and I had met Qutubuddin, a scholarship boy with a masters degree from the University of Calcutta and no job. His father had been a dock worker. Qutubuddin made his money as a mule. Each year he travelled to Hong Kong to carry smuggled goods back to Calcutta to be sold in the Fancy and Five Star Markets in Kidderpur.

Of the over 45,000 acres of closed factory lands in and around Calcutta, a great deal of it is along the banks of the Ganga. Vast swathes of urban space were strewn with the skeletons of its machine-age past. Lush tropical creepers had colonised the sheds inside these compounds. For a while, CITU agitated for reopening factories. Reopening factories was also a populist battle cry for many politicians. It made them seem like heroes, made for good photos in the newspapers. But even when a few factories reopened, often with much government fanfare and ribbon-cutting and press reports, they would close a few months later, far from the public gaze, because they owed money to various banks, lenders and utilities. Typically, the gas company or the electric company would shut the lines, demanding payment for outstanding bills, and the charade would be over.

The conversion of factories to riverfront luxury condominiums is now well underway, but it happens in stages. First, a company buys out the property with promises of reopening the factory. Then the factory temporarily reopens or remains shut. The machinery is moved out and sold off. Then the land is sold off to developers.

By the 1990s, CITU's role changed from fighting to reopen factories, to negotiating the real-estate transactions. CITU had great nuisance power, and of course the ear of the state. It could prove to be obnoxious and obstructive to developers, with its marches, rallies and worse. But as with all Calcutta street theatre that dabbles in the instruments of violence, it could be paid off. In practice, this meant the union would negotiate the payment of outstanding dues to ex-workers, primarily making sure the workers received their retirement savings. Unofficially, it has meant that money sometimes moved into Party and personal coffers. In 1999 police arrested a CITU leader for accepting a 100,000-rupee – or $2,200 – cash bribe from a factory owner at a Calcutta restaurant. The factory, which had been closed for ten years, was being converted into real-estate land to be resold. It was reported that police were tipped off by leaders within the CPM, the work of one faction trying to undermine another.

Our taxi crossed the brace bridge on Garden Reach Road, which is famous because it rotates to let ships pass between the river and the inlet. The bridge rarely rotates any more, said the taxi driver, bemused. After the inlet, the area became an industrial belt. Compounds belonging to ITC, Brooke Bond and MMC, where Pranab worked, lined the road. Some factories had quaint English names like Braithwaite, Balmer Lawrie or Stewarts & Lloyds, but most of them were gone. The factories had been built on land leased from the Port Trust. When the factories closed, unlike everywhere else in the city, the land could not be turned over to a developer to build a mall and luxury condominiums. Some of the spaces had been leased out as warehouses. Most stayed vacant. Taratala was a memorial to the city's industrial past.

We passed the port workers' quarters. The quarters were two storeys high, with long corridor balconies that led to individual apartments. The building was intact. It did not look like the crumbling ruins that dotted the city, with signs that said *Biporjonok Bari* – dangerous dwelling – and were places that had become so uninhabitable that they had to be gradually abandoned. But no one lived in the quarters any more. The doors to the apartments were all thrown open, the insides dark at noon. It looked like a place that had been hit by sudden natural disaster, a place that people had fled.

'Why did they leave?' I asked Pranab.

'Who would stay? The jobs were gone, and there was no electricity or running water.'

The roads in Taratala are long and uninterrupted by the alleys, gullies or lanes that exist everywhere else in Calcutta, unpunctuated by the street architecture of the city, of tea shops, cigarette vendors and pice hotels. Manoj had told me to hire a taxi for this journey and I saw why. It was the only part of the city where there were no buses on the road, no autos, no nothing. It was midday, midweek, and there were no people to be seen.

At one time these streets used to be full of people, twenty-four hours a day, Pranab said, but seeing it now, I found it impossible to believe. In Calcutta, where every space is so layered and dense, Taratala was a lifeless shell. All that remained was what Pranab himself called 'the rubble of the industrial belt'.

On one corner was a field with cows, a meadow in the middle of an industrial zone. 'That was where we had our sports events,' Pranab told me. 'Workers used to play football here.'

He said it like an archaeologist explaining the habits of an extinct civilisation, as if we were wandering through Aztec ruins and had just come upon an imperial ball court. It produced the same reaction of wonder, at how a world so developed could have sprung from this soil and, as mysteriously, disappeared.

Pranab had joined MMC in 1964. 'Did you ever think it would end up like this?' I asked him.

'Does anyone imagine this?'

We drove past godowns that had turned into jungles, down Karl Marx Sarani toward the Fancy and Five Star Markets of Kidderpur. In the days of a closed command economy, when foreign goods were rare, these were Calcutta's smuggled-goods markets, where you could buy coveted foreign consumer goods like the Roos sneakers that we all thought were uber-cool when we were in school. Meanwhile, it provided a source of clandestine employment to Qutubuddin's generation, the children of the dock workers. But now that Reebok and Adidas had stores in Calcutta and there were malls galore, who needed a smuggled-goods market any more? Even the smugglers of Kidderpur had fallen on hard times.

The Communist Party office was at Kabitirtha More – or Poets' Pilgrimage Crossing. It is so named because the homes of three legendary Bengali poets – Hemchandra, Rangalal and Michael – are all nearby.

As Pranab left for the CITU office, he said, 'On the right is Michael's house,' pointing to a one-storey colonial bungalow with white columns where the poet Michael Madhusudan Dutt had once lived. Its facade was blocked by a line of hawkers who had taken over the gates. Along the fence they had hung their inventory of colourful T-shirts and skinny jeans, the visiting cards of today's Indian working class.

***

Manoj lived near Taratala at Old Dog Race Course, a compound with dozens of uniform low-rise apartment buildings that stretched for perhaps a quarter of a mile from the main road. Some of the buildings were freshly painted yellow; others were the collard-green colour that Calcutta flats tend to become after a few monsoons. It was like a Petri dish containing a sample of people who had once been homogeneously lower middle class. In the new economy, as time progressed, some flourished and others stagnated.

Nothing of the race course remained but the name. Manoj moved to the Old Dog Race Course in 1984, though the housing complex had been built much earlier, in the sixties.

'At one time, there were all kinds of athletic events for dogs held here, or so we've heard,' said Manoj, his whole body shaking with amusement.

His home resembled the flat I had lived in as a kid in Bagmari. The sitting room had an almirah, a chair and a single bed. An open door led onto a small caged veranda, where clothes dripped on lines. A calendar with a baby Krishna painting swung on the wall as the ceiling fan whirred above. Manoj was sitting on the chair next to the only window. The morning sun streamed in through the window and the veranda, obscuring his face.

'Please, feel comfortable,' he said, as I sat down on the printed cover pulled taut over the bed.

It was mid-morning and the familiar whistle of the pressure cooker and the aroma of vegetables being fried filled the flat. His wife came in from the kitchen to bring me a tray with four rossogollas and a glass of water. She was neat and trim, her hair and her sari in place, even though she had been cooking. She was the one who had decided to buy this flat, she said. Manoj had lived near the factory most of his life, in Jadavpur. 'His whole world is there,' his wife said, 'I mean, if you walk down the streets there you will find his mother, father, brother, some relative or other. He didn't want to come here.'

But they didn't have a place to stay there, or the money to buy property in the area. 'He was in the union,' she said, by

way of explanation for why Manoj had never made as much
money as he could have.

At Usha, Manoj had been a machine designer. His task was
to draft designs by hand of machines that were to be built. He
had learned machine design at a technical school. Among the
working class, men like Manoj were elites, skilled workers
in demand in a country whose industries ran on reverse
engineering the technology of the West.

In the 1980s, Manoj used to go to the Brooke Bond factory
in Taratala for some freelance work. Brooke Bond made
tea bags that came in boxes of twelve. They had an Italian
machine that used to package the dozen bags into boxes. At
the time, in India's command economy, foreign currency was
scarce and buying Italian machines was a luxury most Indian
corporations could ill afford.

'They came to us at Jay Engineering and took a team of four
of us,' Manoj said. 'They wanted us to see the machine and
copy it.' Manoj and his colleagues did a sketch of the machine,
and when it was built, it worked on the first try.

'The euphoria! They hugged us and shook our hands.'

Now his work, much like that of the typesetters and
designers I had once worked with at the *Statesman,* has been
totally computerised, the skilled handiwork of a department
reduced to the button pushing of one or two men, a victim
of what Marx called the supersession by the machine.

When Manoj started in the 1950s, there were 2,000
workers at the factory. In newly independent India, Usha had
a practical monopoly on the sewing-machine business. At its
peak, 25,000 sewing machines were being made each month as
well as 50,000 ceiling fans, and thousands of new workers were
needed to run the machines that made them. By the late 1960s,
the labour force had risen to 5,000. In the unrest of those years,
the Communists grew politically more powerful, wielding the
weapon of militant trade unionism on the factory floors.

Long before the Usha factory was shut down in 1998, there
had been closure after closure. In 1964, there was a five-and-a-

half-month closure, because the annual bonus had been reduced. 'It was a very silly demand,' Manoj said, thinking of it now.

At the time, he had felt differently. Factories were the theatres for meetings, marches and militant trade unionism.

When I first started at the *Statesman,* the corridors would periodically be festooned with red hammer-and-sickle pennants and posters calling the management 'dogs'. Back then, CITU had a union room down the hall from the newsroom with life-size paintings of Marx and Engels. CITU's reach was vast, from the boatmen on the Ganga to the jute mills, the docks, the port, the factories and the *Statesman*'s presses. In the epic war of capital and labour, the Communists used militant tactics like the gherao with abandon. Escalate crisis to show strength: that was the CITU tactic until well into the end of the twentieth century.

By the early 1970s small factories in northern India started making ceiling fans. They were so small they didn't have to follow the government's stipulated wages for factory workers, so they paid their workers half of what was being paid in Calcutta. Meanwhile at Usha, the workers' wages kept going up while sales kept going down. Initially, to reduce costs, the company decided to outsource – or 'farm out' – some aspects of production. The union protested that too.

'We protested the farming-out system, the changing of various norms inside the factory.' Manoj said, 'A lot of the agitations were not right. They could have been avoided.'

'Why was it done?' I asked him.

'Militant trade unionism!' he said, his eyes twinkling, as if we were talking about highjinks from a misspent youth. 'They were just about militancy. At the time I didn't think so. Now I realise it.

'It was not.' He paused. 'A necessary development.'

'So it is true, what people say, that the militant trade unionism killed the industries?'

'All the industries were not closed by militancy. It was a natural crisis,' he told me. 'There was nothing management could do.' By the 1990s, the production of sewing machines had stopped at Manoj's factory. Fans were still being assembled, but the whole fan was being made elsewhere, and coming in only to get the Usha stamp. In 1998 the unit closed and remaining assembly operations moved to Bansdroni.

'At the time they closed, we used to talk about how management stole money and how they needed to diversify. Probably they stole; all owners set aside more than they show. But that's not why it closed. They were posting losses. We shouted a lot of slogans then. We shouted "diversification". But is it so easy to start a new technology? It requires skilled manpower from outside, and it is risky.'

When Manoj worked at Usha, a group of technicians came from Germany to demonstrate computerised design machines. 'One man just presses a button and sits quietly,' Manoj said. 'That's all the labour required. The computer is more accurate and more perfect. But you can't stop it, no more than you can force people to travel by bullock carts, or ask that they take ships to America rather than fly there in a day. Car production has become totally computerised. There is still some manual production around, lathe machines and so on. Just as there are still some bullock carts.

'As a worker I was privileged. Ours was one of the first offices to have air conditioning. It was a very sophisticated office.' He said this with some relish, recalling his standing in the hierarchy of capitalism. When the union struck in '68, the owners offered to keep him on salary. He says he refused. 'We had respect. But I didn't think of that. I wanted other things. I was doing a job to do a job. My mind was on social change. I had seen people starving in 1943, during the famine in our village.'

Manoj was ten years old in 1943 at the time of the Bengal Famine. His father was a schoolteacher in their village in East Bengal. They were landed people, with a house on the banks of the broad Meghna river. They had food when many did not. 'I remember I was home from school,' Manoj said. 'We had an open veranda and a man came asking for food. Oh, how he ate! We even gave him the food from our own plates.'

Streams of people kept coming across the Meghna river in search of food. Many had walked overnight through jungles, and waded across the river to reach Manoj's home. One day a Muslim boy named Moti was among those who came. He was about Manoj's age. Moti had made it through the woods and across the river to Manoj's house. But a jackal had bitten him on his knee along the way. Within hours of arriving, he was dead.

Almost sixty years later, Manoj spoke of that boy, Moti, as if he could still see his emaciated face.

It happened during wartime. Those were the days when the Victoria Memorial was covered in cow dung, the Empress sheathed in shit, for fear of Japan's bombs. Buses were parked on the Maidan so the Japanese wouldn't use it as a landing strip for their planes. Air-raid sirens went off regularly, and were regularly ignored. As kids, we all learned a ditty passed down through schoolyards from those days:

Sa re ga ma pa dha ni
Bomb pheleche Japani
Bomber bhetor keute shaap
Britain bole baap re baap.

Do re mi fa so la ti
Bombs dropped by the Japanese
Bombs contain coiled cobra snakes
'Oh dear, Oh dear!' Great Britain quakes.

The Japanese attacked Kidderpur Port. A few bombs fell. But their armies never came to Calcutta. No tanks rolled through. The Tommies and GIs stationed in the city lived the good life. The city was teeming with women being sold into prostitution to survive. Each day thousands of people were arriving on foot from the countryside, columns of emaciated bodies begging for food on Calcutta's footpaths.

'*Phaan dao, Ma, Ma, phaan dao.*' There is not a person who lived through that time who does not remember this cry, of starving people begging, not for rice, but for the leftover water in which it was boiled. There was rice in the city, they had heard, the only place in Bengal where one could still be fed. They walked to Calcutta hoping to survive, and died by the thousands on its streets. There were literally piles of corpses accumulated in the streets all over the city. Calcutta had become a necropolis.

Three million people starved to death, and the causes were man-made. The British diverted grain away from the countryside for their war. They cleaned out granaries from village after village and seized boats that transported grain across Bengal's rivers. The only place where food could reliably be found was in the capital city. Calcutta, with its barracks full of soldiers, and its government buildings full of clerks, was fed in preparation for an Axis attack that never came. The Japanese never dropped their cobra snakes on Calcutta. The war against Bengal was waged by the British themselves.

The moral order of society was broken by the famine. When that break occurred, those who had survived sought ways to make it whole. Why did we watch and do nothing? asked the liberals. Why didn't the starving people rob, kill and revolt? asked the Communists. Why did they just wither away?

Before the famine, Manoj's family had supported the Congress. He joined the Communists. He wanted to be on the frontline of a revolutionary movement for social change.

It was a very different party then, he said. 'There was a member of the Party, Sailen Bose, who had a twelve-hundred-rupee-a-month job, who left it to take a sixty-rupee-a-month job as a Party full-timer. He contracted tuberculosis. Still he didn't stop. He was in the Jadavpur CPI.

'There was a major rail-union leader, later CITU vice president, Kanai Banerjee. His younger sister died of cancer. She had a son. The son was handicapped. There were rail quotas for the handicapped. He could have easily arranged for the boy to get a job in the railways. He didn't arrange a job,' he said. 'He didn't arrange a job!

'Where are such people today? I don't see them now. Almost all Party leaders have put their brothers and their families into jobs, helped them into businesses.'

The Calcutta district of CITU used to have 250,000 members, almost all of them factory workers. Now there were about 170,000 members. A majority were hawkers, auto drivers, private security guards – occupations that were mostly off the books, part of the vast sea of India's so-called informal sector.

The proletarian struggle that Manoj had joined was gone. It had failed to make the world anew.

When we came to the end of our conversation, he said, 'Don't give my name.' He was, after all, still the vice president of a CITU unit. Then he changed his mind. 'Give it. Give it. I don't care. What will happen? Most of the people I was with are dead.'

Chitpur Nights

One morning I awoke in a great funk. It was the sort of funk that would ordinarily have led to a shouting match in our house. 'I'll make you a cup of coffee,' Durba said, 'but today you need to decide what it is that you would like to do.'

Before moving back, I had fantasised about long, leisurely afternoons with a house full of friends, two pots of food – one of rice, the other of meat – and adda. Sweet Sunday adda! For the first few months, it never happened. Perhaps it was that our life in those early months had simmered with discontent and flared up with frequent fights. It could be too, I thought, that sweet Sunday adda was just a memory, a habit that had been dropped by people who were busy with their children and careers, busy looking busy, tooling around on their cell phones just like the whole wide world. It used to be, a CPM leader said to me, that you bragged about how little work you got away with doing. That showed how artfully you dodged the thumb of your capitalist boss. Now you bragged about how much you worked, as if the number of hours logged at the office and litany of emails in your inbox showed your worth as a human being. I missed the addas of my *Statesman* days, at Majestic bar on Madan Street, at the tea shop in Chowringhee Square, in Mike's room after office hours or at Sunday lunches at Sumitro's house.

'What I want,' I said to Durba when she returned with coffee, 'is a Sunday adda.' Durba acquiesced: 'If you will it, it is no dream.' And so off I went to buy goat from Mejo Mama's butcher near College Street and shrimp from one of the fishmongers at Maniktala Market. Durba made Kashmiri goat curry; I made *camarao* Mozambique. We cooked together late into Saturday night. For the first time since we'd moved to Calcutta, our friends came over for Sunday lunch.

Sumitro and Nabamita arrived first. Imran and Ayesha came with their young son. Our friend Rajesh came too, while his wife, Beauty, dropped by en route to visit a relative who was in the hospital. So began a full day adda: beer, lunch, tea, more tea, and more tea. Some even stayed till dinner.

How many addas had we had, just loitering on street corners, at the bus stand, or standing for hours in the corridors at the *Statesman,* among the Himalayas of discarded files?

In those days we didn't even need a place to sit. I remember one evening Sumitro, Imran and I kept talking in front of the tram stop at Esplanade until the hookers had propositioned us so many times that we had to move on just in order to keep talking.

'Everything I know,' the great Bengali writer Syed Mujtaba Ali once wrote, 'I have gathered from scraps collected at addas.' Gajendra Kumar Mitra, his publisher at Mitra Ghosh – which hosted its own famed adda – wrote that he once ran into Mujtaba Ali in front of Basanta Cabin and four hours passed in adda before they had even made it inside.

To read Mujtaba Ali is to always feel as if he is talking to you from across the table at Basanta Cabin. Whether he is drawing us into the world of Kabul's markets, Berlin's streets or Cairo's cafés, he can make a reader feel as at home as we are at the local tea-shop adda. Mujtaba Ali was a peripatetic soul. He lived and taught all over the world, including for a year in Cairo.

'From my rooftop you could see the pyramids clearly,' he wrote. 'A tram would whisk you there in minutes – on full-moon nights, they even ran a special service. And yet, six months passed in this café and in that café. For the pyramids, there never seemed enough time. When friends would enquire about this oversight, I would sigh, "All is fate. Ten years in Calcutta and I never managed a dip in the Ganga. Is seeing the pyramids really in my destiny?" (Let me confess: What ephemeral truth is gleaned from seeing a bunch of boulders I have never been able to ascertain, neither before seeing the pyramids, nor after.) I love Hedoa, Hatibagan, Shyambazar. In those places there are no Taj Mahals and no pyramids. And this fact fills me with no grief at all. I love my neighbourhood tea shop. Morning or evening, you will find me in attendance there, next to the neighbourhood's Potla and Hablu, soaking in the pleasure of idle comradeship over cigarettes and banter.

'When fate forced me to nest in Cairo, by the third day I began to suffer from adda withdrawal. I wandered like a vagabond across this strange city in search of Potla, Hablu and Basanta Cabin, the Sahara's warm breath mixing with my sighs. And then, thank God, I noticed it: At my neighbourhood coffee shop, each day five fellows would arrive and rant and carry on Basanta Cabin-style over endless cups of coffee and countless cigarettes.'

What follows is a delightful account of the café culture of Cairo, a whole society laid out before us via adda.

Mujtaba Ali was Sir's favourite writer. Sir now lived with his son's family in Boston, too ill to live on his own in Calcutta. When I was a kid Sir had told me this story:

Over fifty years ago, Sir took a ship from Europe to India. He was single, with lots of time to kill. He had befriended several other young men on board. An adda formed on the ship and soon they were in the middle of a raging card game. The ship travelled through the Suez Canal. The passage took a day, and passengers were allowed to get off and make a day trip to Cairo and the pyramids. Sir stayed put. 'There will always be another chance to see the pyramids,' they said to one another, and kept dealing.

Sir never saw the pyramids. Like Mujtaba Ali, he preferred another kind of worldliness over the mute testimony of the Sphinx. In the best cosmopolitan Bengali tradition, he always maintained an ease with the world, an uncanny ability to make himself at home no matter how far he ventured.

Some evenings as I left my Bengali tutorials, books unopened, I would feel a fleeting pang of guilt: 'Sir, we didn't do any work today.'

'*Shobyi kaaj,*' he would say. 'Everything is work.'

Everything is work in the end, if you know how to pay attention.

Sometime after lunch, Imran said, '*Ektu kaaj ache*' and went off for a half-day's shift at the *Telegraph.* He was back before dinner time. At around 11 p.m. we packed him, Ayesha and their son into a taxi and sent them home. Imran was still talking as the cab sped away.

***

Rajesh and I had become friends through Sumitro. Rajesh made large woodcuts like the nineteenth-century Bengali artists from Battala, full of mythical beasts, Bengal's canonical heroes and characters from the streets, to create images of the phantasmagorical present. During lunch he had been telling us about his trips to Kumortuli when he was a student at the art college. Sometime after the fourth cup of tea, Rajesh asked, 'Do you want to go see witches?'

Apparently the nightlife in Kumortuli this time of year was worth seeing. It was the time when the *dakinis,* or witches, came out to play. A few days later, Sumitro, Rajesh and I met in front of Maniktala Market and took an auto up Beadon Street to Chitpur Road.

Chitpur Road is the oldest street in Calcutta, older than the city itself. Chitpur starts in Dalhousie and leads northward and becomes a commercial strip that cuts through the whole Black Town. At the corner of Beadon Street and Chitpur Road are offices of the *jatra* theatre troupes that travel across Bengal. The buildings at the crossing were covered with billboards that displayed the familiar faces of Bengali TV stars. One billboard advertised a jatra called *Return My Land Unto Me*. In Bengali, the billboard read: 'I don't want industry. I don't want development. Return my land unto me.'

Just after the jatra district is Garanhata Lane, narrow, brightly lit, and full of silver shops. Sumitro led us in. In the Company days a British visitor to Chitpur found on sale 'the jewels of Golkonda and Bundelkhand, the shawls of Cashmere, the broadcloths of England, silks of Murshidabad and Benaras, muslins of Dacca, calicoes, ginghams, chintzes and beads of Coromandel, (and) firs and fruits of Cabul'.

In Garanhata Lane, the silversmiths still sat cross-legged on the floor, tapping metal sheets gently with hammers as they must have a century ago. In the shop windows were silver headdresses, silver plates and silver coins embossed with Queen Victoria's head. We bought cigarettes from a stall among the silversmiths and started walking.

We walked on, past the prostitutes of Sonagachi, garish like prostitutes everywhere but also always with vermilion sprinkled in their hair and conch bangles on their wrists like Bengali Hindu brides. It was from those courtyards, Rajesh said, that the first clay is still collected to make the Durga deities each year at pujo time.

Just as we passed the cluster of strong-box sellers – bang! – a *tubri* erupted in a volcano of blazes, rushing high above the catenary of the tramline. Its fiery bouquet encompassed the whole width of Chitpur, before its embers rustled down through the trees and the awnings of the paan shops to silence.

As we crossed Sovabazar Street, four men approached carrying a Kali deity as if she were riding a palanquin. It had started.

Fifteen-foot statues of Kali were parked right on Chitpur Road. Men were hoisted up to the shoulders of the deities to give the finishing coat of paint. Lined up on the roadside were Kalis of straw, Kalis of clay, Kalis half painted, fully painted, in terrifying black, in sombre blue. The street became an assembly line. We had arrived in Kumortuli.

Just before Durga Pujo, Durba and I had weaved through there during one our morning walks as the tableaus of Durga and the demon were being readied. Hindu deities were being made there at all times of the year. The para was perpetually muddy, like a village set in the heart of the city. I had been to Kumortuli many times, but this was my first visit there at night. The darkness made its activities more frenzied and surreal. Sumitro, Rajesh and I turned into a lane lined with warehouses-cum-workshops-cum-showrooms. Inside each windowless room, bright fluorescent bulbs revealed half-made Kalis. Interspersed were shops selling scimitars made of thin gleaming metal and human heads oozing macaroni brains made of clay. The finished Kali deity held up those heads, as well as the scimitars, in her four hands. A man sat with a box of clay hands and massaged each onto her arms. The cycle-van drivers deftly dodged the half-made idols on both sides as they noisily squeaked through the busy lane. We went deeper. The lane clogged and led into another vein. Now we were in a gully only wide enough for walking. Everything in the gully had the bilious olive hue of wet clay. Even the sleeping dogs were camouflaged. The powerful smell of *bidis* emanated from a corner where loaders played cards. From inside each workshop came the hiss of spray paint. From under a bamboo scaffold on which Kali stood, a rat scurried out, dodging a pint-bottle of Bagpiper Whisky on the way. The light bounced off the walls to create the mood of a theatrical set.

The story goes that Kali was called upon to vanquish a demon, and then, having destroyed it, she kept going, a jhor of unstoppable destruction doing her death dance. It was then that the mortals called on Shib, her husband, to intervene. Shib lay himself prostrate in Kali's path, and when Kali stepped on her husband, realising her mistake, she stuck out her tongue, a gesture we still make to acknowledge a grave error. The tableaus are a freeze-frame of that moment of recognition: The deity is formed in the throes of her dance, naked in mid-leap, with one foot on Shib's torso and the iconic tongue darting out.

'Look,' said a boy peering under a tarpaulin. 'She's eating a leg!'

In fact they all seemed to be eating flesh, a phalanx of cannibals biting into whole bodies, gnawing at legs, arms and the fleshy bits in between. These were the witches, or *dakinis* and *joginis,* that Rajesh had brought us to see. They were fearsome creatures who were part of Kali's battalion. There were witches with frighteningly disfigured mouths in bikini tops and sarongs who looked like contestants for a pageant from another planet. There were headless women, some with bodies emerging out of the bloody mess where heads should have been. There were European phantoms dressed in ties and topcoats, and bhodrolok ghosts dressed in dhuti-panjabis and monsters with golden Godzilla heads who disobeyed any known form.

The witches and phantoms had once been Durga's children, Laxmi, Saraswati, Ganesh and Kartik, part of the Durga Pujo tableaus. Recovered in various stages of dissolution, they were recycled. You could tell this from the sway of a witch's hip that recalled Saraswati, or the size of a sahib phantom's gut, which gave away its first avatar as Ganesh. Upon the basic structure of sticks and straw a whole new garb of clay was added, of skulls and rumps and bloody fangs. Some were sculpted devouring limbs, others in miniskirts with bared midriffs and fangs. Some were skeletons dressed for a party, in three-piece suits or a gentleman's dhoti. Others looked like a cross between Marianne at the French Revolution and a she-male dominatrix. We saw hollowed-out eyes fitted with orange light bulbs that lit up like nuclear egg yolks. Others had miniature skulls in their eye sockets. In their arms they cradled cuts of corpses: a shank, a flank, a rump, dripping with blood. Then there were those who had the entrails of corpses hanging from their mouths, looking like pink bubblegum.

The sculptor who had made those ravenous witches was putting the finishing touches on a set of skeletons bogarting cigarettes. 'No one else has done this,' he said with a smile.

He told us he had made similar skeletons last year, brandishing bottles of booze until the sculptors' trade association leaders told him to stop, saying it would give Kumortuli a bad name. Most of the phantom-makers are not 'kumors' by caste. They do not belong to the sculptors' trade association, but they live in Kumortuli, para people who have other day jobs. The man who made smoking skeletons had been making phantoms for seven years. During the year he worked as a water-filter repairman, travelling the city, seeking inspiration for his fantastic creations amid the banal details of everyday life.

Kumortuli is like any neighbourhood. There are stationery shops, tea shops, nursery schools, the typical architecture of a Calcutta para. A girl was finishing painting a few small phantoms in an unlit corner outside her house. It was a typical slum house. The bed was raised high with bricks so as to create the semblance of two floors, the upper tier for sleeping. A man in a lungi was lying on the bed, a woman was cooking on the floor. Samples of work were displayed on a shelf: an artist's whole world in 10' by 8'.

It was clear that Rajesh had brought us to the city's largest art gallery. At times Sumitro and Rajesh stopped to comment on what would happen if some of these figures were taken as art objects and put in a gallery. At others they mocked contemporary artists, their colleagues, whose work was inferior to the worst specimens in the alleys of Kumortuli.

Sumitro wanted to buy something. Four children were playing carrom on the street. Next to them were sculptures that looked like dolls, each about a foot high. They were dressed not unlike Barbies, except the hair was wild, and the expressions mangled, the bodies splotched with blood.

'The boy who made them will come soon,' one of the boys explained. 'He is a bit slow, that's why this is all he can make.'

Sumitro wanted me to buy one but I had already purchased a decapitated head. Then he bought it for himself and said, 'I'll give it to my wife: "Menstruating Barbie".'

***

How could I explain to the Freudian that the city was the problem between us?

Calcutta was a place of darkness, Durba maintained, the city of Kali. Wasn't that what all the outsiders ultimately said when they took the easy way out, representing the city as a horror show? Even Anita Desai and Günter Grass, who came to live here for a time and wrote books about the city, ultimately fell back upon the trope of an urban hellhole. Kali became emblematic of the dark forces they felt seething here. Shocked and fascinated by Kali, whose long red tongue, black body and garlands of skulls peer out from every sweet-shop calendar and taxi dashboard, they saw in her the embodiment of the soul-crushing force of the city.

I have lived in Calcutta half my life, and only been to the iconic Kali temple in Kalighat twice, both times at the urging of visiting American friends who had read about it in their guidebooks. Just as there were no pyramids in Mujtaba Ali's Cairo, in my Calcutta there is no Kalighat.

My grandmother worshipped an image of Kali in her prayer room, as does my mother in New Jersey. So what? When I read the hackneyed descriptions of Calcutta as a city of Kali, I feel like a man who does not realise he has been speaking in prose his whole life. The city's myriad enchantments and horrors resist such a neat and facile metaphor.

A few days later, I took Durba to Kumortuli. Chitpur Road was already blocked off by police. Kali Pujo was only days away and lorries kept arriving with dozens of para boys, those whom we call 'lumpen' in Marxist Bengali. They had come to Kumortuli to pick up the Kali deities, and accompanying witches, for their para pujos. Young men sat on the roofs of the trucks, looking badass. 'FD Block' said the banner on one lorry, and a man sat on its head, legs splayed like he was a hero in a Bollywood number. FD Block was one of the alphabetised sections of bourgeois Salt Lake. The hero was wearing metal-framed glasses, his light complexion betraying limited exposure to harsh sunlight. Soon he would be back at his desk, studying for his computer science exams, or writing code at his cubicle in Sector Five. Here he played lumpen for a day.

'Hey, follow me if you want to get drunk,' said one to his posse.

We followed the lumpen down Banamali Sarkar Street as it wound towards the river. The road was thick with people today, picking up orders, haggling over prices. From a third-floor window a yellow sari hung down to dry like a festoon all the way to the top of a doorway. A trio of devouring witches stood below. The sari looked like all that was left of their latest victim.

On the street were crowds of witches, clusters of ten to match the posses of boys who had arrived. The witches had wild hair that went straight up, bared teeth, and eyes that popped out of their sockets. Some had enormous zipper mouths full of teeth from ear to ear. Others had worms coming out of one socket, blood running down their cleavage. They were eating body parts with the relish of someone gnawing at chicken wings. One was eating little bodies held upside down, a leg in each hand and some of the soft middle parts inside her mouth. The witches had breasts and hips and asses of the most preposterous proportions, to match every jangled fantasy. Some of the witches were accompanied by skeletons that looked like pimps. They throttled the witches with poses full of nonchalance: one hand on hip, the other at someone's throat.

Banamali Sarkar Street meanders all the way to the river. We crossed the train tracks and were along the Ganga. Inside a parked auto, a few guys were drinking hooch and playing cards in the darkness. Along the embankment, a man was making a tableau featuring two well-dressed children seated on the laps of their smiling parents – a Bengali family portrait in clay. Except the children had no heads. The parents were devouring their brains.

Sealdah

In California, my uncle Ashoke went to bed one night and failed to wake up. Boro Mama died, just like that, with no forewarning. Nine months before, I had seen him in Calcutta at Dida's funeral. The night before he left, Mejo Mama had sent me out to pick up Chinese takeout from a place on Beadon Street. My parents, my uncles and aunt, and Durba and I had had a final family gathering in Dida's house. Mejo Mama presented Ashoke with a watch, 'From us all,' he said, to mark the timeliness of his arrival, because Ashoke had been able to spend time with Dida before she died. He had made it home at the right time.

That night, Boro Mama had said he was only going to stay in America another two years, maybe three, till my aunt retired. And then they were coming back, to his city, his home. He called it 'his refuge'. Nothing in his plans had anticipated the interruption caused by his death. It was not like Dida, whose end seemed well planned. Boro Mama was across the dalan when she died. I had no regrets about Dida's death. She had died at ninety-four, at home, surrounded by her family. To regret her death seemed to me to expect that people should not die. No, her life had a storybook ending. Boro Mama's death was like being on page 237 of a 300-page novel and having the rest of the pages ripped out.

I had not 'given shoulder' to Boro Mama's corpse, had not carried him to Nimtala and rolled him into the maws of the electric oven. By the time I arrived in California, there was no body, only absence.

The absence clung to me when I returned to Calcutta, its pall spreading over our shared city. When I went to D. L. Roy Street, the house felt like a museum. Boro Mama was peering down from the walls, just like his parents and their parents. Phantoms seemed to fill up each empty room. For Mejo Mama, his brother's promise of return was the thing which had sustained him these last few months since Dida died, the promise of the house being peopled again. With that return foiled, he knew now that no one would come back to live in our ancestral house, in our city. Mejo Mama had put up a framed photo of himself on the wall in the courtyard downstairs, just in case there was no one to do the job when his time came.

It was the wrong time, the wrong place for Boro Mama to die. When we were in Calcutta together, Boro Mama made it a point to visit old school friends, and places he knew as a child. He jotted down memories in his pocket diary. He had stopped painting years ago. Now, he was planning to write short stories, he told me. He was collecting material. He remembered being a boy trapped in St Paul's School, unable to go home, when the riots started on Amherst Street in '46. He remembered the Maniktala Market being closed during the riots. He remembered the Rani Bhabani School across the street from their house becoming a refugee camp. There used to be a small parking garage on their street. He remembered how Dida had hid a Muslim chauffeur who worked in that garage in a secret crawl space underneath her prayer room and saved him when Hindu mobs came. Ashoke was going to write it all down.

I never called Boro Mama after he left, never spoke with him or exchanged emails after our last dinner together. I assumed I would see him again. There seemed plenty of time. Surely, I always thought, we would share a roll at Nizam's, kochuris from Ganguram or a peg of whisky at Chota Bristol. What I did not know, had not anticipated, was that the narrative of every human life does not follow a three-act structure. The hero doesn't always exit in the third act, after his triumphal return to the place from which he had set out years before. No, many die the death of extras, blown to smithereens in some inconsequential montage battle scene which does not even hold our attention, three-quarters of the way in.

Nothing felt right. I couldn't work.

Would you feel better, Durba asked, if you went to pray at a temple?

I could think of nothing worse. The frenetic crowds of Kalighat temple or the rows of penitents along roadside shrines made me uneasy. They were entranced by forces which I could not fathom.

Instead, I walked, alone. I went for long meanders along the Ganga. I wandered the lanes of College Street. I got lost down unknown alleys in Chitpur and Sovabazar. In this way, one afternoon, while sleepwalking through the city, I ended up at the Pareshnath Temples off Raja Dinenda Street. I had not been there in years. When I was a kid we used to go there to see the pools of fish.

In the late nineteenth century, traders who came from the parched Marwar region of Rajasthan and got rich in Calcutta had built the Pareshnath Temple, or rather temples, for there were four in all, each of a unique architecture. The Marwaris, as they came to be called, became a dominant, and much maligned, business community in Calcutta. Many of them were Jains. The Jains believe in *ahimsa*, doing no harm to any living being, meaning not only to humans, but to animals and even insects and microbes. It was their ethic of nonviolence that Gandhi had mobilised against British rule. The temples at Pareshnath were Jain temples. At Pareshnath, no one hassles you to buy flowers and incense and chadors as at the temples and *dargahs*. There is no mad rush of fervent devotees. Three of the temples at Pareshnath are beautiful but spare, spaces of contemplation. But the one with the pools of fish looks like a funhouse. In the late nineteenth century, Muslim craftsmen from Rajasthan were brought to build a temple of mosaics and mirrors like a child's lush fantasy world.

It was late afternoon, and families congregated there as at any popular para park. There were old men gathered in clusters doing adda. Housewives walked the grounds in groups, and children were left alone to wander from pool to pool in search of golden fish. I remembered coming as a boy with my parents to marvel at those fish, just like my uncle Ashoke had come with Dida when he was a boy. A trail of memories linked that moment to something larger and eternal. I sat there a long while, watching the fish and the children and felt, for the first time, a sense of peace.

I have been back to Pareshnath many times since. Once I asked the priest there why those Marwari Jain traders had built such a place of amusement when their philosophy was so austere. They wanted to draw people to the temple, he said simply. Just like it brought you here.

***

Camouflaged earmuffs and faux babushka hats were the rage at our sidewalk sales that season, producing Calcuttans attired for the Arctic. From New Jersey, my parents' calls included more and more weather reports of snow storms, the climate to match Calcutta's couture.

At Maniktala Market, Salauddin is Mejo Mama's fixed man for chicken. 'When you enter the Maniktala Market, go left,' Mejo Mama advised me, 'past all the fishmongers and the egg sellers to the very end. The guy you hit is Salauddin. He has the best chickens.'

But don't ask for him, he warned. All the butchers call out to woo you as you pass, just as the booksellers do on College Street. 'They'll all say they are Salauddin. I'm telling you, go left then straight down. Buy only from him.'

Mejo Mama had been buying chicken for close to half a century. I took his advice. The front half of Maniktala Market is dedicated to meat, eggs and the real centrepiece of Maniktala, fish. Outside, on the street, the vendors laid out their merchandise on a tarp on the footpath and squatted alongside their potatoes and onions, just like in our local bazaar. But inside Maniktala Bazar, each vendor sat on a plinth raised about three feet from the ground, like a minor lord. Salauddin sat atop his throne at the far end of the first row of butchers. Behind him, like a backdrop, were several storeys of chicken coops.

Salauddin kept poultry and *deshi,* or country chickens, and equally good counsel. He could advise on how to cook a chicken curry, as well as on the appropriate age to father children. I was to bread the chicken pieces ever so slightly, he suggested, before dipping them into the pan. And I was wise to wait a few years – what's the hurry? – before the kids came. They don't let you enjoy life, he said.

The Hindu butcher in my para places each chicken on a small chopping block – the stump of a tree made smooth by blood – and cleaves off the head, guillotine-style. It falls to the floor and rolls a little way away. The body keeps convulsing, a mass of feather and muscle in the butcher's hand as it thrashes about. The butcher throws the decapitated bird into a wooden crate as if it were a feathery football and attends to other business, talks politics – will the bandh come off tomorrow, where did the opposition burn buses today – while the fight slowly leaves the bird's body.

Salauddin killed chickens the Abrahamic way. He slit their necks quickly and let the blood rush out. There is less drama, less agony in the show. Durba is ecumenical in her horror at fowl slaughter, and so it is my job to buy chicken. I don't mind. If I'm going to eat it, then the least I can do is witness its slaughter. If I am to be a beneficiary, then I feel I should at least carry the suffering that is caused for my well-being on my conscience. You can kill an animal by letting it thrash about headless in a box or you can slit its throat and hold it down in a bucket of water. Either way, it is what must be done so that you can have a pleasurable dinner. Vegetarianism to me is no solution to the problems of ethical living, but rather the fantasy of purity. This life is messy, bloody and cruel. There are only dirty hands, I believe, only complicity and compromise. Now that you know, how will you choose to live?

Winter had set in. Not real winter in the way my parents' phone calls brought news of hailstorms, ice and snow. Calcutta winter meant sixty-degree nights. Salauddin was sitting at his usual perch. 'Come, come brother,' he said. He was wearing a wool hat and scarf. 'Ay, this cold, no one can even wake up in the morning.'

At night he slept on his plinth, his piece of real estate in the market. He was just one man, he said, what was the point of renting a house? Besides, 'The chickens are here and someone has to take care of them. Sometimes they get sick, they need constant care.'

But business was hurting, he said. It was too cold to come to the morning bazaar. 'Curry pieces?' he asked, and I nodded. He fished one of his birds from the coops and slit its throat. As the blood rushed out, he kept chatting away, as if the sheer quantity of words would keep him warm.

***

In New Jersey, Baba had read my descriptions of College Street, and called me: 'This was the world in which I grew up, except I never saw it like you.'

It caught me by surprise, for my father had grown up in Sealdah. I had thought College Street was mine. Musulman Para Lane in Sealdah was the street where my father spent his childhood. Musulman Para Lane – literally Muslim Neighbourhood Lane – was not called that any more, for the Musulmans are gone. The names of all the lanes around there were quietly changed into Hindu ones when my father was a boy. In the heart of Sealdah, his street became Monmotha Mukherjee Row. But the city is a palimpsest. The stories rubbed out and written over still seep through, if you know how to look. Like the political exhortations on city walls that defy a simple whitewash, whose messages are legible between the letters of the newer slogans written with fresh paint, so too my father – Hindu, Brahmin, Bangal – always spoke of home as Musulman Para Lane, not Monmotha Mukherjee Row.

I had been there only once, when I was maybe ten years old, with Baba. How small the road was, he had said then, compared to how large it had seemed when he had played cricket there as a boy. He had pointed out the house, a depressing, ancient-looking building in a depressing, ancient-looking neighbourhood.

It had none of the decadent charm of my mother's childhood home, of genteel, storied decline. The para seemed more like a ghetto, a place anyone would be happy to leave as soon as their station allowed. My overwhelming impression had been of the meanness of its poverty. Perhaps it was the stories my father had fed me, too, of his barren childhood, homework by candlelight, one pair of pants each year, a dozen siblings living in two rooms. I remember seeing that house as a child of ten, American-born, and thinking: This place has nothing to do with me.

After our phone call, one day I walked from College Street down Mirzapur Street, and picked an alley by intuition. Twenty years after that first visit, I remembered exactly how to find Musulman Para Lane. The neighbourhood housed more paper merchants, box makers and printing presses than I remembered, the world of College Street pressing south. I walked past the boarding houses and the egg wholesalers, the shawl repairers and a shop of political paraphernalia that carried the flags of all parties, except for the Naxalites. But I could not find my father's house.

I walked farther south, past Surendranath School, where my grandfather had been a math teacher, and where my father and his brothers had gone to school. I took a lane choked by bamboo scaffolding, which had been erected like an arch of triumph stretching across its breadth. A huddle of young men stood playing carrom beneath the scaffolding. I followed a loaded cycle-van and a mother and son as they gingerly squeezed past the carrom players, and found myself out in the familiarity of Amherst Street. I woke up. My mind recovered control over my body. From Mirzapur Street, my subconscious had done all the leading, from lane to lane, through a para I had visited only once when I was a boy. I came home perplexed at having sleepwalked those lanes. What was I hoping to find?

A few days later, I called my father in New Jersey, and without to planning to, I mentioned that I had been in his old neighbourhood but had not been able to find the house. My father is a man of dotted 'i's and crossed 't's. From two continents away, he immediately began giving detailed directions: the boarding houses and cheap restaurants, or 'pice hotels', that I was to use as landmarks, the eastern approach from the Flyover, the southern route from Lebutala Park. Baba was still talking distances and coordinates, when his voice changed. 'I have a funny story about Lebutala Park,' he said. 'Once we went to play cricket there. I was batting. I was using a homemade bat made by one of the para boys, marking the crease, digging the bat hard. "It's not going to break, is it?" I asked the boy who had made the bat. "I made it out of guava wood," he bragged. Then, of course, the bat broke. Oh, how we ran and ran through those gullies, with those boys chasing us. We ran all the way to Bowbazar!'

Then, quickly, his voice changed back to the familiar matter-of-fact tone. 'OK, talk to you later,' he said, and hung up.

***

My father was the tenth of thirteen children, the first born after Partition. In that vast brood cramped into those two rooms in Sealdah, Baba became the boy who made good, finishing college, then graduate school, to become a scientist. In 1976, when he first went to America on a post-doctoral research fellowship, fifty of our relatives came to see him off at Dumdum Airport. In our family saga of collective ascent, his migration was a crowning achievement.

My parents went to Buffalo, New York as newlyweds. Two years later, they returned to Calcutta with a three-month-old baby and moved into the smaller bedroom of our family flat in Bagmari. The world to which we returned was my grandmother's world. Dida lived in the larger bedroom with her two unmarried children. The Bagmari flat abutted a cowshed and a lumberyard. Farts and factory sirens sounded throughout the day. It was the first house my grandparents could call their own since they migrated. In 1947, their home, their village in East Bengal became part of Pakistan, a nation-state for Muslims. For twenty years, my grandparents raised their ever bigger family in rented rooms in Sealdah, in Jadavpur, in Dumdum. In the late 1960s, my grandfather was finally able to buy a small flat in a teachers' cooperative in Bagmari.

By the time I arrived, my grandfather had died, and his children were keen to efface that past. In our family, only Dida went on speaking in the Bangal dialect with its sizzling 'zzz' sounds and confounding turns of phrase, a phonetic pizzazz that my uncles and aunts had flattened into oblivion. It made Dida anachronistic, this harping on the past, this persistence with the dialect of a land lost. But Dida harped. She strictly followed a Hindu widow's restrictions: she wore only white saris, gave up meat, fish, eggs, garlic and onions and cooked all her meals herself. Her mornings were taken up in prayer to her beloved Krishna, the reigning deity in the altar in her room. Each morning she would put on a fresh sari and lay out an elaborate offering of flowers, Ganga water and fruits as *prasad* to her deities as she sat down to prayer. Murmured incantations, bell-ringing and incense-lighting followed as her idols were worshipped and 'fed' the prasad. I looked upon these daily events as an elaborate form of make-believe. How could she seriously think that those photographs and figurines of Hindu gods and saints would actually eat her food? At prayer's end, she distributed the prasad among us. I was my grandmother's twenty-fifth grandchild. She called me Gopal, the nickname for baby Krishna, a diminutive moulded with love. But I steadfastly refused the morning prasad.

The flat had two rooms, a dining space, a balcony – 650 square feet of caged modern living. Dida's room was like the Sealdah railway station. Pots and pans were stashed below the raised bed. Rolled bedding sat in the corner to be unfurled for the constant parade of visiting relatives. Aside from praying, Dida also cooked, ate and hosted countless visitors in her bedroom. The shutters were perpetually flung open. Stray cats were forever coming through my grandmother's room and seemed as welcome as Dida's endless supply of close relatives. To me the improvised arrangements seemed to belong to some anarchic past that was utterly different from our world.

In our room, I remember the shutters always closed, the room cool on muggy Calcutta afternoons. No one murmured incantations or prayed. In the evenings, we listened to the All-India Radio news on my parents' Panasonic 'three-in-one' system from America, after which my mother played LPs of Indian classical music and songs by Rabindranath Tagore. We stored our valuables in a steel wardrobe under lock and key. When guests arrived, they sat on a little wicker love-seat my parents had managed to squeeze into the room. No one ever sat on the floor, much less slept there.

Between those two rooms were the familiar tussles of a thousand joint families everywhere. On weekends, my grandmother went to the neighbours' to watch Bollywood blockbusters on television, which I was forbidden to see. In those days, when such positions were still possible, my parents refused to buy a TV, fearing that once an idiot box arrived, my grandmother would enthusiastically feed me a steady diet of jungle yelps, gyrating chanteuses and *dhishum-dhishum* fight scenes.

Dida had initially objected to my parents' marriage, since she hadn't arranged the match, and because my parents were of different castes. Even after relenting, as a Brahmin she had never fully accepted my mother's lower status. There were never any screaming matches or arguments between my parents and my grandmother. But we lived on two sides of an unbridgeable chasm. My grandmother had never been to school. She was taught to read and write at home and married off when she became a teenager. My mother did research as a biochemist at the Unversity of Calcutta. My parents' dinner table conversations were about autoclaves and northern blots. My grandmother did not believe in using a refrigerator. Dida's room represented religion, tradition and the anarchic confusion that was the past. In ours was science, modernity and a clear path to the future. The perennial tension between our rooms felt like a clash of civilisations.

When I was a child, sometimes the relatives of cancer patients came to our house in Bagmari to speak with my father, the cancer scientist. Many of them believed that cancer was contagious or the result of having been cursed. In the taxonomy of our two-room universe, I always slotted those people into Dida's room, with her pujos and fasting days and irrational beliefs untouched by the light of reason. To me, they represented a past that would soon disappear. The future belonged to the moderns, to us.

***

'Bagmari, Maniktala, Rammohan, Rajabazar, Sealdah, Sealdah, Sealdah!' The bus crawled along slowly, picking up passengers at a leisurely pace. It was midday and most people were at work or in bed enjoying a rice-belly nap. Even though the bus was not full, I stood close to my father, covering his right side so no one could pick his pocket. My parents had escaped New Jersey's January frost to come and see us. Baba and I were going to Sealdah.

Later, he would say with pride to my mother: 'I rode a bus today after many, many years.'

At Sealdah, we alighted at the foot of the Flyover, and followed the tramline as it curved like a sickle into Mirzapur Street. We marched up Mirzapur, past a phalanx of paper merchants. Baba suddenly stopped. 'This is where the old sweet shop was,' he said, 'and there the old tea shop. And that' – he was now standing in front of a locked gate – 'that was the gully that led straight to our house.'

He stood staring intently at the gate. A woman was looking at us from a nearby threshold. 'Wasn't there a gully here?' he asked her.

'Yes, but that has been closed,' she said, puzzled why these two strangers were so enamored of an alley in the middle of the *bhaat-ghoom* siesta hours.

'That gully led straight to our house,' Baba said again.

Baba led me further up Mirzapur and then turned left. We passed a few houses with printing presses gurgling in their front rooms. Then the lane widened and forked. Baba veered left and kept walking. In a house made grey by faded paint, Baba pointed to a niche in the wall, hardly wider than a man's waist, and said, 'That's where Alauddin would sit all day playing his tabla.' Alauddin ran a laundry from that niche, he explained. 'He would sit there in his laundry and play tabla all day.'

'And there, that balcony,' Baba said, pointing up at a little portico lunging from the second floor of the same house, 'Bablu'da would drop his balloons from there. All the children used to crowd below the balcony to catch Bablu'da's balloons.' This was the house where in two rooms my grandparents had raised an ever-expanding family that eventually ballooned to thirteen children. We entered. The corner room had been subdivided. A part of it had been given over to a 'DTP' or desktop publishing shop, which was run by a man my age, who my father spoke with and identified as Bablu's son. The house, too, was subdivided now, Bablu's son informed us blandly, standing at the door of his shop. Inside, a couple of young men were seated in front of computers on Formica desks. For a moment, Baba's natural caution, his pragmatism, seemed to have abandoned him. Without invitation, he brushed past Bablu's son and marched into the room where he had spent most of his childhood and adolescence, the stares of the DTP employees be damned.

In 'Kabuliwala', one of Tagore's most iconic short stories, an itinerant Afghan hawker in Calcutta returns after many years to the home of one of his favorite customers, to visit a little girl named Mini. But of course Mini is not so mini any more. It is her wedding day. The Kabuliwala has been away for over a decade and time has not stood still. In the pathos of the Kabuliwala is that universal urge to slap time across the face and command it to turn backward, to cease and desist all mind tricks, to revert Mini to herself. Tagore expressed what my father felt right then in Bablu's son's DTP shop, what we have all felt at one point or another, where all the learned defences of adulthood are melted by the flame-torch of memory and we surge ahead, unsure of what propels us or how to stop. We demand that the past restore to us our order, our world, the place where we are not interlopers, but ourselves. Is that not the cruellest cut of nostalgia? To walk into your childhood home, and find that three guys have partitioned your sitting room and occupied it with their computer terminals? Now they are looking askance at you! How dare they dwell in the world you have protected so carefully over all those decades in New Jersey, while shovelling snow and creeping through rush-hour traffic, all that time dreaming of a land of tabla players and raining balloons?

Baba went into the corridor, beckoning me to follow him into the dim courtyard that led to a dank bathroom. From the courtyard, he looked up at what was the landlord's residence above.

'When we were growing up there were fights upstairs all the time. People throwing buckets. Metal buckets,' he said to me. 'We have heard every insult.'

The family still lived upstairs, though Baba evinced no interest in meeting them. When they were not battering each other with metal buckets, by Baba's telling, they were trying to evict his family. They tried many times, but since all the boys in the para had been my grandfather's students, they were unsuccessful. The public of the street was against them.

The landlords were Ghotis, like my mother's family, meaning they were from the western part of Bengal, the part that had stayed in India. My father's family were Bangals, Hindus from East Bengal, who had arrived after Partition when East Bengal became East Pakistan, and eventually Bangladesh.

Later my father said to my mother: 'For us, Ghotis were people who fought with buckets.'

To which Ma retorted that in her para the Bangals were the tenants who would wear towels in public. 'For us, Bangal was synonymous with "uncultured".'

In the Ghoti-Bangal battles that were played like background music in my childhood, sometimes playfully and sometimes with taunts, it was always Bangalness that my father and his siblings held up as a source of pride. There was never any talk of being 'refugees'. Refugees were other people, to be pointed at on the roadside with disdain, the squatters of history.

We walked through the Baithakkhana Bazar that stretches all the way to Surendranath College. The adjoining Surendranath School, where my father and his brothers had been students, and where my grandfather had been a maths teacher, had closed down. Inside the college, everything was as my father remembered it. We wandered the halls, two misfits, as he showed me the union room, the canteen, the physics lecture halls.

Baba wandered into a chemistry lab while it was in session. A room full of students worked at long wooden tables, using cloudy glassware. It was as if Baba had become suspended between the person he remembered being and the person he was now. He wandered from room to room propelled almost involuntarily through the labs and lecture halls of a past life, without reason or control. He was not all there.

'It looks exactly the same,' Baba said, as if speaking only to himself. Everything, even the dirty beakers in the chemistry lab, looked unchanged in forty years, he said. Only the students had changed.

The kids were short and skinny. They wore jeans and one hundred-rupee T-shirts, had gelled hair and cell phones, like all denizens of today's Bengali lower middle class.

They look like Marwaris, he said.

In Calcutta, Baba seemed to see Marwaris everywhere. Marwari *shingara* sellers, Marwari barbers, Marwari cobblers, Marwaris in vocations unheard of among their ilk. Like a soldier who carries a photo of his beloved in a secret flap in his flak jacket, an image he always feels is there, protecting him from the miseries of war, my father carried a mental image of his city. What 'Marwari' stood to mean, I soon realised, was anyone who did not fit my father's image of the city, the image he had carefully nursed within him for decades in suburban New Jersey, dreaming of a balmy world full of faces that resembled his own former self. Perhaps it was no different from a generation ago, when the refugees had flooded the college. Then, too, men of an earlier generation must have wandered these halls in quiet outrage at the sight of my father and his brothers.

Russian Dolls

The Sealdah house in which my father grew up had no electricity until Baba was in class nine. Even in my childhood, in Bagmari, when the situation was not so dire, the struggles of daily existence were always palpable. Dida's room was the headquarters of our federation, whose outposts were spread around suburban Calcutta, of families living in one or two rooms, where towels and lungis hung from bedposts, where meals were cooked and eaten on the floor, and where each night every room became a bedroom, every stretch of floor turned into a place to sleep. Every petty task, every small event, seemed fraught with the possibility of bringing forth disaster. In the future loomed the big worries: would there be enough money to get their daughters married? Would their sons find jobs? Those were houses where families struggled for years to save enough to convert an outhouse into an indoor bathroom. In those cramped spaces, there was so little margin for error or desire.

When India became free, my father's family became refugees, part of a deluge of bodies taking over empty spaces all over the city, turning the pristine metropolis into a slum. This could never have happened in the British time, people said. Then, laws were respected. There was such a thing as discipline, orderliness. The streets were washed every day and the footpaths hadn't been taken over by hawkers and the homeless. What an idyll Calcutta must have been before the coming of the refugees!

Before Partition, my grandparents had been Hindu Brahmin landlords. They lived off rents on land worked by low-caste Hindu and Muslim peasants in Faridpur district. My grandfather lived in Calcutta most of the year as a teacher and hostel warden at Surendranath School in Sealdah. My grandmother lived in the village with the children in their family home. In those days Dida would often visit Calcutta and stay in Dadu's hostel quarters. During summer vacations and Durga Pujo holidays, Dadu would return to the village and distribute gifts from the metropolis: stockings and high-heeled shoes for his daughters, stylish backpacks for his sons. In the city Dadu was a schoolteacher, in the village a feudal lord. This nimble hopping from one place to another, the ability to inhabit the metropolis and the village, to be schoolteacher and landlord, to live with a foot in each world, was slashed by Partition. When Partition came, the monomania of the twentieth century caught up with my grandfather. He was made to choose.

To understand what happened, we have to begin with the famine that Manoj had witnessed. The city was full of girls who had been sold to feed their families and meet the new war-fuelled demand in the whorehouses. Thousands of idle and well-fed Tommies and GIs lived the good life of the White Town, waiting for war. In the Black Town, well-fed Indians with steady government jobs went about their daily lives as if normality had not been breached. All the while, dead bodies piled up in the streets. In the 1940s, the sound of hunger and the sight of dead bodies had become somehow naturalised in the streets of Calcutta in a way that we cannot fathom, because we have no reference point, no way to make sense of the calamity that befell the city. For that perhaps we would have to compare it to Tokyo or Dresden, to the cities of the Allies' enemies, which were firebombed or turned to rubble. What the British managed in Bengal, upon their own subjects, could only be understood in those extreme terms.

At the time, Ian Stephens, the English editor of my paper, the *Statesman*, defied wartime censors to publish pages of photographs of people dying amid plenty. The *Statesman* printed numerous editorials to condemn the colonial government for what it had wilfully wrought. Scholarship has since confirmed what eyewitnesses knew: there was nothing natural about this disaster. The British made the famine, of that there is no dispute. But millions of Calcuttans went along, watching people arrive on the streets to die, and did almost nothing.

An unprecedented inhumanity had descended upon the city in the years of the war. In Calcutta today we pass people cooking, sleeping and begging on the footpaths and ignore them as if their predicament is normal. So too, in that time, Calcuttans must have grown accustomed to strolling past people fighting for scraps with vultures and wheelbarrows full of human carcases. The moral order of society collapsed because of the famine. What followed can only be understood in that context.

The war was ending. The two main political parties, the Muslim League and the Congress, were arguing over the future constitution. Both sides knew the British would soon leave India. But in what state? Would there be one India or two, a Hindustan and a Pakistan? What would be the fate of Calcutta, which was India's largest city and the capital of Bengal, its largest Muslim-majority province? Everything was up for grabs.

Initially, the League's demand for Pakistan – a separate nation state for India's Muslims – seemed more like a bargaining tool at the negotiating table. But when the discussions between Congress and the Muslim League fell through in the monsoon of 1946, the League's leader, Mohammad Ali Jinnah, declared 16 August 1946 to be Direct Action Day.

In Bengal, the Muslim League had formed a provincial government. Its leader Husain Suhrawardy declared Direct Action Day a holiday and called a bandh. The league organised a major rally at the Maidan. On 16 August thousands of Muslim men walked to Esplanade from all over the city and its industrial suburbs. Some of the first clashes of the morning happened in Maniktala as Muslim labourers were crossing the Beleghata Canal heading to the Maidan. In front of Maniktala Market, League supporters fought with Hindu shop owners who refused to close their shops. By afternoon those areas had become war zones. Guns had been plentiful during wartime. A bottle of whisky could get you a revolver from a GI. The strongmen on both sides were ready with arms. About three-quarters of the city's residents were Hindu and one-quarter were Muslim, not very different from what it is today. But back then, the layout of the city was completely different. There were Muslim pockets in Hindu areas, Hindu pockets in Muslim areas, patchworked across the city.

On Direct Action Day, Calcutta was going to be liberated para by para. After the Muslim League's rally, mayhem broke loose. Bands of men went lane by lane, house by house, burning, looting and killing. Smoke them out, burn them down, take over land. Drive the other side out. The strategy was area control. In Maniktala, Hindus drove out Muslims. In Park Circus, Muslims were driving out Hindus. In Kidderpur, Pakistan was being made, in Bowbazar, Hindustan. Barricades went up between neighbourhoods, like international borders that could not be crossed. On Chitpur Road, the buses stopped near the Nakhoda Masjid and detoured for several blocks before continuing onward. That stretch of Calcutta's oldest street had become Pakistan.

In the first two days, the League had used its goons and guns to take the battle to Hindu paras. Worse, Suhrawardy used his power to hold the police back. Then the *goondas* of the Congress and the other Hindu parties had organised their war in Muslim paras. Even the full force of the state could not control the violence for several more days. The killings went on for a week. Hundreds of thousands were forced into refugee camps. Five to ten thousand people were killed; the actual figures will never be known. In the muggy August heat dead bodies began rotting on pavements as they had during the famine. There were so many bodies everywhere that the sanitation authorities could not figure out how to dispose of them. On the streets there were bodies being eaten by vultures. Bodies were thrown into the Ganga. Bodies were burned round the clock at Nimtala. Bodies were buried in mass graves at the cemetery in Bagmari. Bodies were chopped up into pieces and stuffed into drains. The water pressure of the city plummeted until, as the historian Janam Mukherjee wrote, Calcutta could finally 'digest its dead'.

Partition was born on the cannibal streets of Calcutta. After this, there could be no more coexistence. There would have to be two nation states: India and Pakistan.

From August 1946 onwards the killings continued sporadically for months, first in Noakhali, then in Bihar, here and there across the land. It was a time when homemade bombs were going off in the Bengal countryside, when rumours of stabbings abounded. In their village, my uncles remembered Muslim schoolfriends suddenly brandishing knives and talking casually of murder. At that time, Dadu felt that it would be better to take the family with him to Calcutta. Not permanently – after all, his mother and brothers were still in the village, with families of their own – just until the 'Hindustan-Pakistan' troubles died down.

On 15 August 1947, the British partitioned their empire and left. Jawaharlal Nehru, India's first prime minister, delivered the radio address on that day in his clipped English accent:

'Long years ago we made a tryst with destiny, and now the time comes when we shall redeem our pledge, not wholly or in full measure, but very substantially. At the stroke of the midnight hour, when the world sleeps, India will awake to life and freedom.'

At the moment that Nehru celebrated India's half-measure freedom, Gandhi, his mentor, wasn't making sweeping Hegelian pronouncements. He was keeping vigil in a house abandoned by a Muslim family in Beleghata in Calcutta, meeting with Hindu and Muslim leaders and pleading with them to hold back their goons. It was a year after Direct Action Day. Pakistan had come into being; Bengal's Muslim League

government was being disbanded. The Hindu thugs began
the attack, dreaming of a redux of the previous year's mass
killing, only this time initiated by them and not the League.
The violence had resumed in Calcutta.

'A big city like Calcutta is bound to have many thieves and
plunderers. God has not yet given me the power to win them
over,' Gandhi said to the city's leaders. '[But] It is the gentlemen
goondas who are the real creators of trouble.' In Beleghata, he
began a fast unto death until the rival party leaders signed a
pledge that they would stop the killing by risking their lives if
necessary. They signed his pledge and the killing ceased. Then
goondas began arriving in Beleghata, bringing with them Sten
guns, spears, rifles, knives, cartridges and bombs to deposit
them at Gandhi's feet as a true peace offering. Among those
who surrendered arms was a local Congress dada in Beleghata
named Jugal Chandra Ghosh. In 1946, he had organised the
killings in the locality, raising funds from businessmen and
doling out ten rupees for each murder, five rupees for a 'half
murder', as he later put it. The encounter with Gandhi brought
a remarkable conversion in Ghosh. Like Dasyu Ratnakar
becoming Valmiki, for the rest of his life, Ghosh worked to
maintain the peace that Gandhi had forged.

But by then, the Great Calcutta Killings had spread to a
whole subcontinent. Millions were fleeing from their homes,
in Lahore, in Bombay, in Delhi, in Dhaka. The battle in
Calcutta, first fought para by para, had turned into a war across
the hurriedly made boundaries of new nation states.

***

My grandmother never accepted Partition. Even in my
childhood something of her feudal bearing shone through in
the anarchic state of our flat – which was proof of her inability
to do housework – and in the hospitality she offered in her one
room, even when there was so little to be hospitable with. Some
part of her was forever living that old life when she had never

stepped out of the house except in a palanquin. As a child I used to help Dida spool thread through the needle of her gleaming Usha sewing machine. That well-oiled and carefully maintained machine had been given to our family on a state-run scheme for refugee families to earn extra income. That machine was one of the only valuable things she owned. Of all her other possessions, she only had stories, tales of what she had left behind. For years, well into my childhood, she wrote and received postcards to do with 'the land'. The land was a running theme in our Bagmari flat, the lost land, the orchards and fields, the mangos and jackfruits, the ponds full of fish. Bangladesh must be the largest country in the world, the Ghotis used to say, because every refugee claims to have left a small kingdom behind.

At various points, the governments of Pakistan and then Bangladesh had offered compensation to Hindu refugees who had lost land. Compensation in cash, or in land swaps. But few in Bengal got any land or money. In the 1980s someone swindled Dida out of a hundred rupees by claiming to be close to Ershad, the erstwhile dictator of Bangladesh. There were rumours that my grandmother was going to receive compensation – fantastical figures depending on whom you asked – but that various members of our extended family had prevented her from going to collect it, for fear of what would happen when she went back. Those stories were the self-deceptions of little lives trying to make sense of that which was not publicly remembered.

In the early years after Partition, Dadu and Dida both went back to their village in East Pakistan several times, once when my great-grandmother was ill, once taking my father and his brothers to show the boys their country, their *desh*. My father remembered riding a palanquin on that trip.

The migration to Calcutta was a temporary arrangement. There were plans for a full return. Like my grandparents, few believed in the finality of the exchange of populations, the permanence of Partition. There had been riots before, temporary bouts of madness, and like those flare-ups, this, too, would subside. In the thousand years since the coming of Islam to Bengal, in over seven centuries of Muslim rulers and 200 years of the British Raj, never had millions of Bengalis been forced to flee their ancestral lands because of their faith. No ruler had done what the British had accomplished, drawing lines on a map to assign each group its place, Hindus here, Muslims there, tearing a land in two and making millions homeless. Their folly was so unprecedented, their solution of a permanent partition so flawed, that Dadu and millions like him could be forgiven for failing to realise the finality of the schism.

There would be no going back. In time Pakistan itself split, and what had been East Bengal and then East Pakistan became Bangladesh after the 1971 war. Dadu's brothers moved too, until by the 1980s there was no one in our family left on the land. That chapter was closed. What was done was done. It wasn't talked about at family gatherings. My uncles and aunts fought to forget and forged new lives in and around Calcutta.

***

Soon after Independence, Dadu had a breakdown. The life of a teacher and hostel warden, which he had led till Partition, now changed dramatically. The warden's quarter had two rooms. What had been a cosy flat when Dida came for visits was now crammed with eight children. There were ten mouths to feed, and only his income with which to feed them. Dadu went to the homes of wealthy children and gave tuition in the mornings before school. He taught maths in the morning school, then in the afternoon school, then gave tuition again in the evening. His days were fuelled by cigarettes and endless cups of tea. On top of that he had to deal with the daily fracas of several hundred boys in the hostel. He fell ill. He gave up the warden's job and flat. The family moved to a rented house in Jadavpur, beyond the southern boundary of the city.

Adjoining my grandparents' new lodgings was a bamboo grove. One night, refugees who had been squatting in nearby areas came and cut down the bamboo. They planted the bamboo poles on a stretch of fallow land nearby, apportioned plots and built huts. The land belonged to a local landlord. The landlord brought armed guards to drive the refugees out. The guards destroyed the huts and flattened the settlement. The people ran into the night. In Faridpur, my grandparents had had their own guards to protect their property, men just like these who had stood sentry outside their ancestral house. Now people like my grandparents were the usurpers, the robbers, the ones being beaten back.

The guards were no match for the refugees, who had nothing more to lose and nowhere else to go. Soon they returned and rebuilt their grass and bamboo huts and began to live there. A 'refugee colony' was born.

In the first five years after Partition, the population of Calcutta grew as much as it had in half a century. The millions of refugees who arrived at Sealdah station could not be accommodated in rented houses. Thousands of families lived in the station itself, because they had nowhere to go. The only destination that the newly formed Congress government had provided for these people was the refugee camps, to eat the dole, shit in troughs, and catch diseases. Rumours of sexual violence were rampant in the camps; damaged people living in damaged surroundings. Right up to the 1950s, the government kept believing that the refugees in West Bengal had come as visitors and would soon go back. No permanent arrangements were made to accommodate them in the city.

When it became clear that neither the post-colonial government nor the political parties could do anything for the refugees, they began organising among themselves. Among them were Congress and Communist leaders, socialists and Radical Humanists, terrorists and Gandhians. What bound them was circumstance. In the struggle against colonial rule, disobedience had been the backbone of their politics. Many had gone to jail for breaking what were unjust colonial laws. The end of British rule had placed them on the wrong side of the law again. They had to break the law in order to survive.

Groups of refugees formed committees across ideology and party affiliation, to identify fallow lands where they could squat and build settlements. Within five years they established over a hundred and forty squatter settlements, or 'colonies', in the outskirts of Calcutta, in Jadavpur, Belghoria, Baranagar. The tragedy of Independence became most starkly clear in the refugee colonies. The iconic parts of the metropolis, like Esplanade, Park Street and Dalhousie, where brown men now replaced white men, were marginal to their experience. They lived in rooms lit only by lamplight, whose walls were as fragile as their lives had become. This was Ritwikland. In his films, Ritwik Ghatak made the world of refugee colonies visible, the lorries full of people being dumped into nowhere, the blank spaces upon which colonies arose. It was a landscape of mud paths leading to shacks that looked like they could be torn apart in one good jhor. Those shacks became shelter for people rendered suddenly powerless, like the refugee family in his film *Meghe Dhaka Tara*. The father is a schoolteacher, physically and psychically hobbled by history, who is no longer able to provide for his family, scarcely able to care for himself. His children splinter in different directions, unable to hold together the family that fate has uprooted from its true home. In those fragile spaces, families lost one another, literally and psychologically. This was the bamboo frontier where human decency was tested by the heartlessness of the city. For Ritwik, the refugee predicament exemplified the universal human condition, of homelessness and alienation in the modern metropolis.

***

In the early 1970s, when the alleys of the city were again full of bullet holes, the director Satyajit Ray made three films that captured the mood of the time. Satyajit was a filmmaker of drawing rooms, Ritwik of the streets, my father used to say.

And indeed, within the Calcutta trilogy, the film that crystallises that era best is set almost exclusively in a drawing room.

'In Bengal,' begins the film *Seemabaddha*, 'the number of educated unemployed is over one million. How many uneducated unemployed there are I don't know. Many believe all of Bengal's problems stem from this fact. I myself am not one among them. For the last ten years, I have been working in the offices of a foreign corporation ...'

The voice is not of an angry young man, but a bhodrolok of fine features and gracious manners, a man who has made it. *Seemabaddha*, or *Company Limited*, is about a Bengali executive in a British-owned company in Calcutta that produces ceiling fans. Played by the debonair Barun Chanda, it shows a brown man who has risen fast to inherit a post once held only by white men. He has a car, a high-rise apartment, and membership in a club formerly closed to Indians. Now, to keep rising, he has to instigate a labour conflict in the fan factory – a factory much like the one where Manoj worked – to provoke a union walkout. For full effect, a bomb is thrown into the grounds and a nightwatchman is seriously injured. But the executive with his high-rise flat gets his promotion. *Seemabaddha* may be one of the few films which is far better than the book that inspired it, because of its ending. In Shankar's novel, the ending is maudlin – the nightwatchman dies and the executive is found alone, weeping. No one dies and no one cries in Satyajit's film. In the penultimate scene, the elevator in the executive's high-rise is not working, so Satyajit films Barun Chanda climbing up eight flights of stairs in suit and tie, climbing literally and metaphorically to his drawing room in the sky. By the time he reaches the top, he is drenched in sweat. He looks spent.

There are no revolutionaries in the film, no Communists, no slogans, no killings. But they are present like a spectral force. In those rarefied drawing rooms there are whispers of bombs going off, of youth calling for an overthrow of the entire corrupt system. The revolution is like a steady hum from high-tension wires that is heard in the background. But those rooms are so high above the streets that the sounds of gunfire echoing from the alleys can only be heard in the deep, deep lonesome dead of night.

By the 1960s, the young men who had been brought up to salute Netaji's portrait on Republic Day were going to college to find a system that looked largely unchanged from the British time. Poverty and injustice were all around them. Two decades after the departure of the British, the ruling Congress was still cashing in on being the party that had led the movement against colonial rule. But the Congressmen were the status quo, nothing more. All across India, the party of Nehru was being dethroned in state assemblies by local ethnic, caste and language movements. In Bengal, those energies flowed to the Communists. The CPI, undivided Communist Party of India, had been organising schoolteachers and sharecroppers, students and refugees. Their vote share was growing with each election. But by the mid-1960s, for the youth who were both educated and excluded by the system, their patience with the mainstream Communists had run out. The party had split into the CPI and the CPM but both remained committed to a revolution through the ballot box rather than taking up arms.

News of the Cultural Revolution was reaching Calcutta from Beijing. Mao had proclaimed that the first revolution had not been enough. A second revolution was needed to finish the job. In north Bengal, in a village called Naxalbari, peasants had revolted and been violently suppressed by police. Radicals within the Communists declared solidarity with the uprising to form a breakaway faction, dedicated to organising an armed peasant revolution across India. They called themselves the Communist Party of India (Marxist-Leninist), a.k.a the Naxalites.

'Political power flows from the barrel of the gun.' Those words of Chairman Mao began to appear on whitewashed walls around Calcutta, as did the addendum by the Naxalite guru Charu Majumdar: 'No one is a Communist who has not first soaked his hands in the blood of his class enemies.'

In 1971 there were ten to twenty thousand Naxalites across Bengal. Most were young men from Calcutta and its suburbs. The city's colleges were full of recruits. The guerrilla movement, which was supposed to ignite a peasant revolution, had turned into a rebellion of urban youth. They were fighting the bourgeois state, the Congress, the CPI, the CPM, the principals of the schools and colleges where they were being stuffed with fodder to make them sheep. In the tea shops and the canteens, elder boys were blooding younger boys, teenagers battling for respect and fighting for turf.

In 1964, when my father entered Surendranath College to study chemistry, the Naxalbari revolution was yet to come. The CPM had just formed out of the CPI and the college was dominated by the radicals of the CPM. Among his group of friends in chemistry was a CPM 'theoretician' named Surjo, a boy well schooled in Marx, Lenin and Stalin. In 1967, Naxalbari was erupting when they went their separate ways, Surjo to study applied chemistry at Rajabazar Science College, Baba to study biochemistry at Ballygunge Science College. Each became caught up in his own world of new friends and new horizons. They saw each other less and less. By 1970, the guerrilla movement that Charu Majumdar had started in order to spread a peasant revolution across the country had turned into an urban war. The movement was turning murderous. Beneath the slogans and wall graffiti the contours of the conflict were no different from gang wars anywhere in the world and, like all gang wars, it eventually became a battle with the police. Across the city, there were countless stories of young men plucked from alleys by police, beaten up in custody, then released and shot in the back. In the police reports, it was written that they were killed while trying to flee.

Baba had started a PhD in Sir's lab at the cancer institute. Every night he came back from lab prepared not to make it home, prepared for a police cordon and being herded off along with the para's young men in a raid. The police were scared too. The Naxalites thought that if you killed policemen, then you could create dissension in the ranks of the police. One of Baba's friends in Bagmari had a brother who was a police officer. The brother was also a bodybuilder. After the Naxalites started killing police, the officer began riding pillion with another bodybuilder.

One night, news spread through the city of a murder on the Rajabazar Science College campus. A Congress activist had been shot and killed. Baba's friend Surjo was arrested for the murder. He went to prison.

By the time he came out, the Left Front was already in power. By then my father was a scientist at a cancer research institute. Surjo was running a neighbourhood chemist shop. He came to see Baba at the lab once. He maintained that he was innocent, as my father still believes, that he had been framed to get him out of the way. Perhaps, like many CPM ideologues at the time, he was threatening to defect to the Naxalites and was sacrificed, a victim of the Communist fratricide that was taking place in the paras. There would be no way of knowing the truth.

If this were a novel, this would be the moment to reveal that my father, or better yet my mother, had been a Naxalite revolutionary. A dramatic family secret would be let out. But life does not work that way. In those years of torture, imprisonment, death and exile, my parents met, fell in love, got married, moved to America, moved back. Life went on. Everything had changed because of the Naxalite period, but no one spoke of it any more.

***

In New Jersey, my father privately remembered the events of his youth, of Surjo and destruction, playing the tape of memory backward and forward to understand how fate had torn his generation apart. And yet Baba, who was so familiar with the traumas of the city in '71, knew nothing about the people who had been murdered in August '46 on Musulman Para Lane and Hayat Khan Lane where he grew up playing cricket. He had no idea how those events had changed the course of his life. Those carcasses in the courtyards and lanes were the reason Baba was born to poverty in Sealdah and not to relative comfort in East Bengal. How could he have known? Of the history that had happened on his own street, there was no mention in his history books. His life was structured by the trauma he knew nothing about. Unlike the street-corner busts or the Faces You Can't Piss On, there are no memorials to the three million who died in the Bengal Famine of 1943, nor to the thousands who died in the Killings of 1946, nor to the millions uprooted there and displaced here who lost their homes and who arrived as refugees in the city. No monument remembers those pasts, which have been wilfully forgotten.

It is not so easy to remember that time, nor to build its memorials. To do that would be to make the footpaths of the entire city into a memorial. Satyajit Ray had witnessed those calamities with his own eyes and his 'famine movie', *A Distant Thunder*, is one of his most terrible films. It exposed the limits of Ray's visual language. Neorealism made famine look picturesque. The best effort is a film about the impossibility of such filming, by Mrinal Sen, called *In Search of Famine*, which is about a film crew trying to make a movie about the '43 famine. When they go to a village to shoot a period piece about the '43 famine, the villagers ask, 'Famine? Which one?'

In Bengal, there were famines to mark the beginning and end of British rule, and famines in between. The lasting legacy of the British in Bengal was famine. Soon after the East India Company first took over Bengal in 1757, a fixed cash payment was imposed on farmers that caused widespread famine and the Company refused to provide any relief. According to colonial records, a third of the population died of starvation. Whole districts turned into jungle. Imagine that: one in three people just vanished. It marked the real beginning of colonial rule.

An account of the past should help a people to understand its present in order to imagine a shared future. The history we are taught about ourselves is no longer being written by our rulers.

Yet we fill our heads with fantasies about the past, of nationalist history or Marxist history, each time like diligent fly-swatting clerks matching up some European narrative and copying it out in local colours, matching their Renaissance to our Renaissance, their nationalism to our nationalism, their revolutions to our own. The goal of this also-ran history is to pass the biggest exam of all – the test that certifies that we, too, are moderns, that is, that we, too, are human beings just like Europeans.

It is no surprise that this 'history' makes our present look like an *Abol Tabol* nonsense poem. It tells us nothing about the real traumas of our past. It does not help us make sense of those breaks, does not help us reconstruct ourselves. To remember what really happened, to understand how we came to be, we have to rely only on our own wits, only on private memory, a limited, blinkered version of the past. My memory leads back to Bagmari, my father's to Sealdah, as my grandmother once remembered her village across the international border in Bangladesh. My father relives the city of the Naxalite years, just as my grandmother's world was forever in the lost village in Faridpur, just as my world somehow remained fixed in the Calcutta that was being destroyed without flood, famine or riot, a city that my generation was abandoning as if it were a sinking ship, the city to which I returned, from which I fled. Inside each private memory is another private memory, like a set of Russian dolls, in an infinite regression of experiences of longing and loss, each separate and unconnected by any narrative thread that other peoples call a history.

We who were raised on such faith in the nation and progress and modernity, who viewed the future with such confidence, hid away in shame from the most obvious realities about our humiliating condition. How else could the bare fact that freedom had meant homelessness be hidden from plain view? And so we remain strangers to ourselves, our heads filled with notions that have nothing to do with the lives that we are living, and our eyes blind to the most basic truths of our existence.

This Little Corner

'Why did you come back?' I asked the Freudian during one of our therapy sessions.

'My PhD advisor in America had asked me the same question,' she said. 'Why are you going back to *Calcutta*, of all places?'

'I said to him, "I can walk there at ten o'clock at night without fear of being raped, unlike in an American city."'

Then the Freudian looked at me and said, 'Although I don't think that's true any more.'

Each day the papers were full of advertisements for luxury high-rise apartments. In the architects' drawings, the towers were always arising from an empty space that had no people, a *terra nullius*, like Antarctica or the moon. From these towers emanated a fantasy that seemed to have swept across urban India, from Gurgaon to Gujarat, and finally made its way to Calcutta. In those drawings that appeared in the newspapers, I wondered, where were the tea shops, the bus stands, the people sleeping on the sidewalks? Why did they never show the men who drove their share autos past the malls with the behemoth billboards of bra-and-panty models, which seemed to have been erected only to taunt them? Where were the people of the city, the people of the country, the millions of spitting, shitting human beings who did not figure in this fantasy world?

The structure that had held us together for my lifetime was coming apart, releasing some to soar to new prosperity. But that unbinding also caused many to be cast out, rejected from any social order, like the former factory workers no one cared about any more. The city seethed with their humiliation, their shame and their alienation from the new dream worlds that were being beamed from those towers.

Would we be like the Johannesburg I had once visited, with its miles of bungalows with swimming pools, a California in Africa where the rich went to bed each night next to panic buttons and machine guns, awaiting their executioners in the dark?

For my whole lifetime, through the auto unions and para clubs and Party offices and in myriad other ways, the CPM exercised its tight social control. It patronised thugs and intellectuals, pujo committees and football clubs. No one escaped its embrace, regardless of caste, religion or party affiliation. There was no underworld in Calcutta because every world was subsumed in the Party. In this way, for more than a generation, it had kept the peace. Now, when the towers beamed their fantasies, I saw the contours of older, bloodier orders.

On the emptied spaces along the Eastern Metropolitan Bypass arose five-star hotels and luxury high-rise apartments. From Park Circus, the Number Four Bridge whizzed motorists to the bypass, skipping over Topsia and Tiljala. You could live in Calcutta your whole life and never enter those paras, which were poor and predominantly Muslim, unseen and unheard by the Hindu city. The lines drawn on the map by the Great Calcutta Killings in '46 were still there, of Muslims here and Hindus there, even though no one cared to remember how they had been drawn in the first place. If this order collapsed, what would take its place? Every time I crossed the Number Four Bridge, the sight of those invisible lines filled me with fear for the future.

***

The bush-shirt and mud-coloured sari world to which I belonged was still waging an internal battle between schools of leftism. There seemed no memory of the hell this city could veer towards. It was as if they felt a false sense of luxury, of infinite time, which came from living in a society that was suspended for thirty years in formaldehyde.

I was in Beleghata at the offices of a leftist organisation that has compiled report upon report on the fate of former factory workers. One of the group's activists and I were drinking tea and smoking on the terrace in the waning light. I was saying how moved I had been by a documentary they had made that profiled former factory workers.

'Doesn't it bring tears to your eyes?' he said, and began telling me about the backgrounds of some of the men in the movie. 'Thinking of them makes me want to cry,' he said.

Then he said: 'All this information-gathering, all these democratic movements are useless. Because no one cares. What you need to do is get some water bottles full of kerosene and get about ten guys and go through all the floors of each of these malls and take care of things. Then people will pay attention.'

He laughed at the thought. Then he came closer to me, speaking softly so no one would hear: 'We need a Nav Nirman Sena here, like the one in Bombay. It's all Hindi speakers here buying the big houses, taking the jobs. Our boys can't even get into the city to sell potatoes on the pavement.'

He was talking about the right-wing party, which had been terrorising migrants to the city in Bombay, a leftist uttering out loud a fascist fantasy. He was narrating the dream that we have all had, when all else fails, that dream of tearing it all down and starting with a clean slate. In each generation it takes a different avatar, but the dream is the same and its causes are the same. Who of us has not felt that shame at our powerlessness, and that alienation from the world around us that we are unable to change? From that incapacity arises a fantasy, a fantasy born of weakness, to wipe everything clean.

After having been so thoroughly colonised, what faith could we have in our own capacities? We see our society as a heap of failure upon failure, failure to organise our resources effectively, failure to be honest and not corrupt, failure to advance according to the dictates of science and reason, failure to have highways and skyscrapers, failure to not spit and piss everywhere, failure to hold our heads up high and not be pitied by the rich countries of the world, failure to cover our drains, to provide clean drinking water or clinics or schools or the basics of a dignified life. Failure upon sweeping failure. And, unable to cope with this mountain of failure, unable to see through the endless complexity and variety of the society in which we were made, we dreamed the child's dream of purification, hoping for a messianic force to descend and wash all the shit and disease away like a giant monsoon deluge, or burn it down like a fire raging through a slum. When all else fails, let it all burn.

***

From the street, the furniture shop on Rafi Ahmed Kidwai Avenue looked like a Sukumar Ray poem. Clothes horses, cane chairs, wooden desks, beds and armchairs were piled high to the ceiling in fantastic formations. In their midst sat Mihir Choudhury, dressed in a crisp pink shirt with red stripes. His wavy hair almost reached down to his collar and complemented his dapper French-cut beard.

When we moved in to our flat, my neighbour Sugato had referred me to Mihir's shop in central Calcutta. We had rented two desks, a cane sofa set, an armchair, two round side tables, and a dining room set, all for the equivalent of $12 a month. It would have been about $13, but Mihir gave us a discount, perhaps because I was Sugato's friend. Who knew when a policeman would come in handy.

Our flat had marble floors, glass bookshelves and recessed lighting. But it was Mihir's furniture I coveted. Those cane armchairs reminded me of the chairs in Dida's house. The wooden round side tables, which I pulled up when friends arrived for tea, had been ubiquitous in the homes of my childhood. The pieces were old without being antiques, appealing without being ostentatious. They were designed for my kind of people.

'Do you know Amitabh Bachchan rented his bed from here?' Mihir said, when I went to see him to pay my dues. He was referring to the biggest Hindi film star of all time. 'That was back when he was a salesman in Calcutta, before he became "Amitabh Bachchan".'

A few years ago the *Times of India* ran a story about Mihir's Bachchan connection. Fans started showing up, wanting to buy Amitabh's bed. 'One woman offered me twenty thousand rupees for the bed. Twenty thousand!' he said. 'How am I to know which bed we rented out to him? If I wanted to do some "dishonesty" I could have given any bed and said, "This is the one: Sleep in Amitabh Bachchan's bed."'

Mihir fished out the bound ledger for 1967–68. The signed entry revealed that the young Amitabh had rented a bed, a divan, chairs, end tables, over a dozen pieces in all. When Bachchan was hospitalised a few years back, TV cameras arrived to interview Mihir. 'I said, "Oh yeah, a tall guy came once and took all this furniture. But we didn't think anything of him." What was I to think? He was nobody then. Then a while later when I went to see *Parwana,* I thought, "*Arre,* this man rented from our shop."'

Actually, Mihir confided, he had realised nothing of the sort. In fact, his uncle had rented the furniture to Amitabh, and later recognised him on screen. But Mihir was too much of a raconteur to let facts get in the way of a good story. 'What I am good at is adda,' he said. 'That's what saved me.'

At the time when Amitabh had been their customer, Mihir had no intention of ever joining the family business. He was studying political science at Maulana Azad College, only a few blocks down Rafi Ahmed Kidwai Avenue but a world away.

'People were being knifed in trams. I got mixed up in it,' Mihir said. 'I never *knifed-fifed* anyone or anything. I couldn't manage that. But I had to "abscond".'

In those days, Mihir used to go to an uncle's house from time to time for tea and adda. Mihir's uncle had a friend who was a high-ranking police officer. The officer used to come to his uncle's house for adda too. One day, his officer friend told him it would be best if he stayed home from college for a year.

Mihir spent most of 1971 in self-imposed house arrest in Shyambazar. In return, the officer made sure that Mihir was saved from a knock on the door in the middle of the night, prison, torture and worse. Infiltrated by informers and sold out by defectors, the Naxalite movement was decimated within three years of its founding. Across the city there were countless stories of young men plucked from alleys by police, beaten up in custody, then released and shot in the back. There were killings in Jadavpur, in Diamond Harbour, in Beleghata, in Barasat. In that blur of violence, each massacre emerged for a moment and whizzed past into oblivion. Around 2,000 Naxalites were killed. The whole whirlwind of destruction laid waste not only to a movement, not only to a generation, but to a whole society.

When Mihir returned to college, the war was over. He wanted to get a job, any kind of job. He took the entrance exams for the prestigious Indian Civil Service, but he could never conquer the maths section of the exam.

'Numbers have always been my undoing,' he said. 'I had almost secured a bank job. Once I had the job I would marry.' At that time he met an accountant who also studied astrology. The accountant predicted that he would not get a job, and that he would not marry.

'I was determined to marry. And he said, "Produce a wife. Bring a wife for me to see, and I will believe you."'

In the end, he spent a lifetime much like his father and grandfather, sitting amid those columns of chairs and side tables, watching the trams go by. 'All the next generation have jobs and are out of Calcutta,' he said with a sense of satisfaction. 'I'm the end of the line.

'Are you an atheist?' he asked me. 'I was a double atheist. My father was an atheist. I never believed in anything. The things

I would say to people who wanted to talk to me about religion! At around age thirty-five or thirty-six, I totally turned. You see, the game of your life has already happened. You are only watching the replay. My fate was that I would never have a job, never get married. So I have ended up here: a furniture-walla. What else can you say but fate?'

Sugato had told me that he had had his palm read by Mihir several times. Many people came to Mihir's furniture shop to have their fate revealed and left with prescriptions for various gemstone rings. Now you could get your astrological charts read over email, and daily predictions sent by text message. Multiple cable channels were devoted to such call-in shows for tele-astrologers, whose faces adorned billboards.

Everyone I knew seemed to have red thread wrapped around their wrist and a few gemstone rings on their fingers. I always thought of astrology as a relic from my grandmother's room, superstitious mumbo-jumbo that the future would sweep away.

'Now everywhere you see people with rings on ten fingers. Do you know why? Because people have become more ambitious. In my generation we had no ambition. Get a degree, get some kind of job, then get married because that's what everyone does. And live your life. We were believers in high thinking and low living. Our thoughts were up here,' he said, raising his hand above his head, 'but our lives were simple. Today it is the reverse. People's thinking is about what TV to buy, but their ambitions are sky high.'

When your wants increase, he explained, then life becomes much more uncertain. You fear that you won't get what you desire.

'But if everything is fated,' I asked, 'then why wear rings at all?'

'Because, say, you're supposed to be five foot six but you can't get past five foot four. Something can be done if you are not reaching your fate. We can stretch you to five foot six. But we can't make you six foot three like Amitabh Bachchan.'

***

College Street was pitch black. There was a power cut. I followed in the footsteps of three men as they marched down Ramanath Mazumdar Lane. On both sides, old buildings rose above us, forming silhouettes of decay and bygone splendour against the moonlit sky. Dipankar Chakraborty, the editor of the little magazine *Anik* was striding briskly, reciting a poem by Subhas Mukhopadhay about floating in the darkness, as if he were a metaphor.

I had first met Dipankar a few weeks earlier, at a street meeting on Bowbazar Street to protest the CPM's new war against the Naxalites. In Lalgarh, on the frontier of Bengal and Jharkhand, a new generation of Naxalite guerrillas was waging war against the government. Communists were killing Communists, just like a generation ago. But this time, the war wasn't in the neighbourhoods but in the jungles, and the prize was control of villages, of entire districts, of whole swathes of land. The street meeting had been organised by a human rights group to condemn the killing of innocents by soldiers in the name of fighting terrorism. Many of the men on stage belonged to organisations that were all part of the non-CPM left. Many were former Naxalites. For a generation they had splintered into factions and fronts like a dysfunctional joint family. Now the killings of unarmed peasants in Nandigram by the Left Front had brought them out of the woodwork, loosely united by an anti-CPM agenda, as leftists against the Left Front. Dipankar's *Anik* published many of the recent anti-CPM critiques by the left. Dipankar was a retired college professor who had spent years in jail as a political prisoner in the 1970s, though he was never a Naxalite. He had belonged to the CPI, the CPM and then a more obscure faction of the Maoist left. I asked him why there had been almost no protest from these groups for thirty years, why the left had basically become mute during the three decades of Left Front rule.

It was a desire to help the poor and the suffering all around that propelled many to Naxalism, a desire to serve the nation by serving the poor, he said. They saw suffering and poverty in society and they joined. But they had no logic in joining. When they failed, they went the way they came, like Mihir had done. Most of the people came from middle-class, or lower-middle-class backgrounds and when the period was over, they saw their friends and colleagues getting jobs, and many became careerists themselves. Some joined the private sector, others went abroad or joined the government and many joined the CPM when it came to rule. And then there were those whose turn was inward, who didn't do any kind of work for society but who retained a feeling, an orientation, some kind of vision as they went about their banal lives.

'There is no greater instance of such a high level of sacrifice by so many with so much to lose. The tribals fighting today have little to their name, they have little to lose. Those people had middle-class futures and careers before them,' Dipankar had said. 'Nowhere else in Indian history do you see such a large degree of sacrifice. When they were smashed, it was a huge trauma. That is why subsequent people's movements failed, because of the trauma of the failure of the Naxals.'

On Amherst Street we entered an old house, crossed the courtyard and went up the stairs and down a long veranda leading to a row of rooms. Dipankar opened the door to one of the rooms. Just then, the lights came back on. Papers, books and bound volumes of magazines were stacked like a cityscape upon the floor of the publisher's office. The room had high ceilings and even before the fan turned on, a breeze came in from the road and wafted through the veranda. Across the street I could see a butcher chopping mutton under bright lights. Through a window above the shop, a woman was combing her long hair in front of a dressing table. I looked at the street below, past that long veranda that was just like the one in Dida's house, and thought of all the rooms like this one that still existed in Calcutta.

I felt like Alexander Portnoy at that moment. There is a scene in *Portnoy's Complaint*, the great novel of my native New Jersey, where the protagonist, Portnoy, who is all grown up and working in New York, is remembering a Sunday-afternoon ball game in his old neighbourhood in Newark. All the Jewish fathers are out on the field, trading jokes and fielding ground balls. And Portnoy has a fantasy: all he wants to do is stay in Newark forever and play softball every Sunday with those neighbourhood men, family men, Jewish men, to forever belong. At that moment, I wanted that room, that office, that life. I wanted to run a little magazine and to be part of the world of the fathers.

The discussion was about the recent annihilations by the Maoists, and whether an equivalence could be made between state terror and guerrilla violence. They were talking of the Pathan uprising in 1930 in Peshawar, the Jewish rebellion in Minsk, Enver Hoxha's war against the Nazis in Tirana. I struggled to follow the references of their arguments. I felt as if they spoke another language altogether, as if I was listening to a debate between sects whose feuds went back to the Naxalite days. The disputes and refutations had been buried for thirty years and were being rehashed anew. It was as if there was no other way forward but the road that was not taken, the dead end.

For those of us who were born after the Naxalite violence, our lives were structured by a void. We grew up around adults who were shell-shocked for reasons we could never see nor fathom, who rushed home by 10 p.m. Taxis refused to go to this or that para because it was rumoured to be 'notorious', meaning a place where bombs went off, where innocents were stabbed. But there were no more bombs, no more stabbings. When the Left Front government came to power in 1977, it released thousands of political prisoners and expunged their police records so they could find jobs. It called an informal truce to the war in the paras. We were living in the graveyard peace of Communist rule. Yet, like a reaction that remained long after the action had stopped, we still felt the phantom pain of Naxalism.

As a graduate student, I had gone to Spain during one winter break. When I came back to Yale, I met a student from Barcelona, and we got to talking of my visit to her city. I mentioned a church near Las Ramblas when she began giving me directions: if I had walked past that church and into the square and turned right, I would have noticed bullet holes in the wall where the fascists had killed her grandfather in the Spanish Civil War. That had been her society's bargain: they chose not to memorialise, to publicly not remember, as the price of ending fascism. And yet that amnesia meant that you confronted the void everywhere.

***

When the Naxalite vision of the future went bust, it was as if the future itself had imploded. It was as if no collective vision of our society could be imagined any longer. Their failure had doomed all other ways of imagining an alternate future. In my generation, in household after household, there emerged a self-imposed one-child policy. Our cohort was as much a product of that Naxalite terror as the birth-control pill, as much the reactions of mothers seeing boyfriends and brothers put to death, a generation of our boys gunned down in gullies. To achieve what? What did all those slogans and actions, all that machismo and vanguardism accomplish, but parents burning teenage corpses at Nimtala?

Don't look. Don't talk to strangers. We were a generation taught to turn away from the world that unfolded at our door. To us, politics meant ceaseless protest marches chanting 'No Way, No Way', '*Cholbe Na, Cholbe Na*', which held up traffic and made us late for school. Politics was the property of the dada who ruled the street. We were to keep away from that world, and focus on our homework. To value the lives of their young, mothers had to hunker down, have only one child each and coddle it with cottage cheese for breakfast, fish curry for lunch and warm milk during tuitions, in the hope that they would clear one of the competitive exams to enter an engineering college and then land a job behind a big desk in Bangalore or Boston. Those who were raised successfully, who got into the right schools and passed the right exams, were packed off far from Calcutta. The city became a graveyard of dreams.

I finally understood their sentiment when I went to Mexico City years later. We were in the Plaza de las Tres Culturas, as part of a guided tour, to see the Aztec, colonial Spanish and nationalist monuments on each side of the square. In 1968, 10,000 students had gathered at that plaza to protest the government's actions and demand revolution. Soldiers surrounded the square and, in the ensuing chaos, they fired into the crowd and surrounding buildings. Then they cut off power and went house to house through the night. Between thirty and 300 people were killed that night as part of Mexico's 'dirty war'. The truth of what happened is still not known. Our tour guide was a bookish middle-aged man. After we had seen the ruins and the church, we got to talking and it turned out that he had been one of the protesting students at the Plaza in '68.

What did they accomplish, all those careers destroyed, those lives vanquished? he asked. He had raised his children to stay away from politics.

All revolutions eat their children, whether they succeed or fail. And so, just as it was depicted in the family portrait along the riverbank in Kumortuli, the phantoms of our parents' generation devoured our tender heads.

***

At twenty-two, when I had first moved back to Calcutta after graduating from Princeton, I had bought a one-way ticket. I had come to stay. Two monsoons washed all that idealism away. The *Statesman* was sinking. The paper had nothing new on offer. Worse, there was nothing old that it chose to defend.

A few months after I left the *Statesman*, a colleague sent word that the squatters along the Beleghata canal had been removed. The papers played their part and reported the demolition of the homes by bulldozers, and then those lives were forgotten. When I had written about the squatters, I had seen the people only as poor. Their misery was heightened in my telling, in the hope of drawing outrage. But there was no outrage. That way of seeing, of telling, only rehashed a familiar narrative, of people who were 'other', not like us, perhaps not people at all. It was the white way of seeing Africans that Lessing had written about in *The Grass is Singing*. The lived experience of the city told us that that way of seeing was wrong. We instinctively knew that the fabric of our society was woven in a different way. But that truth never found expression on the written page.

When I had returned to America, at first campus life seemed idyllic. There were no deadlines, and attending four seminars a week felt like a vacation. Soon, all I wanted to do was go back to Calcutta. I had walked away and the city followed me. I could not start over.

***

My year in the city was nearing its end. Now I felt as if I was hopping from one political meeting to another, trying to reconstruct a past that was not there. At a rally of former factory workers at the Maidan, speaker after speaker arose on stage to assert that they were neither the ruling party nor the opposition. They were independent voices, they said, though we all knew they were another breed of Naxalites. It was as if, after thirty years of Communist rule, there was no other alternative, no other way to move forward, but to look back at what had spectacularly failed. Charu Majumdar had announced the formation of the Communist Party of India (Marxist-Leninist) at this same Maidan four decades before. This was the same Maidan where Uttam Kumar, the matinee idol, and quite possibly the only Bengali ever to have gone jogging, saw the police shoot Saroj Dutta, the Naxalite intellectual, in the early morning while the actor had gone for his morning run. In '59 – before the joint family split up into the CPI, CPM, Naxalites and then a thousand little pieces – the united Communists had organised their first mass protest right here in the Maidan. At the rally, thousands of people came from the countryside demanding food, in what came to be known simply, poignantly, as the Food Movement. Eighty of them were killed by police, many beaten to death with batons. It was in this

Maidan in 1946 that Suhrawardy, then chief minister of Bengal, had spoken during Direct Action Day, and unleashed killing across the city unlike anything Calcutta had witnessed before or since.

Every year on May Day, I still came to this Maidan and listened to the speeches where CITU leaders mouthed the same slogans about workers and imperialism and globalisation, even now, while their own government was selling off their people's farmland to multinational corporations. Someday soon, I thought, these pageants would go the way of the ribbon-cutting and bridge-inauguration photo-ops that dominated TV news in my childhood – another piece of political theatre consigned to the B-roll of history.

I was sitting at Relax with Mike, JB and Suku'da, eating popcorn and drinking, when the bank manager at our table arose from his rum-fuelled reverie. Can you tell me what they have done in thirty years? Can you tell me one thing?

Did they build roads, did they build schools, did they build hospitals? He went on like this for quite some time. What have they done in thirty years? Can you tell me one thing?

Nobody did. Everyone just kept quiet and let it pass.

Later, as we walked through Abdul Hamid Lane, Suku'da said the bank manager wasn't married. He had joined the opposition party, Mamata Banerjee's Trinamul Congress. There are days when he cries, 'Nobody loves me,' Suku'da said. That was worse.

Can you tell me one thing? Those were cries you heard more and more vociferously on buses and at tea shops around the city. For decades, anyone who had dared to voice such challenges in front of Party loyalists would be cowed down and shut up. Now, faced with such a challenge, Communists quickly mouthed platitudes about land reforms and village democracy, policies enacted in the countryside and learned by city people second hand, as Party pap. To tell the truth, even they could not tell you what they had wrought.

***

In West Bengal, there are no events to note in thirty years of Left Front rule. Between the Naxalites' bullets and until they shot and killed those unarmed peasants in Nandigram, the history of Bengal that we told ourselves was of a place where nothing happened. At Budh-Bikel adda, writers told me that was the reason why no great literature was being produced any more: because there were no great traumas, no great events. Nothing had *happened*. If Calcutta felt like a place where time had stood still, it is because discursively it had. In a city still traumatised by the violence of the Naxalite era, the Party had come to power to keep the peace. It covered its society like the patina of dust that settled over the furniture in Mihir's shop. Meanwhile, we lived on like an unhappy extended family, in ever smaller rooms, partitioned and sub-partitioned, fated to suffer a timeless present.

Calcutta was an impossible place, as Durba had said, full of the sorts of people who fought over strands of Communism while sipping tea served by a ten-year-old boy. There was no life for us to build here. How could we stay here? How could I go? I was left only with memories, which I could never disavow.

When I was a boy, there were giant open drains along the sidewalks in Bagmari. One day on the way to nursery school, my water bottle fell into the drain. I watched it sink into a dark, thick sludge. It was gone. That was the first time I experienced the feeling of irrevocable loss, and I remember it filled me with a deep sorrow, which then turned into fear. Any of us, at any time, could fall into the black river that bubbled below the sidewalks of our city and be sucked into oblivion.

From time to time, the image of being trapped in sludge seeped into my mind like the whisper of a demon. Now I saw the sludge, slow as molasses, dark as tar. My feet were caught and I was slowly sinking. I was trapped.

This swamp city was all there was, all there had ever been. Like so many others, I had believed that I could escape the lanes of my memories by leaping onto another continent, another future, a new dream. All that running, when there was no way to escape. We were all trapped.

The Greek poet Cavafy, citizen of Alexandria and bard of exile, had understood our fate better than most:

You said, 'I will go to another land, I will go to another sea.
Another city will be found, a better one than this.
Every effort of mine is a condemnation of fate;
and my heart is – like a corpse – buried.
How long will my mind remain in this wasteland.
Wherever I turn my eyes, wherever I may look
I see black ruins of my life here,
where I spent so many years destroying and wasting.'

You will find no new lands, you will find no other seas.
The city will follow you. You will roam the same
streets. And you will age in the same neighbourhoods;
and you will grow grey in these same houses.
Always you will arrive in this city. Do not hope for any
other –
There is no ship for you, there is no road.
As you have destroyed your life here
in this little corner, you have ruined it in the entire world.

PART IV

The Fortress of Triumph

It was only the beginning of April and already the midday heat had become unbearable. Nitai Pal was sucking on a popsicle when I met him in the lane leading to his house in Bijoygarh. He recognised me from the earlier times when I had come to see his brother, Gosto Pal.

'Hey!' Nitai yelled up at the sky as he reached the gate of the joint family home. A girl came to the balcony and lowered a key on a string. Nitai let me in. The house had been built in such a way as to maximise the number of bedrooms. We walked down the unlit hallway that ran between the bedrooms like a spine.

'My mother is ninety-nine,' said Nitai as he led me up the stairs. 'She is still alive. You will see her.'

Sure enough, upstairs in one of the many rooms, squatted a woman with short hair and a caved-in mouth. She stared at me wide-eyed and wordless. I could not make out if she was still all there. Nitai showed her to me as if she were a statue of Victoria or a pet pelican, as you might find at the Marble Palace. In her own family, she had become an object of curiosity.

The corridor ended in what looked like a sunroom, bright, airy and open on two sides. Walking through those long dark corridors into the light felt like being born. The women of the house, mothers and daughters, sat chatting and singing, all dressed in bright, colourful housecoats. The floor was covered with hundreds of clay models of the Hindu gods Laxmi and

Ganesh. Some were pocket-sized, others a foot high. It looked like a workshop from Kumortuli had been transplanted into their house. The women were Gosto's daughters, his sisters-in-law and nieces. Each was performing a specific task. Together they formed an assembly line, just as they would in a factory. They were producing gods and goddesses.

In idol-making, the hardest part of the job is *chokh dewa,* literally 'giving eyes'. The eyes are drawn last. It is believed that a clay model only becomes divine upon the drawing of the eyes. One of the girls knew how to 'give eyes', she told me proudly. She was the youngest of Gosto's seven children, all daughters. The one above her is Sarbani, a schoolteacher, who was at work. The other elder sisters were all married.

'Baba is upstairs,' the eye-giver said.

I scaled the steps to the terrace. Set off from the assembly line, Gosto had the terrace all to himself. Beyond it were mango trees and sky. Gosto was squatting on the floor under the shaded part of the terrace, surrounded by unpainted clay models. He saw me and said: 'So, am I any worse off with the closing of the factory?'

With eighteen people living under one roof, the Pal house always feels as if it is preparing for a wedding. Everything happening within those three floors that day was at his command. He was in charge of his own production unit. How could he be worse off than during his days as a factory worker at Bengal Lamp?

'I am far better off,' he said.

The white-hot sun was searing the cement on the terrace. Even under the shed it was hot. Gosto had an ancient table fan going. He angled it away from himself and pointed it at me.

'I don't need it,' he said. Gosto had a hammer in hand. Next to him was a set of pint-sized Ganeshs, the sort merchants put above their cash registers to auspiciously bring in the Bengali New Year. Gosto took each statue and tamped down the nails on its back. Tap-tap-tap-tap-tap, done, then another Ganesh, another five taps, rapid and repetitive.

Then he said it again: '*Ami onek bhalo achi.*' I am far better off.

For Saraswati Pujo, the last big festival, he had made 750 Saraswati deities, but now, for the New Year, he was making far more. He had lost count of how many Laxmis and Ganeshs he was manufacturing. As he did every year, on New Year's Eve and New Year's Day he would set up shop on the pavement by Jadavpur University and sell the deities for twenty-five rupees apiece.

Talking and tapping, in a series of swift, economical movements, he began telling me about his sons-in-law. His middle son-in-law had a clothing business. His third son-in-law was an elevator operator at the Chittaranjan Hospital in Park Circus, where his wife had been admitted for twenty-six days, and where she died.

This was his first New Year as a widower. His wife had died, but his paternal duty was not done. He still had two daughters left to marry off.

Every time his wife had a daughter, the guys at the factory would egg him on, saying, 'Gosto, next time you'll have a son.'

'That's how I ended up with seven daughters,' he said, laughing. 'But now I feel I'm better off without sons. Is my daughter any less than any son?'

He was talking specifically about Sarbani, the schoolteacher, whom I had met before. She would be back in the evening to help him paint the deities. Sarbani had a bachelor's degree in Commerce, he told me, as did his youngest daughter, the one whom I met downstairs.

In Vikrampur, in East Bengal, Gosto had only studied till class four. He came over with his family when he was around ten, after Partition but 'before the visa-passport business'. His father and three uncles each settled in the refugee colony in Bijoygarh. The Pals were kumors, or clay sculptors by caste, just like the sculptors of Kumortuli. When they came over, his father forged a living making clay pots as per his caste profession. Gosto wanted nothing do to with the family trade. Instead, he took a job at the Bengal Lamp factory nearby in Jadavpur. In 1961, when Gosto started as a helper in the cutting department,

Bengal Lamp was one of the largest bulb manufacturers in India. Once the glass for each bulb was blown, his job was to slice off the blown glass as it emerged from the furnace. As he talked, he tapped the Ganesh in his hand with the hammer and it cracked open. He inspected it and said, 'Some crack. Even with light bulbs, we didn't always get a perfect batch.'

Production was booming in the 1960s. He became permanent staff in ninety days. He worked for over a decade in the cutting department and then in the finishing department. Working in front of a furnace all day was hard work, 'Much worse than this,' he said, as we roasted on the hot roof. But it was a good union job.

When the factory closed, he was fifty years old. He remembered the date precisely – 7 January 1989 – like he remembered the day his wife died.

It wasn't a strike that precipitated the closure, though there had been several CITU-led strikes at the factory when he worked there. The union had been skilful in strong-arm tactics and brinkmanship, producing bonuses and pay rises with regularity. For a while after the factory closed, he showed up at the gates to picket like the CITU leaders told him. He went to meetings. But he received no salary, no compensation, not even his retirement savings. When the jobs went, mighty CITU proved powerless. Beyond picketing and meetings, there was nothing further his union could do. Before the closure, he had taken a 7,000-rupee loan, or about six months' salary, from Bengal Lamp. 'The smart thing I did was borrow that money,' he said laughing, 'which I never paid back.'

He said he used that money to finish expanding the family home, and to marry off five of his seven daughters. Gosto told the story of the loan as if he was the one who had hoodwinked Bengal Lamp, and not the other way round. In his telling, he was nobody's fool.

I had met Gosto Pal while searching for workers from the closed factories around Jadavpur. I wondered what happened to the thousands of men who had toiled in the factories that had been erased by the malls and high-rise towers. In the shadows of South City Mall, which had eviscerated all memory of that industrial past, I began to meet former workers. They were men no one kept track of any more but who were everywhere in plain sight. They were the roadside tea-shop owners, the pavement vegetable sellers, the security guards, the men on bicycles who went from shop to shop collecting savings deposits for the banks, or who went house to house giving schoolboys tuition. A cycle-rickshaw ride away from the former factory, through lanes reverberant with temple bells, I met a Brahmin priest who blessed the luxury flats at South City. He had worked for four decades making light bulbs at Bengal Lamp, just like Gosto. He had been lucky to retire a month before the factory closed. He got a wristwatch, a bouquet and a box of sweets, but he never saw a paisa from his retirement account.

When the factory closed, many workers died of malnutrition or worse, he said. 'There are so many "Bengal Lamp suicides".'

As a Brahmin's son, he had kept going by falling back on his father's caste profession, just like Gosto had fallen back on his father's caste trade. The Pals are six brothers, four of whom lived with their families in that house. When the factory job ended, the bonds of caste and family had let Gosto survive. This avatar of Gosto, on the terrace commanding an assembly line of gods, emerged slowly. Between the proletarian and the kumor there was a large gap. For over a decade after the factory closed, Gosto worked as a gopher on construction sites, one of the lowest paid and most dangerous professions in the long line of such jobs available in Calcutta.

'On a day like this,' he said, looking up at the April sun overhead, 'I would be out on a scaffold.'

The nails on the Ganesh idols had all been tamped down. Gosto bathed each statue in *bhela,* a milky clay coating to protect the idols. At four, Sarbani would come home and the painting of this batch would begin. But not before lunch and a siesta. First he would have a bath.

Gosto took a thin red towel, and wearing nothing but his blue lungi, nimbly walked out of the house and down the lane to the neighbouring pond for a dip. It was as if he were still a kumor's son in Vikrampur and nothing in the world had changed.

***

Ranjan Guha Thakurta's house was near the main road in Bijoygarh. We were sitting in Ranjan's living room, on sofas covered with lace doilies. Swami Vivekananda looked down from the wall. The built-in wall cabinet was full of books and his daughter's childhood dolls. Ranjan was elegantly dressed like a thoroughly Calcutta bhodrolok. There was no sign in the room to reveal that we were in a refugee colony.

Ranjan's father Sambhu Guha Thakurta had been one of the founders of the colony. 'You should see some of the pictures of us from those days,' Ranjan said, 'hair messed up, wearing shirts which barely cover our bodies. Just one look and you'll know: These are refugees!'

Ranjan took me out to their backyard to show me the latrine left by American GIs. The hole he showed me had been covered over with concrete, but you could still make out the sizable footholds of a squat toilet.

'What big feet Americans have,' he said.

The sight of those footholds reminded me of a scene in Ritwik's film *Subarnarekha.* The refugee children, who are the film's protagonists, arrive in India and find themselves on an abandoned World War II military airfield. The remnants of a war machine are parked in the middle of a primeval emptiness. The airfield becomes their playground, the place they colonise to make a new life.

The land that became Bijoygarh had been an American military camp during the Second World War. GIs were stationed there for the Japanese attack that never came. When the war ended, the military camp became a ghost town. Some Bangals in the area, like Ranjan's father Sambhu, set up a relief camp in the abandoned sheds to provide food and temporary shelter for the refugees. But the refugees who came had nowhere else to go. Over time, the camp's organisers decided that they had to take over the land. They drew up plans and allotted plots, planned for schools, playing fields, a colony bazaar, a maternity ward, a temple and neighbourhood clubs. Just as Bengal's Chief Minister Bidhan Roy was building the planned suburb of Salt Lake with its Jetsons nomenclatures, water tanks and identical traffic circles, a different kind of planned community was being developed here, with its own organisation, its own order, its own logic. Except everything they were doing was against the law.

Within months, hundreds of refugees came to the camp. Ranjan's family had been living in a house abandoned by a Muslim family nearby. Their father was allotted a plot in the colony. There was no running water, no electricity. For a toilet they used the latrine left by the Americans, covered on three sides by grass. But even that was better than what most people used in the beginning, which was the colony's communal trough. I thought about the squatters I had written about as a reporter, in makeshift huts, shitting in outdoor toilets along the Beleghata Canal. How different had they been from the refugee colonies that sprang up all around the city in the 1950s? The residents of Calcutta at the time had looked upon the Bangals living in shacks and assumed that these people were by nature squatters, as if their condition was not a function of historical tragedy but rather a way of life.

Soon after the military camp was filled, the colony committee decided they had to occupy empty lands surrounding the camp, which belonged to a major businessman. The committee mapped the area and apportioned plots. Refugees began moving in and building their bamboo huts. Then one day, truckloads of the landlord's armed guards descended upon the colony. The refugee women gave ululations and sounded their conches as they would at a wedding, to raise an alarm across the settlement. The boys of the colony's sports clubs came with sticks and knives. The guards tore down many of the shacks. In the ensuing battle, several of the squatters received broken bones and busted heads and were sent to the hospital. But the guards were defeated. Their trucks were burned. The colony had been defended successfully. It was after this fight that the Jadavpur Refugee Camp was named Bijoygarh, literally the Fortress of Triumph.

***

A journalist who lives in Bijoygarh told me this story: a few years ago, a group of thugs chased after a man who lived in the colony. In broad daylight, they trailed the colony boy with a bomb. Inside the colony, hundreds of people filed out into the streets. The public began to chase the thugs. The thugs threw the bomb; the crowd threw the bomb back. It exploded and one of the boys in the group died.

There was a time when even other refugees who lived outside the colonies would not marry their daughters off to 'colony boys'. That reputation for toughness comes from the fact that in the colony, everything had to be fought for, not once but continually. Without any legal papers, colony dwellers' only strength was their physical power, the heft of bodies in the street, and men united with sticks and votes. In a new democracy, that power could be channelled into politics.

Bijoygarh was the first refugee colony in Calcutta. Following Bijoygarh's example, within five years over 140 such squatter settlements or 'refugee colonies' came up all over Calcutta and its surrounding districts. In Baranagar, past the northern edge of the city, Debjranjan Ghosh had seen the founding of Netaji Colony, his home, as a boy.

'Do you remember the scene in Ritwik Ghatak's film *Subarnarekha,* where a colony is being established?' Ghosh asked me. 'Everyone is very busy. People are being brought in lorries and allotted plots according to their home districts. Dhaka people in one zone, Barisal people in another. And in the middle of all that activity a man with a blackboard is setting up a primary school. That's just as it happened here. I saw that scene with my own eyes.'

In Netaji Colony, the colony committee had settled first on fifty acres of land and alloted about 200 plots. Refugees had to furnish 'refugee cards' to prove they were refugees and then pay fifty rupees for a plot. Eventually the colony would grow to 600 plots. The land had to be mapped and planned, and along with homes, plots were established for schools, playing fields, ponds, a bazaar, sports clubs and a temple. A surveyor was hired by the colony committee to draw up plans. They organised the layout on a grid, with roads of equal length, side lanes and drainage, and divided the colony into wards. Each ward had its own ward committee, and each school had its own school committee. The infrastructure of colonies followed a similar template everywhere. A half-century later it made colony spaces seem much more ordered than the areas surrounding them.

From the first squat to getting schools, roads, electricity, sewer lines, running water and postal deliveries to ultimately receiving legal land titles, everything had to be fought for through a permanent politicisation. The Communists took on these battles against the ruling Congress in the legislature. In the colonies, the colony committees, school committees and ward committees came to be dominated by Communists. The colonies became solid voting blocs for the left. When the Left Front came to rule in 1977, they granted land titles in the colonies and turned squatters into owners.

***

The yellow spire of the Bijoygarh temple could be seen from almost any spot along the main road that ran through the colony. Unlike in most paras of the city, all the colonies have a central temple. These temples were the product of politics as much as piety. The Bangals had an idea that if they built a temple, their colony would not be destroyed, not because the gods would offer protection for their community, but because the government always found it more difficult to destroy the houses of gods than to bulldoze the houses of the poor. People can be evicted, gods cannot. Slums, villages, entire regions can be demolished, lives ground to nothing. But if a house of worship is destroyed, a whole community will become inflamed. Better to leave it alone.

Jagabandhu Pal was known in Bijoygarh for his patronage of the Bijoygarh temple. He was also one of the oldest people living in the colony.

'When I first got the plot, my wife didn't want to come because of the snakes and all. There was a big pit here. We filled up the hole and built two rooms with bricks and tin roofs.'

We were sitting in one of the two original rooms of the house. From the walls hung pictures of gods and ancestors, including Jagabandhu's father and stepmother and his Vaishnav guru. There was a gas stove with a handi on the floor, a bicycle parked in the corner, clothes hanging from hooks on the wall, children crying in the background – a scene of shabby Bangal living that was so familiar to me from my childhood.

One of his sons came in and said, 'Sorry it's chaotic here. We are doing construction on the house.

'Take him upstairs,' he told his father.

'Let me have a bidi,' Jagabandhu said.

We went upstairs. Jagabandhu lit a bidi and puffed, relishing the taste and began:

'I was born in a bad year, the year of the typhoon. Thousands of people died in that typhoon. When the typhoon happened I was in my mother's belly. She had lost two children before me. When I was born, three priests from the Jagannath temple in Puri were passing through my village. They gave me the name, Jagabandhu, friend of Jagannath. My mother died within a year of my birth. A fakir came to the house after my mother died. He said to my grandmother: "The boy will live. He will drink your milk." My grandmother was dry, but sure enough I drank my grandmother's milk!'

Jagabandhu was from a village near Dhaka. His family moved to India in 1950. Initially, Congress workers had settled them in a house abandoned by a Muslim family in Muraripukur. Eventually, they moved to Bijoygarh and started a grocery shop in the colony bazaar.

Jagabandhu went on to have nine children: five sons and four daughters. 'All of them are doing well. All of my children are honest,' he said, puffing his bidi. 'Right now I am ninety years old. My whole life I have stayed on the same path. I didn't go on the second path.'

'The path of honesty?' I asked.

'I did Congress all my life. I never joined the other party.'

Three of his sons lived with him, another lived down the street, and his eldest son had just retired from the ordinance factory in Bombay. That son's son was a computer programmer in Houston, Texas. He told me proudly: 'He makes four thousand dollars a month.'

Jagabandhu showed me around the second floor. His two shacks had grown into a bright and airy two-storey house with a dozen rooms. He expanded it slowly.

'What have I not done, brother? I had a gas machine, a rod supplies business, I sold lanterns for pushcarts, made sweets. But what stayed with me was the grocery shop and the candles.'

When he first moved to the colony, he lived with his wife, two children, father and stepmother. He had six mouths to feed. But the grocery shop was failing. The family had no food.

'I couldn't feed my children, what could I do?' he said. He and his wife decided to sell her gold wedding necklace and bought sacks of rice and dal, enough for their children to eat for three months. Then they scouted a secluded spot on the rail line near Jadavpur station. They made a pact. That following Monday, they would jump on the railroad tracks together and commit suicide.

Before he moved to Bijoygarh, Jagabandhu met a man who owned a match factory. Somehow, the factory owner learned of his plan and was moved to help. He took him to Howrah to buy a candle-making machine and three sacks of wax. In those days, every house in the colony used candles, since there was no electricity. His friend acquired a government permit for candle-making. By eight every evening the whole Pal family would be engaged in packing candles.

'With that candle workshop,' he said, 'I rose up.'

He took me to a small front room and unlocked the door. There were five machines in the room, two spools of thread for wicks and thirty-two candles in a packet. He pointed to an iron contraption with levers and cylindrical slots, and said, 'This machine saved my life.'

***

When I was a kid, I had thought that the world of my grandmother and her prasads would soon disappear. But when I returned to Calcutta, two decades after my grandmother had died, every idea, every artifact that I remembered of that agonistic upbringing was still present. After thirty years of Communist rule, no belief, no superstition, no prejudice, had been wiped out. A few years ago, an embarrassing story emerged about Subhas Chakraborty, the popular Communist leader and transport minister. Chakraborty had been caught by the news media offering prayers at a Kali temple. Confronted the next day, he said, 'I am a Hindu first and a Brahmin later and then everything else.'

The Party must have thrown him quite a coming-out party, because a week later he cleared up what he had meant by saying, 'I see everything on the basis of dialectical materialism.'

Looking back, I realise now that the clash between our two rooms was not about civilisations, not between reason versus faith, nor the traditional against the modern. The idea that our life was somehow modern and my grandmother's was traditional was a fantasy. Our conflict was between two sets of beliefs: Dida had her gods and demons, while our side proclaimed blind faith in ideologies of nationalism, socialism, science and progress. We had our own prejudices, no less outlandish than Dida's views on the dangers of using a refrigerator. 'Modern' and 'traditional' were just borrowed words with which we comforted ourselves that we would control the future. But our future never happened because our present had never happened. We had such a poor grasp on our reality, and hence all of the past from which it sprang. We attempted to disavow most of what we saw around us, to turn away from our own society in disgust. We believed in the power of our myths to deliver us to another future. Of the present, we considered only shards and fragments, forcing schisms within homes and within minds, because we had no way to order it into a coherent narrative. But the society in which we lived, of slums and palaces, of demons and demagogues, of autoclaves and fasting days, constituted one civilisation, one whole.

In the last film Ritwik Ghatak made, art imitated life so closely that it could hardly be called a film at all. *Jukti Tokko Goppo* is the most didactic of his films, uneven in quality, with flashes of brilliance, tacked together by a man who knew time was running out. Started in 1971, when the streets were riddled with slogans and bullets, *Jukti* took him four years to make. Though he was only in his late forties, his life was almost over, tattered by alcoholism, much like the main character in *Jukti*, who is always found with a bottle of Bangla in his satchel. By the time it was released, he was dead.

Jukti takes place exclusively on the streets. Its characters are defined by a literal and an existential homelessness. The film follows a middle-aged alcoholic, played by Ritwik himself, who wanders the countryside with a collection of social castaways: a refugee of the Bangladesh War, an educated unemployed youth, and an elderly teacher abandoned by his family. In the climax of the movie, the wandering drunk and his crew find themselves captured by Naxalites in the jungle. The Naxalites are young city boys with guns who are awaiting a police ambush. They decide to let the group go. Ritwik determines that he and his group will stay, because, he says, 'You are the future, you are all we have.'

The Naxalites want to know if he is ideologically on their side. Has he read *Deshodrohi* and *Lal Jhanda*, Che Guevara and Mao Tse Tung? Is he up on Naxalite praxis? When Ritwik demurs, a rebel leader says that it is because of 'worn-out, rotten, washed up, petit-bourgeois intellectuals' like him and their failures, that the Naxalites are in such a situation.

'Yes, indeed!' Ritwik replies. 'Then let's drink.'

And he does.

We are 'confused, utterly confused', Ritwik mumbles, like King Lear on the heath, '*dishahara hoe hatrey hatrey beracchi*', searching for something to grab on to. The film betrays no vision, no way forward, beyond the ramblings of a drunk. *Jukti* is a film about failure – political failure, moral failure, a failure of imagination. The film itself is a failure, for it does not hang together as a coherent work, but rather remains like tattered fragments of inspiration. Yet even the drunk saw clearly the world around him for what it was, and his people for who they were.

'My sons, he says, 'this country of ours, these thousands of years of history, and no matter how much we abuse it, this land has given birth to some of the most luminous philosophical ideas known to man. These are the weapons of villains and scoundrels, but they have to be understood to be ripped up from the earth. They won't vanish just because you say they are not there.'

Ora nei bollei chole jabe na.

Life was not as simple as wiping the slate clean and starting anew in a pristine future. There is no easy way out.

They won't vanish just because you say they are not there. If you fail to heed them, they will haunt every world you live in. The phantoms of the past roamed freely in the breeze, their echoes trailed those who walked away. We heard it louder and louder the further we went, until we could hear nothing else. I had been haunted by those voices each time I had walked away. When the daily distractions of the present disappeared, all that remained in us were the voices that haunted our souls.

You had to listen to them, give them their due. Then, you had to master those voices, and move forward to make another world.

***

When I saw those architects' drawings for luxury highrises in ads in the newspaper, of towers arising skyward upon a moonscape, I wondered, What would the children of those flats be like, who belonged to no street, no para, heard no loudspeakers and spoke no dialect? What kind of jokes does a child raised on the fifteenth floor, in a stratosphere so far from the pavement, learn to make?

It was Sunday *bikel*, or late afternoon, and Bijoygarh was in bloom. At the central green, the old-timers in white were perched all along the boundary wall. Teenagers were playing cricket and football on the same field with imaginary divisions. Several games were simultaneously in progress. I saw boys running up to bowl like Kapil Dev, and a part of me, as always, wanted to play.

My boyhood city was forever frozen in memories of cricket matches. We used to rush home from school, change out of our school uniforms, slurp down rice and dal, and be off by 4:30, bat and ball in hand. One by one the boys would be called down, their names screamed into the houses: 'Jho-ru! Pi-ku! Pi-aaal!'

'Have you no sense of time?' Pial's drowsy grandmother would scowl at us from their balcony. We knew this: for the next two hours, we were our own masters. Bikel was our time.

All those cricket matches, all the pleasures of my childhood were taken away from me on 15 August 1990, the day we moved to America. That time was gone forever. When I lost the city as a child, I lost the capacity to be fully myself. But by coming back, I had not recovered the self that I had left behind. The self, it turns out, is not an inert object, to be lost and found. My childhood is an unreachable city down memory lane, just like yours. But that was never really why I came back, anyway.

Everywhere in Bijoygarh, there were signs of the old yielding to the new. As South Calcutta pressed southward and butted up against Ritwikland, 'PG Accommodation' signs cluttered lamp posts, promising affordable housing to the next generation of newcomers to the city. Few of the *hogla* and bamboo shacks remained. They had become brick houses. Tiled roofs turned into terraces, second floors had been added one room at a time. The houses had been built in pieces, expanded with each wave of need and as funds allowed. Their parts did not always fit seamlessly together. The joints were often still exposed, to reveal an edifice fashioned over time. Those colony houses stood as metaphors for the lives that had been rebuilt in this city. And in that building there was resurgence.

The city had let these people live, as it had millions of those who still came from the countryside, pushed by hunger and hatred onto its streets, its squatter camps and its slums. All that violence was still there, waiting to be triggered. And yet, in spite of the daily struggles, in Calcutta we remade a new peace each day. A tight social order arose from the para clubs and the tea shops and the pujo pandals. This city did not happen by accident. The miracle of what we had achieved together as a people was that those countless little pieces made this present city and let people live together again.

In Delhi, Durba had grown up knowing she always had to be on guard. Travelling after 8 p.m. required a male escort. The capital's empty avenues and deserted traffic circles became prowling grounds for sexual predators. Until she lived in Calcutta, Durba confessed to me one day, she had never imagined that it would be possible for a woman to travel freely in an Indian city after dark. She had thought that such freedom was a privilege, reserved for women in Europe and America. In Calcutta, she said, she felt safe on her own. In a para, on a street corner or in a crowd, there were a thousand little unspoken rituals and codes that made up what can only be called the street-level culture of the city, which was both so extraordinary and so banal that one barely noticed it until it was gone.

The stage was being set at the Niranjan Sadan in Bijoygarh. Ranjan had invited me to an evening's cultural programme organised by a local community service group dedicated to the principles of Swami Vivekananda. A harmonium and a tabla had been set up on the low stage, with mikes craning down. A sound engineer in track pants leaned into them: 'Testing, testing, one, two, three.' The neighbourhood women sat with powdered faces and beautiful Baluchari saris. The colony boys sat with neatly combed, glistening hair and crisp, oversized panjabis. They wore their enforced gentility like overcoats, waiting to take it off to reveal their natural boy selves at any moment. I took a seat behind them, and remembered my own self and could not help but smile. The evening's programme was about to begin.

***

It rained all morning. We stayed under the covers till almost lunch time, pleasantly cocooned as torrents washed the world away.

By afternoon the rains ended. The city had become cool.

'It's such a beautiful day,' Durba said. 'Let's make the most of it.'

She had been reading a novel by Alka Saraogi about the Marwaris, who came from dry, dusty villages in Rajasthan centuries ago to trade. In those days, the streets were washed with the holy waters of the Ganga every day. Such an abundance of water! Calcutta, to them, felt like a city paved with gold.

'I want to see the Ganga,' Durba said.

We hopped from auto to auto to Bagbazar. There were a few afternoon bathers, lovers sitting in twos, idle men staring at the lovers, the typical pastoral scene along the riverbank. The river was, as always, the colour of milky tea.

On Chitpur Road, a tram rushed at us, fresh out of the Bagbazar depot, invitingly empty. The conductor was reclined across three ladies' seats while all Calcutta slept its bhaat ghoom. We latched on. We tung-tunged past the unfinished idols of Kumortuli, past the brass pot sellers of Sovabazar, past the strong-box sellers and the silver shops of Garanhata, past Vivekananda Road, which led to Dida's house. The light of late afternoon streamed in from each lane that arrived from the river to Chitpur and covered the street with gold. The city spooled past like a film strip, each frame illuminating many layers of lives. We crossed Muktaram Babu Street and the Marble Palace, and the worlds upon worlds of Chitpur accumulated rapidly as we entered Barabazar.

The tram stopped at Lalbazar police headquarters. We got off, bound for Esplanade. Near the *Telegraph* office, where Sumitro now worked as an illustrator, is the best tea shop in Esplanade. The tea is served by a man perched in front of a life-sized copper boiler that looks like a potentate with a parasol.

I fired off an SMS and Sumitro materialised for a cup of tea.

'*O bhai, teen-tho chai,*' I said to the tea seller. 'Special.'

'I have come back to the old para, to all the old places where I used to eat, and all the old places where I always meant to eat,' Sumitro said. 'For instance, there's a fellow here who fries excellent jillipis.'

With barely a word, Durba ran to where Sumitro had pointed, and returned with a paper bag full of sticky hot jillipis.

You can never get this sweet and tangy taste in Delhi, Durba said, relishing each bite and badmouthing her hometown. It got later and later as we talked. The sun dipped over the Ganga. Soon the sex-potion salesmen would pick up foot traffic from the office crowd in front of Chowringhee Square. I kept looking past Sumitro to the marquee of Paradise Cinema, scanning the sea of faces along the Chinese shoe shops. Somewhere under that marquee, Suku'da would appear, whistling past the parrots on his way home, followed by Mike.

The traffic was dense as Durba and I crossed Central Avenue in front of Statesman House.

'Your old home,' Durba said.

'Yes,' I said, as I looked through the revolving doors into the dark foyer. I was nineteen years old when I first entered there. And so had started the tugging back and forth between here and there, this oscillating existence.

I realised that my whole adulthood should have been another life really: a job in an American city, a house in the suburbs. Yoga. Thoughtful considerations of vegetarianism. Organic squash by the bushel every summer. That life would have meant living almost entirely in English, with Bengali worn at home like a high-school T-shirt until it faded and fell apart. Once every four years or so, when vacation time permitted, I would have taken a trip to India for a family wedding or a funeral. With each visit, I would find the country more unrecognisable from the one I had left. My India, which had ended on 15 August 1990, would seem ever more diluted from its original pristine self, changed from the world of my childhood into something impure, something hideous, until I would one day recognise it no more. Then I would fall back quietly into one place, one time zone, one language.

Once you fall into the great abyss of assimilation, you become an individual. You have yourself, to love and to loathe, to buy and to sell, just like everyone else, alone. No new society, no ready-made collective life awaits you to replace what has been lost. Instead, you cling to your spouse, your progeny, your pets, like lifebuoys in a fearsome sea of strangers.

But how do we make a good life? Two thousand years ago, Aristotle had asked that question. We human beings are not meant to live exclusively indoors. We need to hear the symphony of the street, feel the pavement at our feet. The life outside our door beckons us to a destiny larger than the lonesome murmurs of our souls. To live the good life, Aristotle had said, you have to make a world in public, with strangers.

Standing at Chowringhee at dusk, I felt gratitude at that moment for the life that I had made. In coming back and accepting this present for all that it contained, I opened myself to the possibility of being made anew. If migration truncates the self, then marriage expands it. That joining together teaches you, slowly, painfully, that you are no longer the self that you were, that you are not a full self any more, that your self is not whole without the one you love.

As we walked past Chowringhee Square, I showed Durba the evening beef-roll sellers, Islam saab's samosa stand, and the greasy joints where I had eaten countless mutton chaaps.

'So this is your para!' she said.

'Have we never come here together before?' I asked her. In all the time that we had been in Calcutta, we had never walked together through these streets at the navel of the city.

'Where's Chota Bristol?' Durba asked.

We crossed the tramline on Lenin Sarani as it entered Esplanade. I led her across the street and into a lane, half dug up. We walked single file past the clothing stores and I showed her the bar where we used to go, where women were still banned.

'What would they do if I tried to go inside?'

'Durba! Keep walking.'

'Down that way,' I said as we made our way to Metro Gully, 'is the Punjabi hotel where I used to eat fish curry and rice lunches with Mike and JB, and that's Anarkali where Imran and I ate after late shifts, and through there is the shop where our office folk would order kochuris when there was something to celebrate. We never came: a peon would be sent, and the kochuris were excellent. And just across from it is Nizam's, whose mutton rolls, Durba, as you know, no words can do justice.'

I was flooded with memories of experiences I could not digest. I let them all wash over me, joyous and true, as I narrated the life I had made. I had walked through those revolving doors to enter countless portals of the city, following streets upon streets, pavements upon pavements, to another life.

Durba and I were swirling in the evening crush of taxi-rickshaw-human traffic of Esplanade. For all these years, I had kept circling back, pulled by forces beyond my conscious control, returning repeatedly to my past. Now, for the first time, I felt the whirl propelling me outward, hurtling me from this orbit to other worlds. I was beginning, I realised only now. Just beginning.

Acknowledgements

At the *Statesman*, my friends and colleagues were like an extended family. Even today, I feel happy and nostalgic when I meet any of them. They were: Michael Flannery, Arunava Das, Esha Nag, Chandidas Bhattacharya, Ajoy John, Sukomal Basak, Ratan Pradhan, Debabrata Chakraborty, Gautam Bhaumick, Kunal Bhaumick, Dipankar Ghose, Arindam Biswas, Santanu Mallick, J. B. Lama, O. P. Rana, Mita Ghose, Nessa Bose, Rina Chunder, Chitralekha Basu, Imran Siddiqui, Paromita Kar, Swagata Sen, Rajrupa Ghosh, Rajib De, Piyal Bhattacharya, Dwaipayan Ghoshdastidar, Gautam Basu. The list could go on and on and I am sorry if I have excluded anyone. From 2009–10, I had an ACLS Early-Career Fellowship from the Andrew W. Mellon Foundation, which enabled me to return to Calcutta to spend a year doing research for the book. During that time, Rajesh Deb and Tridib Chakraborty helped organise interviews and accompanied me during a part of my work. Otherwise, most of the writing and reporting was done alone. I spent more than four years sitting alone in little rooms in Philadelphia and New Delhi, writing this book. I don't think anyone can help you through that process, which is lonely and long. Susan Roth, Lisandro Kahan, Ajay Gandhi, Jacob Dlamini and Durba Chattaraj all read parts or all of the manuscript and gave me excellent feedback. Often they simply offered me the encouragement to keep going. My parents always had faith that I was doing something worthwhile, even if they could not always see the path that I was taking.

Alice Martell, my agent, has always believed in the book. I like to think that reading about Calcutta made her yearn for her childhood in Philadelphia. Faiza Sultan Khan, my editor, has championed the book from the time I sent it to Bloomsbury, unsolicited. Her faith in the work far surpasses my own and I am grateful to them both for their hard work on its behalf. John McPhee, my teacher at Princeton, first suggested I write a book about Calcutta more than a decade ago. He gave me the courage to pursue the writing life. Without him I wouldn't still be writing. I think about the people who I loved who died in these years that I spent writing: Anna Tverskoy, Shefali Kerr, Chhaya Chattaraj, Ashoke Kerr, Rajat Kumar Neogy, and Sumitro Basak. I don't know what Calcutta means to me now that Sumitro is gone. We who loved him did not deserve to lose him so young.